Ideology and Politics:
The Socialist Party of France

Other Titles in This Series

Communism and Political Systems in Western Europe, David E. Albright

The Spanish Political System: Franco's Legacy, E. Ramón Arango

Westview Special Studies in West European Politics and Society

Ideology and Politics:
The Socialist Party of France
George A. Codding, Jr.
William Safran

A case study of a modern political party, this book explores the strengths and weaknesses of the French Socialist party—its history, ideology, organization, and constituency—as well as the reasons the party has remained a viable force in the French political system for over seventy years.

The authors explain the party's past and present role in French politics, and in the process interpret the major changes in French political affairs during the past several decades. They examine the crisis of identity that occurred for the French Socialists in the 1960s—the result of a massive Gaullist majority—and the party's subsequent reappraisal of its role, changed pattern of conduct, ideological compromise, and finally reemergence as a significant force in the French political scene of the 1970s. The concluding chapter compares the French Socialist party with some of its counterparts in other European states. Here the authors discuss perceptively the tendency of European Socialist parties to merge into larger units and to weaken their ideologies in order to attract large numbers of voters.

George A. Codding, Jr., professor and former chairman of the Political Science Department, University of Colorado, Boulder, received his Ph.D. from the University of Geneva, Switzerland. William Safran is also professor of political science at the University of Colorado, Boulder; he received his Ph.D. from Columbia University.

Ideology and Politics:
The Socialist Party of France

George A. Codding, Jr.
William Safran

Westview Press / Boulder, Colorado

Westview Special Studies in
West European Politics and Society

Copyright © 1979 by Westview Press, Inc.

Published in 1979 in the United States of America by
  Westview Press, Inc.
  5500 Central Avenue
  Boulder, Colorado 80301
  Frederick A. Praeger, Publisher

Library of Congress Cataloging in Publication Data
Codding, George Arthur.
  Ideology and politics.
  (Westview special studies in West European politics and society)
  Bibliography: p.
  Includes index.
  1. Parti socialiste—History. I. Safran, William, joint author. II. Title.
JN3007.S6C6   329.9'44   78-17924
ISBN 0-89158-182-0

Printed and bound in the United States of America

To
George III
William
Jennifer
Gabriella
Joshua

Contents

Preface xiii
List of Abbreviations................................. xv
Introduction 1

Part 1
Party Background

1. Historical Background.............................7

   Genesis 7
   Unification.......................................12
   World War I and Its Aftermath 14
   Tours and After.....................................16
   The Popular Front and World War II 19
   The Fourth Republic and *Tripartisme* (1945-1947)......21
   The Socialists in and out of Government (1947-1955) .. 24
   The End of the Fourth Republic and the Beginning
      of the Fifth (1956-1968) 30
   Notes 33

2. The Ideology of Democratic Socialism 37

   The Concept of Man and Society 38
   Economic Theory 42
   Social Doctrine 47
   Order and Social Control 49
   The SFIO and the World at Large 53
   Notes 55

3. Party Organization 59

    Party Structure 60
    Party Discipline 69
    Party Finances 73
    Clientele and Membership 74
    Leadership 80
    Guy Mollet 82
    Notes 85

Part 2
The SFIO in and out of Government

4. The SFIO and Domestic Issues in the Fourth
    Republic 91

    The SFIO and the New Postwar Regime 91
    Nationalization and Economic Planning 95
    The SFIO and Agriculture 98
    Education and *Laïcité* 100
    The SFIO and the Working Class 102
    Preserving the Republic 109
    Notes 114

5. The SFIO and International Policies in the
    Fourth Republic 119

    The Socialist International 120
    International Cooperation and Disarmament 125
    European Union: Toward a Third Force 128
    The Dissolution of the French Empire and the
       Algerian Disaster 134
    Notes 141

6. The SFIO and the New Republic 145

    The Fall of the Fourth Republic and the Accession
       of de Gaulle 145

The SFIO and the New Constitution 148
Qualified Participation or Constructive
  Opposition? 152
The SFIO in Opposition 159
Notes 164

Part 3
Toward Revitalization

7. In Quest of Realignment and Redefinition 169

Looking for Allies 169
The Abortive Candidacy of Defferre 176
The SFIO and the Federation of the Left 182
Opening to the Left 190
The "May Events" and Their Aftermath.............. 197
Toward a New Party and a New Leadership 202
Notes 204

8. The New Socialist Party: Its Problems and Prospects ..211

Two Constituent Congresses 211
The Epinay Congress: The New Shape of the Party ...217
The Common Program and the Revival of the
  Popular Front 221
The Problems of Senior Partnership 226
The *Embourgeoisement* of the *Parti socialiste*........ 231
The 1978 Parliamentary Elections and After 234
Notes 237

9. Comparisons and Perspectives 243

Notes 260

Selected Bibliography 265
Index 273

Preface

This work was begun a number of years ago. It evolved out of extended discussions between the coauthors, each of whom had met and talked with many French politicians and intellectuals in the course of numerous visits to France. We were fascinated by the tenacity with which many of them attempted to combine a "correct" analysis of society with an awareness of the basic conservatism of their compatriots, and to combine a concern about practical reforms for the benefit of the underprivileged with an interest in political power. Although our basic sympathy with the Socialist party is apparent in the pages that follow, we have been realistically critical of its leaders and their tactical maneuverings.

We owe a debt of gratitude to many friends, some of whom, alas, are no longer living. They have helped us by giving us insights, by furnishing us with information, and by questioning some of the statements appearing in the manuscript at its various stages. We wish to express our appreciation to Mme Marie Meller and Mme Françoise Praderie for their unstinting help in obtaining material. We want to thank Professor Vincent Beach and M. Jacques Soulier for their thorough critical reading of the entire manuscript. We recall with gratitude the late André Philip, Marius Moutet, and Raymond Mage.

We want to express our thanks to the Committee on University Scholarly Publications of the University of Colorado for its generous support. Last but not least, we must record our indebtedness to our wives, not only for their editorial help but also for their sympathetic understanding of the inevitable tribulations of coauthorship. In this context, George A. Codding, Jr., had primary responsibility for the Introduction and chapters 1, 2, 3, and 5; and William Safran for chapters 4, 6, 7, 8, and 9. Yet the work is truly a joint product, and we must jointly assume the blame for any errors of fact, omission, or interpretation.

G.A.C.
W.S.
Boulder, Colorado
May 1, 1978

Abbreviations

CAP	Comité administratif permanent
CERES	Centre d'études, de recherches et d'éducation socialistes
CFDT	Confédération française démocratique de travail
CFTC	Confédération française des travailleurs chrétiens
CGA	Confédération générale de l'agriculture
CGC	Confédération générale des cadres
CGT	Confédération générale du travail
CIR	Convention des institutions républicaines
CNO	Commission nationale ouvrière
COMISCO	Consultative Committee of the International Socialist Conference
EDC	European Defense Community
EEC	European Economic Community
FEN	Fédération d'éducation nationale
FGDS	Fédération de la gauche démocratique et socialiste
FLN	Front de la libération nationale
FO	Force ouvrière
FNSEA	Fédération nationale des syndicats d'exploitants agricoles
IFOP	Institut français d'opinion publique
MRG	Mouvement des radicaux de gauche
MRP	Mouvement républicain populaire
OAS	Organisation armée secrète

ORTF	Office de radiodiffusion-télévision françaises
PCF	Parti communiste français
PS	Parti socialiste
PSA	Parti socialiste autonome
PSU	Parti socialiste unifié
RDR	Rassemblement démocratique révolutionnaire
RPF	Rassemblement du peuple français
SFIO	Section française de l'Internationale ouvrière
SOFRES	Société française d'enquêtes par sondages
SPD	Social Democratic party (West Germany)
SUNFED	Special United Nations Fund for Economic Development
UCRG	Union des clubs pour le renouvellement de la gauche
UDF	Union pour la démocratie française
UDSR	Union démocratique et socialiste de la Résistance
UDT	Union démocratique de travail
UGCS	Union des groupes et des clubs socialistes
UNEF	Union nationale des étudiants de France
UNR	Union pour la nouvelle République
WEU	Western European Union

Introduction

This is the life story of a political party, the Socialist party of France. Under various names, the French Socialists have played a critical role in French political life for almost a century, beginning in the turbulent era of the 1890s. In 1920 the party was torn asunder when a majority of its members opted to join the Communist International. Reorganized as the SFIO (Section française de l'International ouvrière), the remaining Socialists were soon able to outpoll their Communist rivals and become one of the major parties in the kaleidoscopic multiparty political system that characterized the Third and Fourth French Republics. The names of its leaders in these crucial years—Jean Jaurès, Albert Thomas, Léon Blum, and Guy Mollet—were known throughout France and throughout the world.

Nevertheless, only ten years after the return of de Gaulle to save France from civil war over Algeria, the SFIO passed into history. The emergence of de Gaulle and his party, the Union for the New Republic (Union pour la nouvelle République—UNR), posed a problem that the SFIO and its leaders could not solve. As one of a number of political parties fairly similar in size, the SFIO was able to influence the events of the day. Confronted by a massive UNR and its dynamic leader, however, the SFIO was able neither to influence political events nor to attract enough strength to challenge the party in power. After a number of months of agonizing reappraisal, it was decided that only as part of a much larger grouping could the SFIO provide an opposition strong enough to compete with the UNR and its leader. With amazing determination, the Socialists reorganized themselves and modified much of the traditional doctrine in order to permit them to make alliances with previous ideological enemies, including the Communists. In the person of François Mitterrand the Socialists found an effective leader.

Under their new leader and new name, the Socialist party of France (Parti socialiste—PS), the Socialists have once more assumed a critical role in French political life. Having succeeded in making alliances, not always permanent, with the Communists on the left and with the elements of the center of the political spectrum, they have made several significant attempts to capture political power.

It is the aim of the authors to provide the reader with a case study of this political party from its inception to the present. Its strengths and weaknesses will be explored, as will be the reasons why it has remained a viable unit in the French political system for so many years. Because of the focal position of the Socialists among French political parties, the study should also furnish the reader with an insight into the major developments in French political life over the past several decades. Finally, it might also supply some clues to the tendency of socialist parties all over Europe to merge into larger units or to water down their ideology, attracting large numbers of voters but losing their traditional identity in the process.

This study contains nine chapters divided into three parts. The first part provides a historical overview of the highlights in the life of the French Socialist party from its origins to the beginning of the Fifth Republic and a more detailed analysis of the unique ideological and organizational apparatus of the party from which its strength flowed during these years. The second part is devoted to an analysis of the success with which the Socialists were able to apply their ideology and tactics to several important domestic and international issues that arose during the all-important Fourth Republic, both as members of the government and as an opposition party, and describes the uncertainties that characterized the SFIO's response to de Gaulle's return to power and the inauguration of a new, quasi-presidential republic. The third part presents the SFIO in temporary eclipse as it reexamined its ideological foundations, searched for allies to help revitalize its electoral base, and made a fundamental change in its leadership to reemerge as a dominant and dynamic political party to push determinedly toward capture of government power. In the final chapter, the authors present their conclusions, comparing the French Socialist party with other socialist parties in the postwar years, especially those of Britain and West Germany, and, to a lesser extent, with the Democratic party in the United States.

Part 1
Party Background

1
Historical Background

Few French political movements have had as impressive a heritage as socialism. The official Socialist party at the present time is only the latest of many socialist political movements dating back to the First International. If one looks carefully, one can find socialists long before the establishment of the International. As far back as the early nineteenth century, writers such as Babeuf, Saint-Simon, and Fourier were laying the foundations.

The Socialists are proud of their long tradition and the principles that have guided their political action over the years. This tradition gives the party a strong sense of continuity, as well as a sense of pride, and has provided it with many illustrious names that it can invoke at election time, names of men who have a strong appeal to Frenchmen of all classes.

However, such a tradition can have drawbacks as well as benefits. It can provide a false sense of security. If the party is not extremely careful, it can find itself acting not as the changing times demand, but as tradition dictates. This, in effect, was one of the major criticisms leveled at the French Socialist party, especially after World War II. Thus, to understand the unique beliefs, methods, and organization of the present Socialist party, we must examine the turbulent early history of French socialist thought and action.

Genesis

The French socialist movement from its earliest days was

closely tied to the International Working Men's Association—the First International. A group of French workers, along with their English counterparts, organized the International at Saint-Martin's Hall in London on September 28, 1864, and the French socialist movement was always its strongest single element. The temporary destruction of the French socialist and working-class movement in the disaster of the Commune was the primary cause of the decline and fall of the First International.[1]

The French trade unionists who participated in the meeting at Saint-Martin's Hall already had behind them a rich tradition of socialist thought. As the inheritors of the utopian socialism of Fourier and Saint-Simon and the primitive socialism of Babeuf, they believed in reason, progress, and the inherent goodness of human nature. With certain exceptions their main concern was with the evolution of a new society rather than the revolutionary overthrow of the old. They were truly children of the enlightenment.[2]

Soon after the establishment of the International, French Socialists began to drift toward one of two divergent groups. The more influential of the two in the years before the Commune was the Proudhonist group (later also called the Mutualists), the disciples of Pierre Joseph Proudhon. They dreamed of establishing a workers' society in which the complete freedom of the individual would be established, resulting ultimately in anarchy. In this society interest and unearned income would be abolished and products would be exchanged on the basis of labor content. Since such an ideal society was admittedly far in the future, the first task of the Proudhonists was to achieve immediate benefits for the worker through mutual aid societies, credit societies, and cooperatives.[3]

The Blanquists, followers of Louis Auguste Blanqui, saw the plight of the workers in a different light. The workingman was considered a tool of the privileged class because of his ignorance, an ignorance fostered by the Church, the army, and the capitalists. Workers' cooperatives and nonviolent methods would never be sufficient to break the grip of these three enemies. Consequently, it was necessary for a small determined elite to seize political power and establish an enlightened dictatorship, the primary task of which would be to educate the workingman and thereby

eliminate forever his subservience. The Blanquists were, therefore, the party of revolution and called for all types of open
resistance to authority.[4]

These two fundamentally different approaches to social
problems were the cause of a great deal of friction among the
French in the First International. The German members and, to a
lesser extent, the English, were unhappy about the fraternal strife
of the French. More than once the French were reproached for
"their unnecessary speeches, their violent discussions, their
'witches sabbath'."[5]

Under the leadership of the Proudhonists and like-minded
groups from other countries, the International followed a
moderate program during its first four years. Resolutions were
passed advocating universal education, shorter working hours,
improved working conditions, regulation of labor for women and
children, and the establishment of workers' cooperatives. The
International grew steadily in membership and its activities were
tolerated, within limits, by the governments in power.

The Brussels Congress of the International, held in 1868,
marked a turning point. A group under the banner of Marxian
collectivism gained the upper hand. Resolutions were passed
advocating the nationalization of both industry and agriculture,
an action abhorrent to the liberty-loving Proudhonists. In France
the government of Napoleon III ordered the dissolution of the
International and arrested many of its leaders.

Organized socialism in France was finally extinguished by the
Franco-Prussian War and the debacle of the Commune. Although
the sanguinary story of the Commune itself will not be described
here, it is necessary to point out that the Blanquists and
Proudhonists participated in it side by side and shared the bitter
fruit of its failure.

Without the French the International managed to struggle
along for a few more years, but its days were numbered. A series of
squabbles broke out among the remaining factions. British
elements became frightened by the French experiment of the
Commune and demanded a less unitary organization. The
Bakunin anarchists, an important group, were excluded for their
revolutionary ideas. After several more years of pointless activity,
the First International was officially dissolved in 1877.[6]

For years after the Commune, true socialism did not exist as an important political force in France. Most of the socialist leaders had been killed, imprisoned or sent to penal colonies, or had fled to other countries. Those who remained felt that the bloodshed and suffering they had recently experienced had failed to improve in the least the material state of the worker. They agreed to concentrate on peaceful, nonpolitical agitation for increased wages and for the creation of producers' cooperatives. The word *socialism* was shunned and no voice was raised against repressive measures enacted by the government. As late as 1876, a meeting of French workers proclaimed that better working conditions could only be achieved through cooperation between the employer and the worker. Political action was completely ignored. Even the most conservative newspapers of the time were lavish in their praise of the "wisdom" of the French workingman.[7]

The odd phenomenon of apolitical socialism could not, of course, be expected to last indefinitely. Dynamic socialist doctrine was heard again at a national labor congress held in Marseilles in 1879. For the first time since the Commune, Socialists were able to speak their minds in an open meeting. Not only were they again vocal, but the voice was that of revolutionary Marxism. The Marxists, who had been steadily gaining ground in Europe outside of France, were able to obtain the backing of an enormous majority of the delegates for a program of (1) collectivization of the means of production, (2) revolutionary action, and (3) the formation of a workers' party.[8]

The workers' party founded at the Marseilles Congress, the Parti ouvrier, was the first French political party to claim to represent the proletariat as a class. Essentially a revolutionary Marxist party, it was based on a constitution written by Jules Guesde and Paul Lafargue in collaboration with Marx and Engels.[9]

The Parti ouvrier was not to remain the sole voice of socialism in France, however. Soon after the Marseilles Congress, the government rescinded the laws exiling the Blanquists, and the repatriates established their own party, the Comité révolutionnaire central. The amoeba-like Blanquist party then split in 1882, and a new party, the Parti socialiste révolutionnaire, emerged under the leadership of Edouard Vaillant. Similarly, the Parti ouvrier fell prey to doctrinal splits. Dissatisfied with the revolutionary trend of the party, a group under the leadership of Paul Brousse broke away in the same year to form the Fédération des travailleurs socialistes. This new party, also called Possibilists, was willing, as the Parti ouvrier was not, to collaborate with the government if such action would improve the living standard of the French workingman.

The dizzy doctrinal and methodological conflicts continued apace, and by 1899 the following socialist political parties were contending for the favor of the worker:[10]

Le Parti ouvrier français (Guesdists)
Le Comité révolutionnaire central
La Fédération des travailleurs socialistes (Broussists)
Le Parti ouvrier socialiste révolutionnaire (Allemanists)
L'Alliance communiste révolutionnaire
Les Indépendants

A countermovement toward reunification of all socialist parties was temporarily thwarted by an important doctrinal schism on the question of socialist participation in a bourgeois ministry. The question was posed in 1899 when Waldeck-Rousseau formed a Radical government for the avowed purpose of defending the Republic against the division caused by the Dreyfus affair and invited Alexandre Millerand, a leading member of Les Indépendants, to participate in his ministry. The acceptance of Millerand marked the first time a Socialist had entered a cabinet of any country, except for the short period of service of Louis Blanc during the Second Republic. Although Millerand defended participation as necessary to safeguard the Republic in its hour of danger, it brought about a series of heated discussions among the Socialists. In July, 1901, the Parti ouvrier, the Parti socialiste révolutionnaire, and dissidents of the Alliance communiste issued a joint manifesto completely hostile to collaboration. This faction, known as the Parti socialiste de France, was soon opposed by another group of Socialists known as the Parti socialiste français, which openly supported the Republican ministries of both Waldeck-Rousseau and Combes.

Before going on to consider the successful unification of the two factions under the influence of the revived International, one must deal with another significant development. Although the era of the creation of socialist parties coincided more or less with that of the creation of the trade union movement, the French Socialists were never able to turn the trade union organizations into subordinate allies.[11] This phenomenon had four interrelated causes. First, the French government placed important legal restrictions on trade union participation in politics. Second, the First International had been based on individual, rather than group, membership and considered itself to be the inspired leader of the mass workers' movement rather than just one of its parts. Third, when the trade union movement was created, the French Socialists were divided into a number of contending groups. Finally, there was a powerful anarchist-Proudhonist tendency in the trade union movement that resulted in a declaration by the largest of the trade unions, the Confédération générale du travail (CGT), that it was permanently opposed to all political alliances. As a result, although the French Socialists often influenced, and sometimes inspired, the trade unionists, the two complementary movements developed side by side essentially independent of each other.[12] This separation proved to be a grave weakness for the French Socialists. In Britain, where the Socialists dominated the trade unions, and in Germany, where the Socialists and trade unions were allied, the cooperation of the two groups provided a source of strength.

Unification

The disunity and resultant weakness of the Socialists in France was glaringly obvious to other European Socialists, who soon put pressure on their French comrades to stop squabbling. At the Amsterdam Congress of the Second International in 1904 (the International had been reorganized in 1899), several major leaders of the European socialist movement, including Adler of Austria, Bebel and Kautsky of Germany, Ferri of Italy, and Troelstra of Holland, introduced this resolution aimed at the French: "The Congress declares that, in order to provide the working class with all possible strength in the fight against capitalism, it is indispensable that in all countries . . . there should be only one socialist party just as there is only one proletariat."[13] It was consequently the duty of all Socialists to use all their power to achieve unity. The resolution was almost unanimously approved. Vaillant, in the name of the Parti socialiste de France, and Jean Jaurès, in the name of the Parti socialiste français, accepted the verdict and themselves signed the resolution.

The following April at the Salle du Globe in Paris, the French Socialists hammered out a unification agreement that created a single French Socialist party, the Parti socialiste unifié (PSU). This meeting also created the party organization that remains the basic structure of the French Socialist party to this day.[14]

Jean Jaurès (1859-1914) assumed the leadership of the newly unified party. From the unification in 1905 to his assassination in July, 1914, Jean Jaurès was the undisputed chief of the PSU and was largely responsible for creating and maintaining its effective cohesion. In the words of Daniel Halévy:

> Ce parti qu'était-ce donc? Je le définirai d'un mot, c'était l'oeuvre de Jaurès, et son reflet. C'est lui qui l'a créé et qui l'a soutenu. Il est mort, le parti se défait.[15]

Under the leadership of Jaurès, the PSU had become an influential element in French political life. The number of dues-paying individuals jumped from 35,000 in 1905 to 90,000 by his death in 1914. The influence of the party was even more apparent in the votes that were cast for its candidates. The year after its formation the party polled 830,000 votes. In 1914 it polled 1,400,000, and its representation in parliament rose to the imposing figure of 103. The period under the leadership of Jaurès was one of unparalleled expansion for the Unified Socialist party.[16]

The waters were not completely calmed by unification, however. Debates, sometimes quite heated ones, occurred over such problems as the policy toward nationalization, the relationship of the party to the trade union movement, the proper amount of cooperation between the party and bourgeois republican governments, and the use of the general strike as a means of pressuring the government. For example, at the Congress of Nîmes in 1910 the Socialists split over a bill to establish workers' pensions proposed by Minister of Labor René Viviani. Jaurès supported the law, despite its obvious imperfections, because he saw in it the beginning of a much larger system of social insurance; it was at least a step in the right direction. The more orthodox Guesde, on the other hand, condemned the proposal because it was based on the capitalist system and because the salary deduction it entailed would, in his view, be simply another form of theft, this time performed by the government rather than by the employer. Finally, with great difficulty a common approach was found. And in fact none of the doctrinal splits that occurred during the leadership of Jaurès seriously threatened the newly found unity of the Socialist party.

As tensions in Europe mounted during the second decade of the twentieth century, more and more of the party's time was devoted to defining socialism's duty to prevent war or, if war should occur, the proper socialist attitude toward it. During the five years immediately preceding World War I, the French Socialists consistently denounced war as an instrument of national policy. At the last prewar party congress in 1914, the clamor for adopting a policy of a general strike in the event of war became so great that even such moderates as Jaurès felt compelled to acquiesce. Until July, 1914, the French Socialists were in complete accord with the Second International's opposition to war.

The situation changed completely in less than a week's time. On July 31, 1914, Jaurès was assassinated in a Paris café by a young nationalist fanatic; Germany declared war on France on August 3; and on August 4 the Chamber of Deputies voted unanimously, with the Socialists concurring, on the necessary war measures. The French Socialists were solidly in agreement that the Germans were to blame for the outbreak of war, and they willingly joined the government under the banner of the *Union sacrée* to fight for the defense of the *patrie*.[17]

World War I and Its Aftermath

The first years of World War I found the French Socialists abandoning many sacred doctrinal positions. Cries of revolution, uttered at prewar national and international congresses, gave way to appeals for governmental support. Suspension of certain liberties was defended. Prominent Socialists, such as Guesde, Marcel Sembat, and Albert Thomas, forgot earlier scruples and accepted important ministerial positions in bourgeois governments. Indeed, the great majority both of the leadership and the rank and file of the party dutifully accepted the discipline imposed by the exigencies of the times.

As the war continued beyond its first years, however, opposition to it gradually developed among French and European Socialists alike. In September, 1915, a rump conference of European Socialists was held in Zimmerwald, Switzerland. Although the French, German, and Swiss Socialists were not officially represented, a declaration was issued stating that World War I was not a workers' war and called for a cessation of hostilities. Opposition also began to materialize within the party between the prowar *majoritaires,* headed by Pierre Renaudel and Albert Thomas, and the antiwar *minoritaires,* whose chief spokesman was Marx's grandson, Jean Longuet. At a National Congress in Paris in December, 1915, a manifesto was issued calling for party unity and condemning any actions that would weaken the national war effort. The manifesto received an overwhelming 2,759 affirmative votes, but 72 delegates opposed it and 92 abstained. In April, 1916, a motion declaring that conditions necessary for a revived International had not yet materialized was opposed by 960 members of the congress. Those who felt that Socialists should no longer aid in the war effort continued to gain, and by December, 1916, they were almost equal in strength to those who still supported the nation's war effort.[18]

A new element was inserted in 1917 when the French Socialists were confronted with their first genuine case of revolutionary socialism: the Bolshevik revolution in Russia. The *minoritaires,* in addition to condemning the *majoritaires* for collaborating in the war effort, became the fervent champions of the Russian Revolution. Under the new red banner the minority was able to turn the tables in a meeting of the National Congress in Paris in October, 1918. They introduced a resolution declaring that only through the International could socialism be established, condemning all collaboration with bourgeois governments, proclaiming that the party was ready to reply to any convocation of a congress of the International, and stigmatizing the action of France and her allies against the revolution in Russia. The resolution passed by 1,528 votes to 1,212 (a centrist motion received 181 votes). As was the custom, the spokesmen of the ex-minority took over the important party positions. Marcel Cachin replaced Renaudel as party spokesman and L. O. Frossard became the secretary-general of the party. Both of these men were to lead the movement that ultimately culminated in the formation of the French Communist party.[19]

Two other situations contributed to the downfall of the old party majority. First, the assassination of Jaurès in 1914 and the death of Vaillant in 1915 left the party without the dynamic leadership that it needed in such a trying period; not until late 1919 did Léon Blum emerge as a strong and effective party leader. Second, the PSU had lost some of its contact with the problems of the workers. Wartime shortages, inflation, large-scale introduction of women into industry, and the changing nature of industrial production all influenced the attitude of the French workers. They wanted a positive platform and dynamic leadership; the Socialist party could offer neither.

Tours and After

Although the news of the successful Communist revolution in Russia was received with unrestrained joy by the French Socialists, they were soon forced into a position regarding Russian leadership in the socialist movement that precipitated the great Schism of Tours. The Second International having fallen into almost complete disuse during World War I, the Russian Communists, soon after the October Revolution, came up with the idea of establishing a new, strong, central socialist organization, the Communist International. At the first Comintern convention in Moscow in March, 1919, the Russians decided to exert pressure on the socialist parties of the world to join. The dominant problem of the French Socialists during 1919 and 1920, therefore, became whether to join the Comintern or to help revive the Socialist International.

The question of adherence to the Comintern was presented to the party congress that met in Strasbourg in February, 1920. The

Strasbourg meeting was divided roughly into three sections. A very small group wished to reestablish the Second International. A larger group, but still a minority, wanted to go along with Moscow without delay and without conditions. The majority of the participants, lacking any effective leadership, vacillated between these groups. A motion to leave the Second International was adopted by 4,330 to 337, but the succeeding motion to join the Comintern was backed by only 1,621. A third motion, garnering a respectable majority of 3,031 votes, proclaimed agreement on principle with the Comintern, but called for the formation of a new International in which all socialist parties, including the Russian, should participate.[20]

Although temporarily thwarted, the partisans of the Comintern were not defeated. They launched a propaganda campaign to bring the important French Socialist party into the Communist International. In March the PSU's Administrative Commission sent Marcel Cachin and L. O. Frossard to Moscow to get first-hand information on the Comintern. In June the National Council of the PSU authorized the two envoys, at their request, to remain in Moscow to attend the Second Congress of the Comintern as observers. During this Moscow meeting, the Comintern drew up its famous Twenty-one Conditions for admission.

The Twenty-one Conditions exemplified the spirit of the new organization. In general the document was divided into three parts. First, it established a highly centralized organization. Strict allegiance to the executive committee of the Comintern was required, as well as subordination of parliament members to the central organs. Second, it initiated a new, intensified program to obtain the dictatorship of the proletariat in all countries. Renewed agitation was called for in the army, among the farmers, in labor organizations and cooperatives. Both clandestine and legal action in all fields was demanded. Third, and the most important as far as the future of the French Socialist party was concerned, all reformist and centrist activities were to cease. Reformists and centrists were to be excluded from all posts of responsibility, and all cooperation with bourgeois governments was to end. Any who found fault with these conditions were to be excluded.[21]

In September, 1920, after the French delegates returned from Moscow, the PSU convened in Tours to make its decision. The discussions at Tours were arduous and turbulent. Those who wished to accept the Comintern conditions were violently attacked by the reformists, some center groups, and many of the legislators, but when the motion finally came to a vote, the delegates agreed to the Twenty-one Conditions by a three-to-one majority. The decision did not cause an immediate split, however, since many still felt that party solidarity could somehow be preserved. The controversial Zinoviev telegram finally brought matters to a head. The telegram, sent from the Comintern headquarters in Moscow, congratulated the party but stipulated in unambiguous terms that "the International can have nothing in common with the members of the center."[22] This message, as far as the minority was concerned, added insult to injury. Unable to carry a motion denouncing the telegram and calling for the solidarity of the party, the minority factions, including most members of parliament, left the congress. The unity that had been achieved with such difficulty in 1905 thus came to an end.

The defeated minority of the French Socialists reorganized themselves under the name Section française de l'Internationale ouvrière (SFIO), reaffirmed their faith in the 1905 charter, and, after some hesitation, joined the recently revived Second International. Of the 180,000 effectives that had gone to the party conference at Tours, the SFIO came away with a mere 30,000. Under the leadership of Léon Blum, however, the SFIO began a hard-fought campaign to rebuild its strength. SFIO membership increased to 72,000 by 1924, and surpassed 100,000 the following year. The resurgence of the SFIO brought gains in popular votes and in National Assembly seats. In the 1928 elections the Socialists received 1,700,000 votes and 104 seats in parliament. In 1932 over 2 million ballots were cast for the SFIO, winning them 112 seats in parliament. Within a very few years the Socialists had overtaken and outclassed the Communists.[23]

Throughout the twenties, two major problems confronted the party: participation in bourgeois governments and collaboration with the Communists. The latter temptation was resisted. Despite many overtures, the SFIO persistently refused to associate with the Parti communiste français (PCF).[24] Even when Blum cooperated with the Radicals against the National Bloc in 1924, the party remained firm. The SFIO did not contemplate collaboration until the Groupement des gauches of 1934, just before the Popular Front, and this move was made only because the Socialists believed democratic government to be endangered by fascism.

The problem of participation in bourgeois governments plagued Socialist leaders continually, for "the champions of collaboration are never disarmed."[25] Although the party cooperated with the Radicals at various times, it maintained its independence. At a 1926 congress at Clermont-Ferrand, for example, the party acknowledged the vote of confidence given the Briand cabinet following the Locarno Pact but insisted that refusal to participate is the supreme law and governmental support does not exclude strict independence. This attitude soon caused the factions to the right that had remained faithful to the party in 1920 to become restive. By 1932 the position of the "Participationists," also called Neo-Socialists, became untenable. They felt that the time had come to abandon some basic socialist doctrines in favor of a nationalist policy including collaboration with bourgeois parties and the approval of military credits. After reproaching the majority for maintaining a sterile and passive attitude and denouncing its *immobilisme,* the Neo-Socialists withdrew from the party to form their own independent party. The Neo-Socialists took with them some 20,000 members and 35 members of parliament.[26] In 1933 the French Socialist party found itself at last free of its extreme left and right factions, and ready to face the future with a single voice.

The Popular Front and World War II

The rise of fascism in France before World War II forced the Socialists into a short period of renewed cooperation with the Communists and gave the SFIO a brief term in power. Fascist riots broke out in Paris on the sixth of February, 1934. There was shooting in the Place de la Concorde and an assault was made on the Chamber of Deputies across the Seine. Reaction was immediate. Labor unions and all of the parties of the Left called for popular demonstrations against the Fascists. On the twelfth, over a million workers in the Paris area alone went out on a general strike called by the Confédération générale du travail, the Socialists, and the Communists. The peril from the extreme Right caused the parties of the Left to think in terms of unified action.

A unity pact was signed by the Socialists and Communists in July, 1934, which developed by the following year into the Popular Front of Socialists, Radicals, Communists, and Republican and Independent Socialists. The Popular Front presented a united program for the 1936 election calling for dissolution of Fascist leagues, greater freedom for labor unions, nationalization of war industries, regulation of corporations, reform of the Bank of France, tax reforms, and armament reduction. The Popular Front elected an overwhelming majority of members to parliament; the Socialists 148, the Radicals 109, the Communists 72, and the Republican and Independent Socialists 29. Veteran Socialist Léon Blum was called to form a cabinet.[27]

During the years under Socialist leadership, social reforms not unlike the early legislation of the New Deal in the United States were promulgated. Laws were passed providing for such advances as paid holidays, pay increases, the forty-hour week, and legalization of collective bargaining, but as welcome as they were, many of these social reforms were not fully implemented. Moreover, they were not enough to stop the rise of Hitler or the coming of World War II. As a noted observer of the French political scene stated: "Perhaps the final tragedy of the Third Republic is best symbolized in the cruel dilemma of Léon Blum who, backed by an apparently overwhelming majority, attempted to effect the long overdue social program just at a point at which the country's greater need was not reduction of working hours but an increase in plane production."[28]

In the confused days following the fall of the Socialist ministry in 1938, the Socialists, unlike their Communist comrades who had already gone underground, again faced the problem of positive action in the face of a German threat. The Socialists participated in the wartime cabinets of Daladier in 1939 and Reynaud in 1940. When the National Assembly was asked to grant full powers to Marshal Pétain in 1940, the Socialists provided nearly half of the votes cast against the marshal, but three-quarters of the Socialist members of parliament either voted in his favor or abstained.[29]

Marshal Pétain's assumption of power marked the beginning of a period of political persecution and clandestine activity for the French Socialists. After the arrest of Léon Blum by the Nazis and his famous trial by a collaborationist kangaroo court, the party went underground. From 1941 until the end of the war, the Socialists maintained a clandestine Executive Committee under the direction of Daniel Mayer and Henri Ribière to coordinate Socialist activities in the French resistance. Other representatives of the Socialist party regrouped in London, followed General de Gaulle's provisional government to Algiers, and finally returned to Paris in 1944.[30]

The Fourth Republic and *Tripartisme* (1945-1947)

Even before the last of the Nazi troops were driven from French soil, the Socialists had already begun an energetic and purposeful attack on the difficult tasks of party reconstruction and preparation for peace-time political activity. Despite the fact that many Socialists had voted to give power to the Vichy government, the gallant roles played in the Resistance by many Socialist leaders and the courageous stand of Léon Blum at his trial in a Pétainist court helped the SFIO to eradicate much of the odor of collaboration. The party fully eliminated the last traces of shame when it mercilessly purged all of those who had in any way collaborated with the Vichy regime.[31]

Many felt that socialism's day in France was not far off when the reorganized Socialist party won 150 seats in the First Constituent Assembly by polling about 4½ million votes in the first postwar general election in October 1945. But despite this electoral success and its party membership's reaching an all-time high of 335,705 in the same year, the SFIO was not the largest party in France— the Mouvement républicain populaire (MRP) tied the Socialists in winning seats while the PCF; obtained a healthy 161. The SFIO was very influential, however, seated in its tactically advantageous position between the MRP and the PCF.

The SFIO was thus able to play an important role in the confused days leading to the establishment of the Fourth

Republic. The Socialists firmly supported the provisional regime of General de Gaulle and backed his successful plan to create a Constituent Assembly with limited powers. The Socialists also held five ministerial posts in de Gaulle's short-lived de facto government of November, 1945, to January, 1946.

When de Gaulle discarded his executive power in January, 1946, the SFIO took over the reins of government for the duration of the First Constituent Assembly. Félix Gouin was elected to replace de Gaulle with the support of both the Communists and the Catholic MRP. His cabinet, made up exclusively of Socialists, Communists, and members of the MRP, marked the beginning of the period of *tripartisme.*

The first task of the Gouin government was to draft a new constitution for France. On the issue of the form of government, the Socialists found themselves supported almost exclusively by the Communists, an alliance feared by the draft's opponents as giving too much strength to the Communists. The people rejected the first draft in a referendum and voiced their opposition again in the June elections for the Second Constituent Assembly, where the SFIO lost more popular votes than any other party.

As a result of the elections the MRP became the largest party in the Second Constituent Assembly and was chosen to lead the government. The Socialists were given six ministerial posts and the Communists seven. A second draft constitution, incorporating a great many concessions to the opponents of the first, was adopted by the Assembly over Communist opposition. The Socialists attempted to recapture popular confidence by supporting the new draft and attacked the Communists for their intransigent views. The new constitution was approved by the voters on October 13, 1946, in spite of the personal opposition of de Gaulle.

General elections were immediately called to choose the National Assembly that was to remain in power until 1951. Despite their revised position the Socialists were again the principal losers. From the all-time high of 4½ million votes in October, 1945, popular support in November, 1946, fell to a little less than 3½ million. The Socialists remained the third largest party in the Assembly, with 105 seats, but their prestige and confidence were shaken.

The Socialists were becoming increasingly unhappy with *tripartisme*. Their electoral losses seemed to be the result of their identification with the Communists in the fight for the first draft constitution or their subsequent concessions to the MRP, or both. At the party congress held at Lyons just before the August elections, the SFIO issued a statement declaring that the subjugation of the PCF to the Russian state made alliance with the Communists impossible.[32] Notably, however, that same congress saw the defeat of the humanist leadership within the party by the election of Guy Mollet, then a strict Marxist, as party secretary.

Despite SFIO losses of Assembly seats and popular support, the veteran Socialist Léon Blum was elected the first premier of the Fourth Republic. Blum was elected because of increased antagonism between the Communists and the MRP rather than because of any special confidence in the weakest of the three partners in *tripartisme*. All of the ministers in the Blum cabinet were also Socialists, since the new government would in principle remain in power only until the election of the new president of the Republic, and since the MRP could not agree to the Communist demands for ministerial posts. Although the Blum government lasted only one month, it is interesting to note that, according to a 1947 public opinion poll, 62 percent of the people considered it the most successful government since the Liberation.[33]

Another Socialist success was the election of the Socialist candidate Vincent Auriol, a veteran of the prewar Popular Front, as the first president of the Fourth Republic. Another Socialist, Paul Ramadier, became premier with the backing of both Communists and the MRP. The Ramadier government, made up of ministers from the *tripartisme* parties, with the addition of five members of the Rassemblement démocratique révolutionnaire (RDR) and two Moderates, prepared to grapple with the mounting problems of postwar France.

During the ten months of the Ramadier government, France saw the final dissolution of the *tripartisme* formula and, in the opinion of the Socialists, the rise of a new threat to democratic government, General Charles de Gaulle's Rassemblement du peuple français (RPF). The split with the Communists came in May, 1947, over the question of wage stabilization, a policy inaugurated by Blum to which the Ramadier government was pledged. After the Communists voted against a confidence motion approving the government's policy of wage stabilization, Ramadier ousted the Communist ministers from his cabinet.[34] The next day the Socialist National Council upheld Ramadier's decision by a vote of 2,592 to 2,125. The expulsion destroyed *tripartisme* and ended for a time active Socialist cooperation with the Communists.

The Socialists in and out of Government (1947-1955)

Disturbingly for France and the friends of France, even the most delicately coddled and carefully nurtured majority was not able to survive the insalubrious climate of the Fourth Republic for more than a few halting months. After the downfall of *tripartisme*, the Socialists were particularly disturbed by the constant and persistent drift to the right as government replaced brief government. Consequently, the Socialists supported centrist governments against the menaces of the Gaullist Right as well as the Communist Left. For five years the SFIO participated in almost all governments, making increased concessions and sacrificing more significant socialist objectives as the governments became more and more oriented to the right. But by the election of 1951, as we shall see, the movement to the right had gone further than the Socialists were able to tolerate, and the SFIO became a nonparticipant in the government from 1951 to 1956.

The Ramadier government continued in power for a time after the expulsion of the Communists in 1947, leading the more optimistic to foresee greater permanence in the Fourth Republic coalitions than in those of the Third. This illusion did not last. When the Ramadier government fell, it was due not only to the discord in the coalition over domestic problems, but also to a lack of support from his own party. While Ramadier was manfully trying to hold his government together, Guy Mollet and others made a public appeal for the formation of a new Third Force under the banner of Léon Blum. Mollet felt that "Blum offers the last remaining chance to save democracy in France and doubtless also the peace of this corner of Europe, since a civil war, which is certainly threatened, probably would become international like that in Spain."[35] This attitude from his own party secretary forced Ramadier to hand in his resignation.

This tactic failed, however, as Blum, opposed by the Communists and the Gaullists, failed to obtain a majority, and Robert Schuman of the MRP formed a cabinet on November 24, 1947, giving the Socialists five ministerial posts. The new socialist minister of the interior, Jules Moch, took on the painful task of putting down Communist-led strikes that soon became widespread throughout France. He did his job vigorously, not hesitating to use troops to prevent sabotage and violence. On December 9, realizing that they had failed to bring about the collapse of the government, the Communists called off the strikes. The Socialists supported Moch in the conviction that the Communists had declared war on the French Republic and therefore had made such drastic action necessary, but many strongly suspected that this action would lose them working-class votes.

The Socialists continued to support the Schuman government throughout the winter of 1947-48 and the spring of 1948, despite their objections to the government's policies on nationalization, lay education, and the position of France in the cold war. What finally caused them to break with the government in July, 1948, was the issue of the size of the military budget, and without Socialist support, Schuman was defeated by a vote of 297 to 214.[36]

In the three-year period from the fall of the Schuman cabinet to the general elections in the summer of 1951, France had seven heads of government. The Socialists participated in most of these cabinets and on two different occasions provided unsuccessful candidates for the position of premier. Justifying their participation on the ground that they were primarily interested in saving the Republic from the extreme Left and the extreme Right but, unenthusiastic about the legislative policies of the coalitions, the Socialists were uneasy partners. As stated in a resolution passed by the Forty-first National Congress held in Paris in 1949:

> The Socialist party desired, in the first place, to save the Republic from the two dangers that menaced it. On this point it has been successful.

Neither the Stalinists nor the Gaullists have obtained their objective. On the one hand, the Communist party has not been able to paralyze the French economy. . . . On the other hand, the difficulties occurring with the RPF are evidence of its decline.[37]

But the Socialists were not silent partners. They demanded concessions to their policies, especially on the question of living conditions of the workers. Several times, when they knew it could be done without a subsequent shift in political power to the right, the SFIO brought down cabinets that refused to give due consideration to social reform. For instance the SFIO was instrumental in the downfall of Queuille, whose tenure as premier was the longest of this period, when his cabinet rejected a plan by Daniel Mayer, Socialist minister of labor, to grant a round of wage increases. On June 24, 1950, the Bidault cabinet fell when the Socialists suddenly withdrew their support. Guy Mollet declared, "It must be recognized that there is no majority in this assembly unless it takes into account the social claims we have been setting forth."[38]

When the time for new elections to the National Assembly came in 1951, the SFIO was in a state of confusion. Although Jules Moch, as minister of defense, had withstood a Communist-led impeachment attempt on November 30, 1950, over the 1949 "affair of the generals," Socialists were afraid that some of the electorate had been influenced by the charges. Perhaps the greatest blow occurred with the death of Léon Blum on March 30, 1950. With him the party lost its most able, experienced, and popular member of parliament. In addition the party was coming to the conclusion that, as the junior partner in coalition governments more and more oriented toward the right, they were losing both influence and prestige. Although the participation of the Socialists in coalitions had successfully defended the Republic against the Gaullists and Stalinists, the party had been able to implement very few of its social and economic reforms. "It has been proven too often," reads a resolution of the party's Extraordinary National Congress of December, 1949, "that of all the parties in the coalition government, the SFIO is the one that has made the greatest sacrifices to the common cause."[39]

In 1951 a new electoral law was passed that the parties of the

Center, including the Socialists, hoped would weaken the Communists without at the same time strengthening de Gaulle's dangerous RPF. Most importantly, this resulting "bastard proportional representation system" provided for *apparentement* and a majority-take-all rule. Anywhere outside of the Paris region, parties were permitted to form an *apparentement,* or alliance. Any alliance winning an absolute majority of the votes cast would take every seat. Proportional representation would then be used to distribute the votes within the alliances and when an absolute majority was not obtained.[40]

As a result of the new law, the Socialists were able to gain a few Assembly seats in the elections of June 17, 1951, despite a loss of more than 700,000 popular votes. The Communists, however, lost only about half as many popular votes as the Socialists but were reduced from 183 to 101 seats in the Assembly. As for the Gaullists, nothing could stand in the way of their popular success; they gained over 4 million votes, but the electoral law did some of its duty and held them down to 120 seats in the Assembly.

Seeing a definite swing toward the parties of the Right, and aware that future coalitions would of necessity lean more heavily upon such parties, the Socialists decided that their principles would be better served if they remained outside the government and so assumed the role of critical opposition. In the four years that followed, the SFIO was not represented in any ministry and, with one major exception, remained in opposition.

During the administrations of the first two postelection premiers, the SFIO was preoccupied with the task of defining its objectives as an opposition party. Although the Socialists voted for the investiture of René Pleven (Union démocratique et social-iste de la Résistance) as premier in August, 1951, they refused to accept any ministerial posts in his government. On many major issues, such as the November vote of confidence on Pleven's foreign policy, they abstained from voting rather than take a definite stand. Two months later, however, the Socialists joined in opposition—with the Gaullists and the Communists—to bring down the Pleven government on a question involving minor changes in the social security system. Evidences of a lack of firm policy were also apparent in the Socialist treatment of the second premier, Edgar Faure (Radical). After voting for Faure, the

Socialists voted against approval of his cabinet. They supported Faure's conciliatory policy on nationalist outbreaks in Tunisia and voted for his attempt to establish the European Defense Community (EDC) on the condition that German forces would be excluded until the pact was ratified by all the other European governments. But they helped precipitate the fall of the Faure government in February, 1952, on the question of raising taxes to pay for augmentation of the defense program.

By the advent of the third postelection premier, Antoine Pinay (Independent), the policies of the SFIO had become fairly clear. The SFIO would be opposed to any attempts to decrease the postwar government control over the economy, to any action that would lower, even temporarily, the standards of living of the workers, and to any attempt to appropriate funds for Church-controlled educational institutions. On the other hand, the SFIO would back all measures to grant more autonomy to members of the French Union (colonies in the Orient and in North Africa) and would support the European Defense Community. As far as cooperation with other political parties was concerned, the SFIO made it clear that it wanted nothing to do with the Bolsheviks or the Gaullists, and in a resolution of the National Council denounced the "hypocrisy of the Gaullist group in declaring that they are ready to participate in a government, when their leader has frequently taken antirepublican attitudes."[41]

This period also saw the alienation of the Socialists and the Mouvement républicain populaire. As long as the Socialists felt that the concept of secular schools was in no danger, it was possible to maintain a certain degree of cooperation with the Catholic MRP. With the adoption in September, 1951, of the Barangé Law to subsidize Catholic schools, the situation was changed. The agitation of the SFIO to amend the Barangé Law and to prevent any more concessions to Catholic schools erected a substantial barrier between the two parties which precluded any cooperation for some time.

Although the SFIO voted against Antoine Pinay and abstained from voting on his right-of-center cabinet, the new government was approved 290 to 101. As the Pinay government's tenure continued throughout the summer and fall of 1952, the SFIO became increasingly active. On November 16, the Socialist

National Council approved a motion condemning the "reactionary trend" of the Pinay government and attacking most of its
program.[42] However, the Socialists did agree with Pinay's strong
measures against the French Communists, including the arrest of
their leader, Jacques Duclos. According to the *Comité directeur*
(Executive Committee), parliamentary immunity did not mean
that members could act with irresponsibility and impunity
toward the laws of the Republic, for "no man can pretend to be
above the law."[43] The Socialists did not go so far as to advocate
outlawing the French Communist party, however. That would be
undemocratic and "a great gift" to the Communists.[44]

The resignation of Pinay on December 23, 1952, precipitated a
long and disheartening ministerial crisis. René Mayer (Radical)
formed a center-right cabinet in January, 1953—with the
Socialists, Communists, and Gaullists in opposition—that lasted
only four months. In quick succession four more men—Reynaud
(Conservative), Mendès-France (Radical), Bidault (MRP), and
Marie (Radical)—also failed to form acceptable cabinets. In the
case of Reynaud, it was suggested that he be given the power to
dissolve the Assembly if his cabinet were not approved. The
Socialist floor leader, Charles Lussy, blocked that move by a
statement denying support to any premier who wanted to
threaten the Assembly with dissolution as a means of forcing
through legislation. Likewise, the socialists were instrumental in
preventing Bidault and Marie from forming cabinets.

Finally, on June 26, Joseph Laniel was voted in as premier,
despite Socialist opposition, by a vote of 398 to 206. During the
Laniel regime one of the more important issues was the
paralyzing general strike of August-September, 1953. The strike
had not been organized by any union or political group but was
an almost spontaneous nationwide protest against the general
economic conditions prevailing in France. The Socialists, led by
Jules Moch, were opposed to the strike but could not afford to
appear completely unsympathetic to a demonstration in which so
many of the working class were participating. Therefore, on
October 9, 1953, they introduced a motion in the National
Assembly to censure the government's handling of the strike. The
Laniel government was shaken but had too much support from
the Right to be overthrown.[45]

The opposition role of the SFIO was reversed with dramatic suddenness when the Radical Pierre Mèndes-France replaced Laniel as premier on June 17, 1954. Whereas the Socialists had voted consistently against Laniel's legislation, they voted consistently in favor of Mèndes-France during his seven months in power. Moreover, Mèndes-France offered the SFIO six cabinet posts, including defense, commerce, and the merchant marine. The Socialists agreed to participate in the Mendès-France cabinet on the proviso that the premier agree to certain economic and political principles that the Socialists considered the necessary minimum. The question was still pending when the Mendès-France government fell on November 30, 1955, wholeheartedly supported by the SFIO to the end.

The new premier, Edgar Faure (Radical) also invited the Socialists to participate in his government but was refused. With certain exceptions, such as the programs concerning North Africa, the SFIO found in Edgar Faure another bête noire that deserved nothing but the consistent opposition of all good Socialists. By June, 1955, the Socialists regarded the Faure administration as "the most rightist" government since the Liberation.[46]

Although the period 1947-55 was a difficult one for the Socialists, events were brewing in North Africa that would boil over into trouble for the party as well as for all of France.

The End of the Fourth Republic and the Beginning of the Fifth (1956-68)

The last two and a half years of the Fourth Republic were a time of opportunity and trial for the French Socialists. Of the five ministries during this period, the Socialists participated in four and led the one that endured the longest of any in the entire Fourth Republic. Although they were responsible for a number of internal reforms initiated at this time, the Socialists were unable to cope with the forces from outside that threatened the very existence of France. In the end they were forced by circumstances to help pave the way for the de Gaulle republic, but as events developed during the new republic the SFIO quickly turned from full support to full opposition—and in the process lost its own identity.

The election of 1956 was carried out under the same electoral law used in 1951, but the results were quite different. An alliance was formed by the democratic Left around Mendès-France and the Socialists, as was done by the moderate Right under Edgar Faure, but due to the tremendous pressures of the extreme Left and the extreme Right they were not able to take advantage of the majority provision of the electoral law. In all but eleven districts, Assembly seats were thus distributed by proportional representation. Although the Socialists ended up with some 400,000 additional votes, the number of seats assigned to the SFIO dropped from 107 to 99. The Communists, however, jumped in popular votes from 4.9 million (in 1951) to 5.5 million and increased the number of their seats in the Assembly from 101 to 150. The big surprise, as it turned out, was not the strength of the Communists nor the collapse of the Gaullist RPF, but the capture by the extreme right wing Poujadists of 2½ million votes and 50 seats in the new Assembly.

Despite their losses, however, the Socialists found themselves in an even more commanding role in the new Assembly. In view of the strength of the Communists on the left and the Poujadists and other parties on the right, the 99 Socialist votes were absolutely essential to any moderate government. In recognition of the situation, the Socialists were called upon to provide the first government following the elections.

The Mollet government, however, ran into trouble almost from the start. In his investiture speech, Premier Mollet announced a new program of expanded social legislation and a liberal policy toward Algeria. When he went to Algeria in February of the same year to announce personally his new policy, and to introduce General Catroux, his new minister for Algerian affairs, he was greeted by a barrage of garbage and cries for his death. Mollet beat a hasty retreat from Algeria both literally and figuratively. Back in Paris, convinced that none of the Europeans in Algeria, from the highest to the lowest, were in favor of his liberal policy, he exchanged Socialist Robert Lacoste for General Catroux and a policy of pacification for one of negotiation. The Algerian rebels reacted in a predictable manner, and the Algerian war became a war in the true sense of the word.

To Mollet's credit (or discredit, depending upon one's point of view), he did attempt to win the war in Algeria. He sent more and more men to North Africa to the point where over 400,000 troops, including conscripts, were involved. But as the force increased, the determination of the Front de la libération nationale (FLN) to achieve independence from France grew proportionately. Help came to the FLN from other areas of North Africa, and by the end of the war France was condemned by almost every nation.

In the search for victory, Mollet's coalition government became responsible for, or assumed responsibility for, acts that an observer of the French scene would not normally attribute to a Socialist. One example was the fall 1956 Suez action carried out with the British and Israelis against Egypt's Nasser, who was heavily aiding the FLN. Former Socialist ally Mendès-France was almost alone among those of the Center-Left and Right in his condemnation of the Suez venture. The kidnapping of Ben Bella was another example. Although in this case the initial decision did not come from the premier, after some hesitation he accepted responsibility. Within France itself, the climate became more and more that of a police state. While many of the repressive actions in metropolitan France were a reaction to the terrorist attacks of the FLN and its sympathizers, others were those of a state in the process of losing an important war.

Most serious of all was the government's loss of control over the military and the colonists in Algeria. The primary cause was giving the army ever increasing powers over Algerian affairs. This resulted in a growing number of decisions being made by the army and its colonist allies who finally ceased to bother consulting Mollet's ministry. In some cases they even refused to carry out specific instructions from Paris. As the cleavage between these two power factions and Paris continued to grow, the collapse of the Mollet government became unavoidable.

When the government was finally brought down in May, 1957, it was not by the Left as one would have anticipated, but by the Right. The pretext used by the Right was the "excessive" social and economic reforms introduced by Mollet, but in reality the protest was sparked by high taxes and the weak economic position of France that had resulted from the war in Algeria. Further, despite assertions by the Socialist government that it would not negotiate with the Algerian rebels until the war had been won, the Right was fearful that the Socialists might prefer to back down and negotiate. In any case, despite several important domestic achievements, including higher old age and retirement pensions, longer paid holidays, a progressive policy for black Africa, and the preparation of the way for the creation of the European Economic Community, the Mollet government passed unceremoniously into history.[47]

The centrist governments of Bourgès-Maunoury, Gaillard, and Pflimlin followed in rapid order. Because of its size, and the antagonism of the far Left and Right, the Socialist party was important to all three of these governments. In at least one case, the Socialists were influential in choosing the man to lead the government, and in all three cases the Socialists accepted cabinet posts.[48] However, these three governments were no more able than the Mollet government to recapture control over France's destiny. Nor were they able to stem the collapse of the Fourth Republic and to prevent the reentry of General de Gaulle into the French political scene.

Notes

1. G. D. H. Cole, *Socialist Thought: Marxism and Anarchism, 1850-1890* (London: Macmillan, 1954), p. 211.

2. G. D. H. Cole, *Socialist Thought: The Forerunners, 1789-1850* (London: Macmillan, 1953).

3. Paul Louis, *Histoire du socialisme en France*, 5th ed. (Paris: M. Rivière, 1950), pp. 137-43.

4. Ibid., pp. 126-31.

5. Alfred Rambaud, *Histoire de la civilisation contemporaine en France, 1789-1912*, 4th ed. (Paris: A. Colin, 1926), p. 778.

6. Elie Halévy, *Histoire du socialisme européen* (Paris: Gallimard, 1948), pp. 158-60.

7. Louis, *Histoire du socialisme en France*, p. 239.

8. Marcel Prélot, *L'évolution politique de socialisme français, 1789-1934* (Paris: Spes, 1939), p. 83.

9. Louis, *Histoire du socialisme en France*, p. 244-45, and

Halévy, *Histoire du socialisme européen,* pp. 190-91.

10. Louis, *Histoire du socialisme en France,* pp. 246-47.

11. The various French trade unions merged in 1902 to form the *Confédération générale du travail* (CGT).

12. For an excellent work on the problem of the French labor movement and political action, see E. Drexel Godfrey, Jr., *The Fate of the French Non-Communist Left* (Garden City, N.Y.: Doubleday, 1955).

13. Prélot, *L'évolution politique,* p. 154.

14. It should be noted that the name Parti socialiste unifié (PSU) was appropriated by a group of left-wing Radicals in 1960. See p. 157 of this study.

15. From the *Revue de Genève,* March 1921, p. 241, as quoted in Prélot, *L'évolution politique,* pp. 177-78.

16. Louis, *Histoire du socialisme en France,* pp. 290-96.

17. Louis, *Histoire du socialisme en France,* pp. 325-26. See also Milord M. Drachkovitch, *De Karl Marx à Léon Blum* (Geneva: Droz, 1954), pp. 51-54.

18. Louis, *Histoire du socialisme en France,* pp. 337-38.

19. Ibid., pp. 351-52.

20. Ibid., p. 362.

21. Ibid., pp 363-65.

22. Ibid., as quoted on p. 367. For a more complete text of the telegram, see Alexandre Zévaès, *Histoire du socialisme et du communisme en France de 1871 à 1947* (Paris: France-Empire, 1947), p. 382.

23. Louis, *Histoire du socialisme en France,* pp. 383-87, and Maurice Duverger, *Les partis politiques* (Paris: A. Colin, 1954), pp. 88-89. On the revival of the Second International, see also Drachkovitch, *De Karl Marx,* pp. 55-63.

24. In 1922, only two years after Tours, the executive committee of the Comintern called for a "common front" with the Socialists. Prélot, *L'évolution politique,* p. 254.

25. Louis, *Histoire du socialisme en France,* p. 384.

26. Ibid., p. 389.

27. Zévaès, *Histoire du socialisme et du communisme,* pp. 397-99, and Louis, *Histoire du socialisme en France,* pp. 402-403.

28. Edward Whiting Fox, "The Third Force, 1897-1939," in Edward Mead Earle, ed., *Modern France* (Princeton, N.J.: Princeton University Press, 1951), p. 136.

29. Philip M. Williams, *Politics in Post-War France* (London: Longmans, 1954), p. 61. For a very emotional account of the turnover of power, see Paul Ramadier, "Vichy (Juillet 1940)," *La Revue Socialiste*, no. 203 (May 1967), pp. 443-50.

30. Paul Marabuto, *Les partis politiques et les mouvements sociaux sous la IVe République* (Paris: Sirey, 1948), p. 114.

31. The Extraordinary Congress of 1944 expelled 100 out of the 150 men elected to serve in the Vichy government. Louis, *Histoire du socialisme en France*, p. 426.

32. François Goguel, *France Under the Fourth Republic* (Ithaca, N.Y.: Cornell University Press, 1952), pp. 15-16.

33. Williams, *Politics in Post-War France*, p. 22.

34. *Journal officiel de la République française, Débats parlementaires, Assemblée nationale* (hereafter *Journal officiel*), May 4, 1947, pp. 1473-1474.

35. *New York Times*, Nov. 20, 1947, p. 11. See also *Journal officiel*, November 22, 1947, pp. 5120-22, and November 24, 1947, pp. 5129-30.

36. *Journal officiel*, July 19, 1948, pp. 4861-62. See also, *Bulletin intérieur du parti socialiste*, no. 42 (May 1949), p. 120 (hereafter *Bulletin intérieur*).

37. *Bulletin intérieur*, no. 48 (April 1950), p. 128.

38. *New York Times*, May 27, 1950, p. 4.

39. *Bulletin intérieur*, no. 48 (April 1950), p. 147.

40. For a comprehensive discussion of this electoral system used in both the 1951 and 1956 elections, see Philip M. Williams, *Crisis and Compromise: Politics in the Fourth Republic* (Garden City, N.Y.: Doubleday, 1966), pp. 324-31.

41. *Bulletin intérieur*, no. 60 (April 1952), p. 177.

42. Ibid., pp. 157-58.

43. Ibid., p. 179.

44. From a speech by Jules Moch at the United Nations on May 29, 1952, as reported in the *New York Times*, May 30, 1952, p. 9.

45. *Journal officiel*, June 26, 1953, pp. 3170-3171 and Oct. 9, 1953, pp. 4190 and 4209-4210. During the winter 1953-54 the Socialists suffered one defeat and achieved one victory. In December, 1953, both houses of the French parliament met jointly to elect a new president of the Republic. Marcel-Edmond Naegelen, the Socialist candidate, led all others on the first two ballots. Despite Naegelen's Communist support, which became

more and more embarrassing as the balloting proceeded, he was deadlocked with Joseph Laniel, his chief opponent, at the sixth ballot. In a last-minute attempt to break the deadlock, the Socialists tried unsuccessfully to substitute the name of Vincent Auriol. Finally, René Coty, an Independent who was sufficiently unknown to have many enemies, was elected on the thirteenth ballot. This Socialist defeat was partially balanced by the victory of the Socialist candidate for president of the National Assembly, André Le Troquer, on January 6, 1954.

46. *Bulletin intérieur,* no. 78 (May 1955), p. 77.

47. In a way the experience of the Mollet government was strangely reminiscent of that of the Léon Blum government before him. While both were able to bring about many long overdue domestic reforms, neither was able to cope with the larger outside events of the day.

48. Writing of the time immediately after the fall of Mollet, MacRae states: "Pflimlin tried next to form a cabinet but was prevented by the Socialists' unwillingness to participate. Mollet then influenced President Coty toward the nomination of Maurice Bourgès-Maunoury, a young Radical who had been Mollet's Minister of Defense, and persuaded the Socialists to enter the cabinet." Duncan MacRae, Jr., *Parliament, Parties and Society in France, 1946-1958* (New York: St. Martin's Press, 1967), p. 161.

2
The Ideology of Democratic Socialism

The SFIO was a highly traditional party. Except for the Communists, no other French political party depended so heavily on its doctrinal heritage as a guide to action. This respect for philosophy was both a source of strength and a source of weakness for the SFIO. The strength lay in the continuity and sense of purpose granted to followers of a doctrine that was clear and steadfast through good times and bad. The weakness lay in the difficulty of modifying doctrine to meet the changing conditions that from time to time confront all believers in a rigid interpretation of political dynamics.

While both the Socialists and the Communists claimed to be Marxist parties, there was an important difference in their doctrinal development. The French Communist party, true to its obligations to the Comintern, accepted Lenin and Stalin as the proper interpreters of Marx; consequently there are few, if any, outstanding independent thinkers in French Communism. The Socialists, despite their long history of association with the Internationals, developed their own French interpreters of Marx. It is these men, many of them known worldwide, who gave to the SFIO its unique spirit and particular quality.

In this chapter the philosophic heritage of the SFIO is analyzed in five parts: (1) party doctrine, (2) economic theory, (3) social doctrine, (4) political philosophy, and (5) world perspective. The first section serves as an introduction to the other four sections. The subdivisions of this chapter, although necessary for purposes of description, are not meant to indicate that French socialist philosophy is a collection of unrelated planks in a party platform;

a coherent and consistent seminal philosophy is meaningful only as a whole.

The Concept of Man and Society

The tradition of the Socialist party stems directly from the Compromise Declaration of 1905, which resulted in party unity for the first time. This declaration, clearly permeated with Marxist theory, defines the party as follows:

> 1. The Socialist party is a class party whose aim is to socialize the means of production and exchange, that is to say, to transform the capitalist society into a collective or communist society through the political and economic organization of the proletariat. The Socialist party, although it must attempt to realize the immediate reforms demanded by the working class, is not a reform party but, in its aims, its ideals, and by the means it employs, is a party of class struggle and revolution.
>
> 2. The members of the party elected to Parliament shall form a single group in confronting all bourgeois political factions. The socialist group must refuse the government all the means that could assure the domination of the bourgeoisie and its maintenance in power. Consequently, it must refuse military credits, credits for colonial conquests, secret funds, and the budget in general. . . .
>
> The Socialist group in parliament must devote itself to the defense and the extension of political liberties, the rights of workers, and to the pursuit and realization of reforms which tend to ameliorate the living and fighting conditions of the working class.[1]

Prior to the 1905 unification, all factions within the socialist movement were essentially in agreement regarding the goal of socialism: a society in which the instruments of production and exchange would no longer be at the service of a capitalist minority, but at the service of all men for the fulfillment of their needs. These factions, however, did not agree on how to achieve this end. The Guesdists emphasized the end and refused to compromise the means to attain the end, and so became militant revolutionaries. The Possibilists and the Broussists, on the other hand, held that the goal was of secondary importance to obtainable social reforms.

The unification of the French Socialist party and its successes immediately preceding the First World War were due largely to the dynamic personality and inspired leadership of Jean Jaurès. It was his concept—that social reforms could provide the frame-work, or the means, to clear the way for the coming of socialism to which all Socialists should direct their efforts—that became the accepted doctrine of the unified party. Since the aim of socialism was a profound transformation of the whole of society, Jaurès rejected the Blanquist thesis that the battle could be won by a militant minority. Rather, the socialist revolution must be the work of "the immense majority of the nation," working within a democratic society. Future social organization was to be determined by legal legislative methods.[2]

Jaurès' point of departure was that of an orthodox Marxist. As he stated in his *Histoire socialiste:* "We know that economic conditions, the means of production, and the type of property are the essence of history. . . . We will note the influence of the status of economics on governments, on literature, on systems."[3] Jaurès adhered to the whole corpus of Marxian polemics, including the philosophy of history, historical materialism, the theory of surplus value and profit, capitalist concentration, and the class struggle. However, he so enlarged and modified the basic concepts of Marx that he ended by denying much of their validity.

Why did Jaurès accept and reject Marxism at the same time? Because the essence of Marxism was repugnant to the humanistic and humanitarian spirit that formed the true basis of his philosophy. "Socialism is the supreme affirmation of the right of the individual," Jaurès wrote in the *Revue de Paris* in 1898, and "nothing is above the individual."[4] He emphasized the highest dignity of the human spirit and maintained that a long physiological evolution, in which humanity had predispositions of an aesthetic nature, preceded economic determinism. "It could not be better said [in denying the exclusiveness of Marxist historical materialism] that the Idea commands economic evolution rather than being its product."[5]

Jaurès similarly modified other Marxian economic principles. Having a great deal of foresight, he did not believe in the necessity of economic concentration leading inevitably to a revolutionary catastrophe precipitated by a struggle between the classes. In his effort to understand capitalism, he recognized its utility and persistence, although he insisted on changing the character of property. He felt that capitalism was collectivist by nature and through the tax system it could limit competition and anarchy.[6] To Jaurès, the metamorphosis of capitalism was leading to collectivization and organization. By becoming the regulator and arbitrator of conflicting class interests, the democratic state would provide the framework in which the numerically predominant proletariat would gain political maturity and political power. The democratic state would cease to be the tool of the capitalist class and become the servant of all.

Democracy must be the essence of the new socialist society—an industrial republic based on decentralization and universal suffrage. The legislature will determine the organization of society within the framework of democracy. "The new society cannot and will not be *étatisme, anarchisme* or *'fonction-nairisme,'* rather it will be a civilization of free men."[7] Actually his philosophy is much closer to the federated society conceived by Proudhon than it is to Marxism. "The true inspirer of French socialism," Elie Halévy wrote, "is not Marx, but the individualist Proudhon."[8]

Jean Jaurès gave the party a strong, viable tradition, and his followers continued in essence his interpretation of the proper role of the party. Léon Blum, for instance, affirmed *pleinement et sans reserve* his belief in historical materialism as well as the Marxist philosophy of history.[9] He accepted Marx's concept of the weakness of capitalist society, the theory of surplus value, and the class struggle. He often reiterated his belief in the international organization of workers under the banner "Workers of the World Unite" and the need for revolution. Like Jaurès, however, he relied on democratic means to attain the socialist end. To Blum there was an indissoluble union between socialism and democracy—without socialism democracy was imperfect, and without democracy socialism was powerless.[10] The legal conquest of public and political power became the necessary method of transforming society. It was in this sense that the revolutionary aspects of the party doctrine were to be carried to fruition. "The reform is revolutionary, the revolution is reformist."[11]

Blum also subscribed to the humanist element in the Jaurèsian interpretation of true socialism.[12] "The maintenance and development of the rights of the human person, within a society completely conceived and organized for the collective good, is the very formula of socialism. This is what is contained in the two words social-democracy which were not brought together by accident."[13]

These two themes are essential elements in the Declaration of Principles of the French Socialist Party adopted in 1946, which Blum himself helped to write. The first sentence of the Declaration reads: "The objective of the Socialist party is to liberate the human person from all of the bondages which oppress it and, as a result, to assure to man, woman and child, in a society founded on equality and fraternity, the free exercise of their rights and their natural capacities."[14] And further on: "[The SFIO] is a party which is essentially democratic because all of the rights of the human person and all forms of liberty are indissolubly bound together."[15]

Although Guy Mollet was known as a neo-Guesdist before he became head of the party because of his more orthodox Marxian views as to the role of the party in preparing for the proletarian revolution, upon assumption of power he was soon converted to the more flexible Jaurèsian principles of democracy and humanism. In a discussion devoted to the creation of a socialist program vis-à-vis modern forms of capitalism, Mollet, speaking of a book in which the author used the term *democratic socialism,* scathingly commented that this was a very audacious use of terms: "As though there could exist any socialism other than a democratic one!"[16] At another point in the same discussion he added his support to the party objectives of liberating "the human person" from all of the bondages which oppress it and aiding each individual to develop his own personality.[17]

Perhaps more to the point is the Preamble of the SFIO's Fundamental Program adopted in 1962 after several years of debate under Mollet's stewardship. The first sentence of the Preamble reads: "The Socialist party remains faithful to the Declaration of Principles composed by Léon Blum on the morrow of the Liberation which remains one of the foundations of its doctrine."[18] And, a little further on: "It proclaims today as it did yesterday that its objective is to liberate the human person from all of its bondages and at the same time to assure its improvement by building a society which is completely democratic, without classes and without wars."[19]

In effect, the SFIO's basic philosophy represented an effort to reconcile the individualist spirit of the French with Marxian collectivism. Whether the general principles of Marxism can actually be applied to countries such as France as they and the world change and develop will become clearer as we proceed. The question to be answered here is whether the SFIO was right in claiming that it was Jaurès and his followers, and not Lenin, who correctly applied Marxist principles to the contemporary world.

Economic Theory

Marx's economic principles have proven to be one of the SFIO's heaviest burdens. Though the 1905 Socialist party declaration still emphasized class struggle, revolution, and collectivism, it was not long before many Socialists began to realize that capitalism was not developing according to the simplistic Marxist scheme. The resulting problem was to account for these changes in development and to adapt party doctrine accordingly.

In 1952 Jules Moch wrote a book in which he maintained that modern capitalism was very different from that of the 1850s with the result that Marxism was facing a very different adversary in the twentieth century.[20] Writing the year after Moch, Pierre Bonnel expanded this idea and isolated five aspects of twentieth century capitalism that differentiate it from the capitalism envisaged by either Marx or Lenin:[21]

1. Capitalism had not destroyed itself through wars, depressions, and the like. In fact, the leading capitalist state, the United States, was stronger than ever.
2. The division of society into two antagonistic classes had not occurred. Out of 20,540,000 producers in France, 36½ percent were in agriculture; 30 percent in industry; 15½ percent in administration and professions; 10½ percent in commerce; and 7½ in transport. Out of 5 million industrial

workers, over half were employed in industries with less than 100 employees.

3. In many large industrial centers, the number of proletarians had become stabilized or was on the decrease. Rather, there had been a significant increase in the middle, salaried sector.

4. The economic exploitation of the worker in the capitalist society had been modified. In fact, the standard of living of the proletariat in industrial nations had improved materially.

5. The class struggle had not developed in the uncomplicated, simple manner predicted by doctrine either in France or the world at large. For instance, the proletariat had failed to constitute itself a world revolutionary class. Proletarian internationalism sank in 1914 and since then had not played a significant role in world politics. It had become rent by national and ideological schisms.

With the heart thus torn out of Marxist economic doctrine, something had to be found to replace it. Capitalism obviously could not be embraced without wreaking havoc with the entire idea of socialism. The same was true with communism. Something had to be salvaged from Marx that would maintain continuity and at the same time provide a rallying point for the party. The notion of public ownership of the means of production was not adequate to the task. The capitalist system was no longer based only on private ownership of the means of production. In addition, there were numerous capitalist institutions not founded in the exploitation of man by man and hence not necessarily susceptible to condemnation by good Socialists. How, for instance, could you condemn such things as the lone artisan with his tools and shop, or the cooperative, or the kibbutz? Most importantly, if only the idea of private ownership were condemned, the natural conclusion would be that only nationalization was necessary to bring about the ideal socialist state. The problem with this script, of course, was that state ownership of the means of production and exchange by itself would not automatically mean the liberation of the working man. The Soviet Union had substituted state ownership for private ownership, but the worker in the Soviet Union was still a slave.[22]

The doctrinal solution finally arrived at was to focus attention on Marx's surplus value theory of labor. While offering a logical explanation for the evils of both capitalism and communism, it also provided the foundation for a socialist plan of action. In the capitalist system the difference between the value supplied by the worker and the wage paid was diverted by a minority to their own personal uses. In the communist system the same thing occurred, the minority in this case being the Communist party. Thus both systems perpetuated the classic exploitation of man by man. Surplus value itself, however was not inherently bad; in fact it had an important function to play in any modern society. The evil lay in its improper use—its use for the personal whims of a minority. The job of the Socialist, therefore, was to create a system in which the proper uses of surplus value would be determined in a democratic way for the benefit of all peoples, not just the favored minority.

This new emphasis in the SFIO's economic doctrine was spelled out officially for the first time in the party's Fundamental Program adopted in 1962. Because of its importance to the development of socialist ideology, it will be investigated in some detail. The Preamble notes "the changes that have occurred in the operation of the capitalist regime since 1945[23] and Section 2, the largest single section of the program, provides the details. "The capitalist regime is founded on the accumulation and improper use of surplus value: the portion of labor which is not paid for, even though it may appear to be paid for."[24] A fraction of this appropriation is necessary and legitimate when democratically agreed upon, because it insures collective social investment and buys equipment. But in a capitalist economy an important additional fraction is diverted to the profit of a minority that has arrogated to itself the means of production and exchange. That fraction of surplus value is not necessarily assigned to investment corresponding to the collective will or the general interest. Consequently, the benefits are unevenly distributed and at times even against the best interests of society.

Since the capitalist system does not permit a central and permanent coordination of its programs, an orderly development of society is impossible. The state intervenes in the capitalist system only intermittently and then without the guidance of an overall plan. Rather than the harmonious development of the economy in the collective interest or the increase of production to satisfy human needs, the aims of intervention are the "socialization" of losses incurred by private enterprises and the palliation of demands by producers organized into powerful pressure groups.[25]

Another problem has been created by the fact that the capitalist system is no longer founded on competition between small independent units. Instead it is characterized by large concentrations, technical and financial, which have profoundly modified its structure. Giant units, monopolies, trusts, cartels, holdings, and the like dominate most sectors, creating combines to the detriment of the consumer and sovereignly dividing the markets among themselves. Where there exists an apparent competition between capitalist enterprises, the result is not the lowering of prices but product specialization, the excessive multiplication of products, the expansion of sales services, and a massive barrage of advertising to create artificial needs. The resulting disorder, restrictions, and waste are a brake on the orderly progress of the capitalist system. Over the long term, the average rate of growth remains insufficient to raise the standard of living in terms of real human needs and technical possibilities.

Section 2 of the Fundamental Program then indicts the other enemy of the Socialists, the Russian Communists. "The Soviet system has done away with the capitalists but not the essential blemish on their economy, the exploitation of the workers."[26] Even though profits are no longer paid to individuals in the Soviet system, the rate of profit and its use is not democratically determined. The rigid, integral, dictatorial Soviet planning has so increased the power of the political bureaucracy that the state could be confused with a technocracy. The bureaucracy has formed itself into a dominant group, progressively differentiating itself from the masses, and has thus taken on the characteristics of a new ruling class. Economic development has occurred in Russia, but its price has been terror, propaganda, and the sacrifice of an entire revolutionary generation. Moreover, despite scientific and technical successes, Soviet economic development has never been balanced. Crises, tensions, contradictions, and inadequate use of means available to increase production have imposed on the workers unjustified suffering.

Thus "the two regimes, in spite of their differences, possess common characteristics."[27] Both exploit, and at times even oppress, the worker by creating heavier and heavier bureaucratic and technocratic organs—private for the one and public for the other—which impose a similar conformism on society. The communications media in the capitalist system are controlled by powerful economic groups and in the Soviet system by a single party. In both systems freedom of information thus remains a delusion. Both systems preclude the emancipation of the worker and the true liberation of man.

The SFIO, of course, offers a better alternative. "Opposed to both the capitalist and the communist systems, socialism assures the democratic administration of the economy for the collectivity while maintaining and extending human freedom."[28] This goal will be attained by "socialist planning" ("planification social-iste"), elaborated and realized by workers' groups such as labor unions and cooperatives, directed toward the balanced expansion of production and the full satisfaction of collective and individual needs.

According to the precept of socialist planning, wherever economic oppression exists, ownership of the means of production or exchange should be transferred to the collectivity. This collective appropriation can be on a national, regional, local, or cooperative level. In addition, where judicial proceedings or technical circumstances have in fact disassociated the power of administration from the property itself, the exercise of this power should also be transferred to the collectivity. Taking a lesson from its two adversaries, however, the Fundamental Program warns against the formation of any bureaucracy that would substitute a routine, heavy-handed, or possibly irresponsible administration for democratic planning or that might oppose the direct administration by the workers of enterprises under the control of the collectivity.

As essential as collectivism is to party doctrine, the idea of socialist planning does not require that all means of production and exchange be collectivized.[29] Private property will be abolished only when it exploits other people's labor or results in such exploitation. The private production of goods therefore remains as long as it does not result in exploitation or in economic regression—an exemption applying to agriculture, marketing, the manufacture of small products and handicrafts, and especially to any cooperative venture.

Social Doctrine

The economic objectives of socialist doctrine were not ends in themselves. They were only a part, albeit an important one, of the overall goal of the emancipation of man from any and all types of bondage that might in any way hinder his quest for the achievement of his fullest potential. The elimination of surplus value through socialist planning, for instance, would permit a more equitable distribution of the national revenue. By proper planning there would be an increase in the production of socially valuable goods, consequently a lowering of the price to the consumer. The purchasing power of the individual would be further increased by a planned simplification of the methods of distribution and the elimination of wasteful and unproductive procedures inherent in capitalism. Ultimately the time would come when compensation would be more than just adequate for each individual's physical needs (and those of his family); ideally it would be sufficient for everyone to achieve the full life of a truly free citizen. Or, as stated in the 1962 declaration, the final objective of socialism remained for "each to produce according to his ability and to receive according to his needs."[30]

Another block to man's achieving his full potential is social bondage. Because society is divided into fairly rigid classes, some people have special privileges that the others are not permitted to enjoy, such as the right to choose an occupation. Although proper economic planning can weaken the class system by ending exploitation, economic solutions alone are not enough because class privilege is derived largely from inequalities of condition originating in the accident of birth. The remedy, therefore, became the democratization and improvement of the educational system. The years a young person could attend school should be lengthened, and the content of classes should be diversified "in order to reveal and encourage all vocations."[31] This education would be free and open to all without discrimination of any kind.[32]

Another factor that the Socialists felt might impede the rational development of man was *spiritual oppression.* The great religions of the world had at one time played an important and constructive role in the affairs of man, but the modern Church, according to Jaurès, was standing in the way of science and free inquiry, and "no force, either interior or exterior, no power, no dogma should limit the perpetual effort and the perpetual research of human reason."[33] Although science was not perfect, Jaurès insisted that its uncertainty and errors were no warrant for the Church to paralyze all progressive thought—"to plunge us into darkness."[34]

Since the separation of church and state in France in the early 1900s, there has been little political conflict between the two. The Socialists therefore concentrated their efforts on the field of education. Of all the French parties the SFIO took the lead in the fight for better state schools; it became famous for its willingness to combat, whenever necessary, any attempt to subsidize or in any other way aid church-run schools. Secularization was an essential slogan, almost a dogma, to the French Socialists.[35]

A more modern impediment to man's development identified by the SFIO was *technical oppression.* Since modern means of mass production tend to dehumanize the contributions of the working man, threatening to atrophy and thus destroy his personality, the state must use all available modern techniques to "ameliorate the condition of the worker at his place of work, diminishing his fatigue and the monotony of his tasks, and [to] augment and organize his leisure."[36]

The most recent form of bondage to be criticized by the SFIO was what might be labeled *the oppression of modern advertising.* "The most serious alienation," according to Guy Mollet in 1966, "is found in the fact that the attention of the worker is being diverted by turning all his interest now towards consumption, an oriented consumption."[37] In so doing, the individual ceases to think of himself as a producer and thus loses interest in his own destiny, progressively failing to involve himself in the administration of his own affairs. This renunciation of control over his own destiny was the worst form of social alienation. To the observation by another Socialist that the consumer makes an important contribution to society by choosing the better and more needed goods and rejecting others, Guy Mollet responded: "No, my dear friend Vedel, it is not correct that the housewife each morning casts her ballot in choosing one product or another, because the intoxication of advertising, by all of its modern methods, changes everything. In effect, production is directed towards gadgets sometimes without any interest for the collectivity, and this at a time when our society has a need for so many other things."[38]

Order and Social Control

The attitude of the Socialist party theoreticians toward political organization of the state was an important area separating them from their Communist colleagues. Although both accepted the Marxist contention that the state has always been an instrument of domination and exploitation in the service of the ruling class, and both hope that the bourgeoisie, and ultimately the state, might wither away to be replaced by some sort of volunteer associationalism, the Socialists tended to view the transitional period much more realistically. For instance, the experience in Russia had showed that the transition period may well be of long duration: decades after the revolution there was still the need for a governmental apparatus. To prevent the governmental apparatus from being transferred from one elite to another, as had occurred in Russia, the state must have a truly democratic base. However, in order to carry out the extensive reforms that were needed, such as restructuring the economy, there would have to be a massive intervention of public authority. The task of the Socialist theoreticians, therefore, was to come up with a plan providing both efficiency and democratic control. An organization was needed that could cure the major abuses of the current regime, provide a vehicle for the ultimate socialist victory, and at the same time protect the individual from exploitation by government or by private enterprise. In Blum's terms, the "false and feeble bourgeois democracy" of pre–World War II France must be replaced by "a true democracy," a popular democracy, yet one that is at the same time "energetic and efficient."[39]

This "true democracy" had popular sovereignty as its cornerstone. Universal suffrage, therefore, was always an important plank in the Socialist platform until it was finally

introduced everywhere on French soil. Universal suffrage was not
enough by itself, however, as true democracy also "requires the
active participation, direct or indirect, of everyone in the public
discussion of communal problems, in the elaboration of the
major political options, and in the choice between these
options"[40] on all levels, national, regional and local, and even in
the administration of collective enterprises. Further, it was the
duty of the state to guarantee this public discussion of the issues.

The second major cornerstone in the true democracy sought by
the Socialists was the guarantee by the state of the fundamental
rights of man and citizen. These rights included: (1) respect for
privacy; (2) freedom of religion; (3) freedom of the press; (4)
freedom of information; (5) freedom of association, especially the
right to form labor unions and cooperatives; (6) the right of
assembly; (7) the right to strike; (8) universal, equal suffrage with
the secret ballot; (9) the supremacy of political power; (10)
government by majority; (11) control of power at all levels by the
representatives of the people; (12) the right of opposition in a
multiparty system; (13) the equality of citizens before the law; and
(14) the independence of the judiciary.[41] Only with the guarantee
of these rights would the quest for economic and social justice
remain humane.

The third cornerstone to the edifice was the duty of public
officials to stand for reelection, to be judged anew at frequent
intervals. In this way the true "collective will" could be
determined, and public officials would be kept aware of the
desires of the people.

It is only within this context that the socialist use of the term
dictatorship of the proletariat can be understood. The Socialists
have been willing to guide the republic toward the socialist
utopia, but their leadership—unlike Communist rule in Russia—
would be democratic, representative, and responsible. As
expressed by Léon Blum, the French goal would be a dictatorship
"exercised by a party resting on popular will and freedom and
consequently an impersonal dictatorship of the proletariat," not
a dictatorship exercised by a centrist party or any other special
group that had seized power by nondemocratic means. "Dictatorship of a party, yes; dictatorship of a class or a dictatorship of a few
known or unknown individuals, no."[42]

The French Socialists were less precise concerning the exact form their ideal government should take, mostly because the SFIO was never close enough to actually supplying a dictatorship of the proletariat to run the French government. Nevertheless, from the party's reactions to suggested changes in the existing French system and from various general pronouncements of party leaders we can piece together at least the vague outline of the ideal government of the Socialists.

To begin with, the basic unit of any political system should be the legislature. Ideally all power should be vested in a single representative assembly whose members would be chosen (or subject to reconfirmation) at relatively frequent intervals by a system of proportional representation. The aim, as mentioned earlier, was to provide an institution that might truly reflect the popular will. The addition of a nonrepresentative upper house would only tend to impede the free manifestation of that popular will.

The Socialists had a much more difficult time in deciding on the ideal type of executive organ. In the early days of the SFIO there was more or less agreement on the desirability of a parliamentary system in which the cabinet is clearly subordinate to the single assembly. The prime minister and his cabinet should be chosen by the assembly and should remain in office only as long as they clearly enjoyed the support of a majority of that assembly, a system not unlike that used in the Third Republic. After experiencing the relative instability of the Fourth Republic and the stability of the Fifth, however, there was a decided shift among the Socialists. Although few were openly willing to embrace the system imposed on France by de Gaulle, they did look for alternatives that might provide more stability than experienced under the Fourth Republic system.

One interesting concept aimed at such stability is contained in the joint Declaration of the Federation of the Left and Communist Party of 1968. The basis of the plan was a legislative contract (*contrat de législature*) whereby the majority of the legislature, when investing a prime minister and his cabinet, contracts to support that government for the duration of the legislative session. The government, for its part, would continue in office for the same duration and would remain faithful to its announced program. Provisions were also made for a vote of censure, which if successful would result in both the fall of the government and the dissolution of the legislative assembly.

On paper the Socialists were consistent in their dislike for the dual executive. The office of president had no place in the dictatorship of the proletariat. A president in addition to a prime minister and his cabinet would have no useful function and would tend, as in the case of an upper legislative house, to impede the free manifestation of the popular will. A weak president would be just a useless expense, whereas a strong president could be dangerous in view of France's Bonapartist tradition. Blum did look with interest at the presidential system of the United States and the collegiate executive system of Switzerland, but he concluded they were suited only to federal systems where political power is decentralized.[43] Nevertheless, in spite of their antipathy to the idea, the Socialists did at last agree to having a president for the Fourth Republic. Moreover, the 1968 joint declaration of the Left mentioned above failed to call for the abolition of the presidency of the Fifth Republic and instead confined itself to condemning anyone who would seek inordinate personal power and to adding a few restrictions on presidential power, such as the elimination of Article 16 of the Constitution of the Fifth Republic. Interestingly, although the PCF was the only party to advocate abolishing the office of the president, its view was shared by a very large number of individual Socialists.

As a general rule the Socialists championed the simplification of governmental structures. Several Socialist writers, for instance, suggested that a number of ministries be consolidated to improve coordination and liaison within the unwieldy French cabinets. Unfortunately, when the Socialists were in power, it was difficult for political reasons to make much headway in this matter.[44] There have also been numerous proposals to rationalize the administrative map of France. In an article in 1954, Pierre Rimbert advocated eliminating all administrative units between the commune and the departments so that the boundaries could be redrawn forming a few large departments unified by geographic and democphic factors. The traditional geographic subdivisions made the coordination of activities difficult and were no longer needed in view of modern means of communication and transportation. According to Rimbert, the French state reorganized in this manner would be in a better position to attack the serious problems of the day.[45]

The SFIO and the World at Large

Internationalism was almost as important to socialist theory as it was to Communist theory. To a large part it stemmed from the Socialists' acceptance of Marxist economic theory, at least in its broadest outlines. As stated in the 1946 Declaration of Principles, the party was essentially universal "because economic laws have a universal character."[46] "Internationalism," as explained by Léon Blum, "is based on the postulate that among all nations at the same stage of economic development there exist a certain number of common ideals and interests. The activity of an international working-class party is based on the conclusion that if one looks far enough below the surface and far enough into the future, the interests of every country will be seen as inseparable from the deep and long-term interests of the other countries of Europe, and even of humanity itself."[47]

The humanist tradition of the SFIO dictated that it was the duty of the party to work with the socialist-proletariat parties of other countries, sharing the lessons learned from their experience in the struggle with capitalism, and helping them devise effective means of bringing down the capitalist system. Only when the proletariat were free all over the world and working together in a socialist world, could the SFIO consider its task complete. This then was the basis of the SFIO's enthusiastic use of the slogan: "Workers of the World Unite."

There was one immediate problem that the Socialists of the world faced, and that was war. Wars, according to the accepted Marxist doctrine, were the result of the scramble of capitalist-dominated nations for raw materials and markets, of the Krupps of the world for profits, and even now and then of the desire of capitalist states for "a place in the sun."[48] "Yes," laments Jaurès, "in the capitalist world war is permanent, eternal, and universal, it is war of all against all, of individuals against individuals within class, class against class within a nation, nations against nations, and races against races within humanity."[49]

In order to protect the proletariat, and mankind itself, from the ravages of war it was necessary for the Socialists to declare war on war. While the final cure for war lay in the destruction of the capitalist system, it was possible to make temporary gains against the despoilers of the proletariat. Any and all action that would prevent war was welcome, both parliamentary and revolutionary, as long as there was action. Even fighting against excessive military budgets and large mercenary armies could help. The Socialist must remain at all times conscious of his duty and his power and be willing to throw himself into heroic events as did his forefathers when they gained the first human rights.

The earlier SFIO philosophers, at least, were conscious of the nature and power of nineteenth century nationalism and therefore did not advocate the elimination of national frontiers. To the contrary, Jaurès and even Blum highly praised the cultural differences between nations and recognized the need to preserve them through maintaining autonomous independent states. Jaurès reminded his colleagues of the Stuttgart Congress of the Socialist International in 1907. In addition to affirming the duty of the proletariat to fight for peace, the congress had proclaimed "that the independence of all nations and that the freedom of all fatherlands is inviolable and that everywhere the proletariat must organize to defend the necessary independence of all nationalities against all violence and all aggression."[50] In other words, "autonomous nations have the right and the duty to defend their autonomy energetically."[51] Blum remained in favor of preserving national autonomy at least up to World War II, writing that "it is free people of independent nations who form the unalterable base of any international edifices. Any international community has as its primordial objective the guaranteeing of the freedom and the independence of the nations of which it is composed."[52]

Consequently, in its earlier manifestations socialist doctrine was not necessarily supranationalist. Socialism would of course cross frontiers, just as religion and science tended to ignore national boundaries, but action in the international realm would be carried out by autonomous independent states on a purely voluntary basis. Examples of the projects that individual states should carry out to help preserve the peace, according to Jaurès, included disarmament and the creation of an effective mechanism for the arbitration of disputes between states.

Socialist doctrine did manage to keep pace with events, however, and little by little it took on a more internationalist tone. By August, 1945, Blum was declaring that no party "was more constantly and forcefully attached to the concept of supra-sovereignty, of the voluntary renunciation by each State of a necessary portion of its own sovereignty."[53] The Fundamental Program of the SFIO of 1962 went a big step further and proclaimed that in its present form the "sovereignty of state" could have no other effect than to slow down the social and cultural development of mankind and increase the risk of war. "That is why," continues the program, "the Socialist party has as its ideal a Universal Community in which all people, reconciled and allied, pursue the blossoming of their respective talents."[54] Since this ideal was not necessarily attainable in the foreseeable future, the program set forth some interim goals, including (1) the fight for disarmament; (2) the creation of an international institution with the power to enumerate and apply international law and to enforce its decisions by economic sanctions and, if necessary, by recourse to an international police force; and (3) the limitation of national sovereignty as necessary for the creation of a true international market in the interests of all people. These steps, of course, were only the beginning; the Universal Community would be the end.

Notes

1. Louis, *Histoire du socialisme en France*, p. 272.
2. Jean Jaurès, *Anthologie de Jean Jaurès*, ed. Louis Lévy (Paris: Calmann-Lévy, 1946), p. 217ff.
3. Prélot, *L'évolution politique*, p. 182.
4. Jaurès, *Anthologie*, p. 329.
5. Prélot, *L'évolution politique*, p. 184.
6. Ibid., p. 186ff.
7. Jaurès, *Anthologie*, p. 241.
8. Halévy, *Histoire du socialisme européen*, p. 294.
9. Marabuto, *Les partis politiques*, p. 120.
10. Léon Blum, *For All Mankind*, trans. William Pickles (New

York: Viking Press, 1946), pp. 144-45.

11. "Léon Blum parle de Jaurès," *La Revue Socialiste*, no. 37 (May 1950), p. 397.

12. The humanism of Blum was of such importance that it is an essential part of the title of Joel Colton's *Léon Blum: Humanist in Politics* (New York: Alfred A. Knopf, 1966).

13. Léon Blum, "Les devoirs et les tâches du socialisme." Speech given on May 20, 1945, in Paris at a conference of the secretaries of socialist federations, *L'Oeuvre de Léon Blum, 1945-1947* (Paris: Albin Michel, 1958), pp. 8-9.

14. "Déclaration de principes, adoptée le 24 février 1946, à Paris, par l'Assemblée Nationale du Parti ayant pouvoir de Congrès," in Guy Mollet, *Bilan et Perspectives socialistes* (Paris: Plon, 1958), p. 108.

15. Ibid., p. 109.

16. From a discussion March 29, 1966, on "Les fondements d'une politique socialiste contemporaine," part of a larger debate March 18-29, 1966, on "Le socialisme face aux formes modernes du capitalisme," contained in a special issue of *La Revue Socialiste*, no. 195-96 (July-September 1966), p. 278.

17. Ibid., p. 277.

18. "Le programme fondamental du Parti socialiste," in *La Revue Socialiste*, no. 155 (July 1962), p. 126. This article also includes some of the discussion leading up to the adoption of the program. The program itself is found on pp. 126-38.

19. Ibid., p. 127.

20. Pierre Bonnel, "Signification du socialisme démocratique," *La Revue Socialiste*, no. 70 (October 1953), p. 296ff.

21. Jules Moch, "Confrontation entre Pierre Rimbert et Karl Marx," *La Revue Socialiste*, no. 70 (October 1953), pp. 276-95.

22. See the discussion on the subject in the party's National Council as reported in *La Revue Socialiste*, no. 155 (July 1962), pp. 113-26.

23. Ibid., p. 128.

24. Ibid.

25. U.S. progress toward an annual guaranteed wage evoked much excitement among French Socialists. Etienne Weill-Raynal stated that "the example of the United States can be validly followed by the working class of any nation" in "Deux victoires du socialisme," *La Revue Socialiste*, no. 89 (July 1955), pp. 129-134.

26. Ibid., p. 130.

27. Ibid.

28. Ibid., p. 131.

29. Some of the specific areas the Socialists would be willing to see nationalized, according to the 1968 joint declaration of principles made by the Federation of the Left and the Communist party, were industrial development banks, armament and space industries, industries that are in effect monopolies, such as steel, and industries that depend to a great extent on public funds, such as news agencies and pharmaceutics. The Communists would also include electronics, aeronautics, air transport, petroleum, nuclear industries, automobiles, and the principal insurance companies.

30. Weill-Raynal, "Deux victoires du socialisme," p. 132.

31. Ibid., p. 133.

32. As a complement to the attack on social oppression, in 1962 the SFIO advocated "a policy of generations": "To the family, the right to exist and to evolve while respecting the personality of the individuals of which it is composed. To all the young, the same chance and the same hopes in life, while preparing them in all areas for their future responsibilities. To all the aged, the guarantee of a just share of the national revenue."

33. Jaurès, *Anthologie*, p. 71.

34. Ibid., p. 72.

35. See, for instance, *Programme d'action: Elections législative du 17 juin 1951* (Paris: SFIO, 1951), p. 10. Writing in 1967, André Rey points out that secularization of education is not an attitude hostile to religion itself, but hostile to any attempt by an educator to propound any special set of values. After all, according to Rey, "is not one of the most important tasks of mankind and religion itself the elimination of ideological divisions which set man against man?" André Rey, "L'éducation nationale, priorité des priorités," *La Revue Socialiste*, no. 199-200 (January-February 1967), pp. 119-20.

36. See "Le programme fondamental," in *La Revue Socialiste* (July 1962), p. 133. See also Pierre Bonnel, "Signification du socialisme démocratique."

37. "Les fondements d'une politique socialiste contemporaine," *La Revue Socialiste*, no. 195-196 (July-September 1966), p. 280.

38. Ibid.

39. Blum, *L'Oeuvre, 1940-1945* (Paris: Albin Michel, 1958), p. 468.

40. "Le programme fondamental," *La Revue Socialiste*, no. 155 (July 1962), p. 135.

41. Ibid., p. 136.

42. From a speech at Tours by Léon Blum as quoted in Roger Quilliot, "Le pouvoir et le parti," *La Revue Socialiste*, no. 212 (April 1968), p. 391.

43. See Blum, *L'Oeuvre, 1940-1945*, p. 469.

44. See Colton, *Léon Blum*, pp. 142-43 for Blum's experience in this matter. For more recent plans see Pierre Rimbert, "Esquisse d'un programme socialiste," *La Revue Socialiste*, no. 57 (May 1952), p. 510, and Jean Minoze, "La réforme de l'Etat," *La Revue Socialiste*, no. 75 (March 1954), pp. 253-58.

45. Rimbert, "Esquisse d'un programme socialiste," p. 512.

46. "Déclaration de principes," in Mollet, *Bilan et Perspectives*, p. 109.

47. As translated by Byron Criddle in *Socialists and European Integration: A Study of the Socialist Party* (New York: Humanities Press, 1969), p. 22.

48. See Charles Rappoport, *Jean Jaurès*, 2d. ed. (Paris: L'Emancipatrice, 1916), p. 264.

49. Jean Jaurès, *Oeuvres de Jean Jaurès*, vol. 5, ed. Max Bonnafous (Paris: Rieder, 1933), p. 129.

50. Ibid., p. 124.

51. Ibid.

52. Blum, *L'Oeuvre, 1940-1945*, p. 484.

53. Blum, *L'Oeuvre, 1945-1947*, p. 178.

54. "Le programme fondamental," *La Revue Socialiste*, no. 155 (July 1962), p. 134.

3
Party Organization

The constitution approved at the party congress of Chalon-sur-Sâone in 1906, a year after the various Socialist elements in France were united for the first time, laid the foundation of the Socialist party organization. Although modified in the era of Jaurès and Blum and again after World War II, the 1906 constitution remained the basis of the organization of the SFIO until it dissolved itself in 1968. This document conferred on the SFIO three major characteristics: it was democratic, it had a direct party structure, and it was a mass party.

The democratic spirit was evident throughout the organization. Discussion of important issues was encouraged on all party levels from the village section to the National Congress. As in any truly democratic organization, the rights of the minority were protected. Not only was a person who questioned policy decisions encouraged to make his views known, but representation of minority opinions was mandatory on major policymaking organs. In effect, the structure of the SFIO, the power of its organs, and its financial system were all designed to give the rank and file a great deal of influence in everyday affairs.

The SFIO had a direct party structure; its entire machinery was based directly on the individual member. From the individual in the basic section, party organs progressed directly upward in a hierarchial formation to the National Congress. The leadership of the party always looked with envy at the indirect party structure of its sister organ, the British Labour party, and its happy merger with the major British labor organizations. The failure of the SFIO to gain control of, or create a working partnership with, the largest French labor union, the CGT, has been previously described. As a result, the SFIO with its direct structure was reduced to treating French labor unions on a basis of equality and to relying on the personal prestige of individual Socialists in the enterprises in which they were employed.[1]

The SFIO was also a mass party, based on including the greatest possible number of dues-paying members. From this membership came the required financial support, recruits to be trained for positions of party or parliamentary responsibility, and a large number of individuals to carry on the education of the electorate. All that was necessary for membership was to complete and sign a membership card, pay the monthly dues, and participate more or less regularly in the activities of a local unit.

Party Structure

The structure of the SFIO contained three levels: the local, the departmental, and the national. The basic unit was the section. A section corresponded to one of the smaller administrative units of French local government: the ward, canton, or commune. Although sections were given a rather free hand in establishing their own organization, most included an executive committee elected by a majority vote, and the usual officials—secretaries, treasurers, and assistants. Sections met regularly, usually once a month, to discuss local policy, doctrinal problems, and points of general party interest. The section was also responsible for recruitment, collection of dues, the political education of party members and the general public, and the election of representatives in the next higher level of the party hierarchy. Each member was under an obligation to join a socialist labor organization relevant to his profession, if there was one, and to participate in the activities of the educational and service groups organized by his section and federation.[2]

A great deal of freedom of action was permitted at the section level. Large sections could form subgroups for organizational convenience, but these groups were not permitted to undertake public political activities. Small sections could unite with other sections for electoral purposes. Because of the distribution of Socialist strength, in a great many communes there were no functioning sections. In these areas, the members of the party joined the section nearest to his place of residence.[3] Membership in the section varied from ten to several hundred with an average of around fifty.[4]

In each *département* the sections were combined into a federation, the middle level between the section and the national organization. Each federation had deliberative and executive bodies similar to those of the national organization. Federal congresses, made up of delegates from sections, met regularly to discuss policy matters and issues of party doctrine, and to elect delegates to the National Congress and National Council. All decisions were made by majority vote, except that minority factions had to be provided representation in the National Congress proportionate to their strength.[5] Before the annual meeting of the National Congress, the federal congresses met to discuss proposals from individuals or sections, and to draw up motions to be presented to the National Congress. Federations were permitted to instruct their delegates how to vote in the National Congress on specific issues. These instructions were not usually binding if the issue was changed or modified during the debates, although the delegation could be required to abstain. Despite the fact that federations were obliged to respect the decisions of the national organs, a great deal of independence was granted in practice.

The chief governing body of the party was the National Congress *(Congrès national)*. As stated in the party regulations, "The direction of the party belongs to the party itself, that is, to the National Congress."[6] The congress had exclusive power to amend the party's constitution and was the final authority on the activities of party organs. The congress determined policy, decided on questions of doctrine and general election strategy, and elected the membership of the *Comité directeur*.[7] Unlike the Communist party congress, which meets to approve policies already decided upon by the Politburo, the Socialist congress was essentially democratic. In the National Congress of 1946, for example, the policy of the party leaders was rejected and the dissident wing captured the majority of seats on the *Comité directeur*. The leader of the new majority, Guy Mollet, became the new party secretary.[8]

The National Congress normally met annually and was composed of delegations elected by the departmental federations. A federation had to have at least 100 members and include at least five sections if it was to be entitled to representation in the National Congress. There was a fairly complicated criteria for establishing the number of votes and the number of delegates to which a federation was entitled in the National Congress. Each federation had one vote, plus one vote for every 25 members who had paid their dues for the past year. The delegates were apportioned on the basis of 1 delegate for each 15 votes granted the federation (or major fraction thereof), except that every federation was entitled to at least two delegates.[9] Thus a federation with 725 dues-paying members of one year's standing would have had 30 votes and 4 delegates. At the 1955 National Congress, the Nord federation, the largest, had 409 votes and 28 delegates; the Orne federation, one of the smallest, had 5 votes and 2 delegates. Under this system, the size of the National Congress varied, of course, with the size of party enrollment. In the 1950-55 period, for example, there were usually between 300 and 400 delegates at congresses.[10]

Decisions at the National Congress were normally taken by a voice vote, but one-tenth or more of the delegates could request that a roll-call vote be taken. Since party rules provided for minority representation, the federation predetermined how much of its voting strength was apportioned to each faction. Consequently, roll-call votes usually showed at least a few delegations split on major issues. For instance, on an unsuccessful proposal to change the party rules at the 1955 National Congress, the delegates of the federation of the Seine cast 10 votes for the motion, 222 against the motion, and 14 votes in abstention. Even the little federation of Loire-Inférieure split its votes. The two delegates cast 7 votes for the motion, 8 votes against, and 1 vote in abstention.[11]

"In the interval between the meetings of the National Congress, the administration and the direction of the Party are entrusted to the *Comité directeur* [Executive Committee] controlled by the National Council [*Conseil national*]."[12] The council was composed of one delegate from each federation, but each delegate had as many votes as his federation had in the National Congress.

All of its decisions had to be ratified at the next National Congress. The National Council was supposed to meet every three months and could be summoned to a special meeting whenever it was necessary to make an immediate policy decision. The council was created to provide contact between the *Comité directeur* and the party membership and to assure fidelity to the principles of the party and to the regulations and decisions of the National Congress.[13] The council had the advantage of meeting readily and as freqently as necessary to deal with problems that were beyond the scope of the *Comité directeur*. In practice, if the issue at hand was of any real importance and could not be handled by the *Comité directeur*, an Extraordinary National Congress was usually called to make the necessary decision. For instance, in the interval between the Forty-sixth and Forty-seventh National Congresses, July, 1954, to July, 1955, three Extraordinary National Congresses were convened, while only two meetings of the National Council were held. The Extraordinary Congress made the important decisions.[14]

The *Comité directeur* was without a doubt the essential organ in the party structure. The *Comité* had vast powers. It had the authority to make immediate and binding decisions on any question concerning party policy and tactics between the meetings of the National Council and the National Congress. The *Comité* was in charge of the execution of the decisions of the National Council and the National Congress. It also controlled the party's propaganda and press. Furthermore, it was the task of the *Comité directeur* to decide on the time and place of the annual meetings of the National Congress, and it had the power to call extraordinary meetings of the National Congress. Besides extensive powers regarding discipline, which are discussed at length in a later section, the *Comité directeur* had the power to dissolve a recalcitrant federation or to exclude parliamentary rebels from the party.[15]

The *Comité directeur* was composed of forty-five members elected by the National Congress. It met as often as was considered necessary, averaging forty to fifty times a year after World War II, and elected its own officers. The secretary-general, the recognized head of the party, appointed the assistant secretaries-general, the treasurer, and the assistant treasurer. The secretary-general and two appointees constituted the Permanent Bureau, which was responsible for day-to-day party administration.

In order to assure the dominance of the party rank and file over members elected to office, a limit was set on the number of "parliamentarians" who could become members of the *Comité directeur.* The limit seemed to achieve its aim throughout most of the Fourth Republic until the Socialists provided the government in 1956-57 and the secretary-general became the prime minister. Then, with the increased influence of the Socialist deputies, the *Comité directeur* fell in importance.[16] André Philip in *Le socialisme trahi* states that the *Comité* was reduced to meeting once a month and these meetings were devoted primarily to administrative details. The entire Suez operation, according to Philip, was carried out without any discussion whatsoever by the *Comité.*[17]

Before World War II the *Comité directeur,* then known as the Permanent Administrative Committee (CAP), was even weaker. Not only did it have fewer powers, but a proportional representation system of electing its members led to enervating factionalism. Factions were represented on the committee in proportion to their voting strength at the National Congress, and between congresses these separate wings waged major campaigns in the various federations—some even had their own newspapers and collected extra dues. The later system of election, whereby the delegates to the National Congress voted as individuals for committee members under a simple majority voting method, was introduced in 1944. Although this method tended to overrepresent the smaller federations, it seems to have weakened the previous tendency toward internecine rivalry. After reorganization, there was only one major successful internal revolution. In that dispute, which occurred in 1946, the leftist partisans of Guy Mollet gained an immediate, decisive majority on the *Comité directeur* and elected Mollet to the post of secretary-general.

Two other major national organs deserve some attention: the Finance Control Committee (Commission de contrôle des finances et des comptes) and the Socialist Parliamentary Group (Groupe socialiste au Parlement). The former, composed of nine members, was elected anew at each annual meeting of the National Congress. No more than three of its members could be parliamentarians. This body acted as a watch dog over party finances between meetings of the National Congress.[18]

The Socialist Parliamentary Group was made up of all Socialists elected to the Assembly and the Council of the Republic. In contrast to other major French parties, except the Communists, the power of the SFIO parliamentary group was, in principle, greatly restricted. It could not "even in the most exceptional case" engage the party without the party's express consent.[19] Furthermore, whenever the *Comité directeur* so demanded, decisions on party tactics in parliament had to be made by the two groups acting together. Any decision which achieved a 60 percent majority was immediately effective. In the case of a majority less than 60 percent, the decision was referred to the *Comité directeur* alone. If a majority of the *Comité* then agreed with the original decision, the decision was in force. If the decision of the *Comité directeur* was contrary to the original decision of the two groups acting together, it was necessary to call a meeting of the National Council to make the final binding decision.[20]

As pointed out by Charles Micaud in 1963, the basic party structure contained some essential weaknesses, especially when compared to the French Communist party structure. The basic weakness identified by Micaud was the lack of communication stemming from "the peculiar combination of decentralization and majority rule of the true democracy of militants."[21] At the bottom, the section failed to compare with the Communist cell as a basis for agitation and propaganda. Sections lacked the effective organization, leadership, and systems of punishment and reward that made the Communist cells alert and active. There was little attempt to organize local enterprises and thus there was a failure to keep in touch with the grass roots sentiments of the French worker. A section, really active only during election times, resembled a "club of initiated comrades getting together now and then around a banquet table to exchange jokes and impressions and renew the ties of friendship. They are *bons vivants*, the men of the bistro, very different from their rivals, the men of the cells."[22] All efforts to link the sections directly to the central organization and thus make them the basic unit for the origination and control of party activities were failures.

The federation thus remained the main center of party life. The federation however, according to Micaud, also had its problems. It was "overburdened with too many responsibilities in terms of its resources in men and funds, and it [was] too remote from the people to do effective work in organization and propaganda. Despite its best efforts, it [could] in fact, be only a loose federation of sections, reflecting the attitude of local militants and transmitting them to the higher levels of the party, and distributing information and propaganda coming from above."[23] Individuals and groups who wished to dominate the National Congresses, and thus the life of the party, had to cater to the federations, especially the larger ones.

In addition to the major party organs, throughout the life of the SFIO there were a variety of auxiliary organs of varying importance. In the enthusiasm and optimism immediately following World War II, the party formed a large number of specialized bodies designed to propagandize, recruit members and leaders, and provide the governing bodies with specialized information in almost all fields of human activity. Only a few survived to the end, however. One of the survivors, and a healthy one at that, was the Jean Jaurès Circles (Cercles Jean Jaurès). These groups, scattered throughout France, were made up primarily of educators who met with regularity to discuss the problems and issues facing French education. Tied to the party through party officials at the federal and national levels who were responsible for their activities, the Circles provided an efficient means for finding out the needs of French educators and the educational system, for recruiting educators into the party, for propagandizing them, and for obtaining their support in political campaigns. The Circles were so important that they were given one seat on the executive committee of the Federation of the Democratic and Socialist Left.[24]

The SFIO was not as successful in organizing other specialized areas of the electorate. An attempt was made after the war to create a number of Socialist Enterprise Groups in factories and other enterprises whereby the worker would be educated to socialist aims and could be used in political action. Party members were required to participate in the group corresponding to his own profession. These groups were controlled by federal and national executive committees but were not an integral part of the party in the manner of Communist work cells. An attempt was made to use them as a counterforce for the Communists in the CGT, but they were never very successful. There was no mention of the Socialist Enterprise Groups in the 1966 annual reports. The National Worker's Committee (Commission nationale ouvrière, or CNO) was created to provide a linkage to the party, for the Socialist Enterprise Groups outlasted them and in the end provided one of the only information gathering and policy elaboration mechanisms of the party in the worker's world. Also of marginal importance were the Young Socialists, the Socialist Students, and the Socialist Women. The Young Socialists had on paper a complex organizational structure paralleling its parent organization on the local, departmental, and national levels. Open in principle to young people from fourteen to twenty-five years in age, its purpose was to recruit, socialize, and propagandize. From a high point of some 54,641 members in 1947, when the *Comité directeur* of the SFIO disbanded its national bureau and forbade it to debate party policies because it had been captured by leftist leaders critical of the SFIO's leadership and direction, it fell to around 5,000. In 1956 it rose temporarily when the SFIO provided the government of France. The SFIO failed badly in its attempt to involve French youth. As stated by Simmons: "In many cases the adults were unwilling to let the Young Socialists assume responsible tasks in the organization, and they frequently took advantage of the young members by using them to perform menial secretarial tasks."[25]

The SFIO fared no better with the students and women. The Socialist student organization, Etudiants socialistes, was never very large, especially after its reorganization in 1957. In 1957 its national bureau was dissolved because of student radicalism, especially after the group publicly disagreed with the Socialist Algerian policy. Further, the statutes of the Socialist student organization were revised to add membership of students from French lycées, thus watering down its opposition to official SFIO policy. The Socialist women's organization, Femmes socialistes, also a propaganda and recruitment organ, played a very minor role in the SFIO hierarchy. Again according to Simmons: "The Socialist women's group met with either indifference or lack of comprehension from many of the male members who thought the National Commission of Socialist Women was an organization devoted primarily to charitable activities."[26]

Two other auxiliary organs merit some attention, the National Léo Lagrange Federation (Fédération nationale Léo Lagrange) and the National Studies Commission (Commission nationale d'études). Named after a minister in the prewar Blum cabinet, the Lagrange federation had as its purpose the organization of the leisure time of French youth. In 1966 there were some 350 individual Léo Lagrange centers and groups throughout France made up of some 40,000 members engaged in a wide variety of sports and other leisure-time activity. The federation was aided in 1958 when it was recognized by the French government as being of public importance and thus eligible for government aid, and again in 1961 when it was decided that communes could apply to the government for subsidies to construct youth facilities and to help pay for their administrative expenses. Socialist mayors throughout France encouraged the construction of Lagrange Clubs or the expansion of existing ones. Although the Lagrange Clubs tended to de-emphasize propaganda and socialist doctrine, they tended to be politically important because their directorates were staffed by active Socialists. Thus, when staffers ran for office they could be assured of the support of the local club. The SFIO considered the Lagrange groups so important that the club's federal executive committee always contained a number of top Socialist party leaders.

Also of importance, especially when the SFIO came to power, was the National Studies Commission. Made up of Socialist parliamentarians, members of party executive organs, and experts in various fields, it was originally created to coordinate the activities of the party's various auxiliary organs. Later, as the number of these organs diminished it was turned into a legislative study group. Organized into a number of subcommittees representing the major areas of legislative concern, it was responsible for the preparation of draft legislation for submission by Socialists to the French parliament.

For purposes of information and propaganda, the SFIO maintained a number of internal and general publications. The SFIO's daily newspaper was *Le Populaire,* which dropped from a circulation of some 52,000 in 1949 to less than 15,000 in 1957. Of greater temporary success was the SFIO weekly, *Le Populaire Dimanche,* patterned after the popular French weekly *L'Express,* which started in November, 1948, with 35,000 subscribers, rapidly rising to 70,000 where it leveled off.[27] The national party also issued three internal publications, the *Bulletin intérieur du parti socialiste,* four times a year; *Documentation politique,* which was in theory a weekly; and *Arguments et ripostes,* as the need arose. Various auxiliary organs also had their publications. The National Léo Lagrange Federation published *Jeunesse;* the Jean Jaurès Circles published a bulletin, *L'Université socialiste,* in addition to the widely known *La Revue Socialiste;* the national women's organization was responsible for the journal *Femmes;* the National Studies Commission issued a monthly *Bulletin mensuel d'informations;* and the Socialist Enterprise Groups, a monthly bulletin entitled *Le Lien Socialiste.* Many of these publications managed to be lively and informative and some were of real literary merit. None, however, with the exception of *Le Populaire Dimanche,* ever achieved a circulation of any great importance, although all were considered an important part of the SFIO's propaganda effort. Party rules permitted freedom of discussion by its press on matters of doctrine and procedure but did not permit criticism of the decisions and actions of the major party organs and the International.

Party Discipline

According to Léon Blum, "Discipline is a normal state for a political party, and its unity should be strictly maintained against selfish defections inspired by personal interest, ambition, or other forms of temptation."[28] With the obvious exception of the Communists, the Socialists were, at least on paper, the most disciplined of the major French parties.

Individual party members were normally under the disciplinary control of the federations. For disciplinary purposes, each federation established a conflict committee composed of seven or nine members, all of whom had to have been members for at least five years. They could not have been members of any of the federal organs, and no more than a third of the committee members could have been parliamentarians. The federal conflict committees heard any complaints made against their own members by individuals or groups and had the power to acquit or to punish by private or public warning, censure and temporary suspension of the offender from party office, or expulsion from the party. Federal conflict committee decisions were binding except in cases of suspension or exclusion, which were strong penalties for extremely serious offenses, such as a grave breach of principles or regulations of the party, or misconduct of a type that would reflect seriously on the good name of the party. A suspended or expelled member could appeal within thirty days to the National Conflict Committee. Once a member was excluded he could be readmitted only by the decision of a National Congress after consultation with the federation and section of which he was originally a member.[29]

The National Conflict Committee was composed of nine people, all of whom must have been party members for at least ten years. No member of a national organ could serve and no more than one-third of the committee members could be parliamentarians. This committee had jurisdiction over cases appealed from federal conflict committees and disciplinary cases involving two or more federations. The national committee could impose any of the penalties within the competence of the federal committees, and in all cases its decision was final. In all cases the accused had the right to appear and present his side of the case. If either the federal or the National Conflict Committee found the accusations unfounded, it had the right to punish the complainant.[30] As an illustration of the work involved, in the year July, 1952, to July, 1953, the National Conflict Committee considered seventeen cases, fifteen new and two carried over from the previous year. After fourteen sessions, the committee disposed of the fifteen new cases and postponed the two carry-over cases. The disposition of the completed cases included eight sentences of expulsion, two of suspension, two of censure, one rejection of an appeal, and two dismissals with the agreement of the complainant. As a general rule the national committee confirmed the decisions of the federal committees unless there had been some irregularity in the proceedings.[31]

Party organs could be disciplined as well as individuals. With

Comité directeur approval, a federation could dissolve a recalcitrant section. A federation in turn could be dissolved by a decision of the *Comité*. In either case it was the duty of the disciplining body to lay down, as soon as possible, the conditions for readmission to membership. Although dissolution was not a common occurrence, during the winter of 1950-51, two sections and one federation suffered this fate.[32]

Easily the most difficult problem, either real or imaginary, was the conflict between the party members who had been elected to public office, especially the Socialist Parliamentary Group, and the rank and file. The latter, the *militants,* always strove to control the former, the *parlementaires.* Although in the history of the SFIO the parliamentarians had many times proven to be the more stable element, the conflict was a natural outcome of two major fears. The first was a worry that Socialist parliamentarians would succumb to the French tradition of political careers starting on the left and progressing steadily to the far right. The second, which was linked with the first, was the tendency of parliamentarians to place primary emphasis on their allegiance to their constituents rather than to party policy when party actions happened to be unpopular in their districts. These fears resulted in a number of actions that were designed to keep the parliamentarians subservient to the party militants.

First, as mentioned earlier, a limit was placed on the number of parliamentarians permitted to sit on the *Comité directeur.* Before 1913, when the problem was obviously not acute, no members of parliament were allowed to belong to the *Comité's* predecessor, the CAP, or to represent their federations on the National Council. In 1913 the regulations were amended to permit ten parliamentarians to belong to the thirty-one member *Comité directeur,* and in 1956 it was raised to twenty out of forty-five. Second, there was the early postwar decision to raise from three to five the period of consecutive years of party service necessary before a member of the SFIO could serve on a major party organ or be nominated as its candidate at legislative elections.[33] While this regulation did result in assuring that parliamentarians were imbued to a certain extent with Socialist tradition, Professor Duverger comes to the conclusion that the most important effect of this decision was the rupture between the SFIO and the

National Liberation Movement, which cost the party badly needed young blood. "The loss to the Socialist party was very considerable," Duverger points out, "for the elimination of its reserve teams is one of the prime causes of its decline since 1946."[34]

Finally, the *Comité directeur* was given responsibility for disciplining the parliamentarians. It had the power to warn offenders, censure them formally, suspend them, and even exclude them from the party. Except for expulsion, the decision of the *Comité* was final. In exclusion cases, an appeal could be made within fifteen days to the National Congress or National Council, whichever convened first. Once excluded, an individual parliamentarian could regain his membership only by decision of a National Congress.[35]

A mass disciplinary action took place on December 30, 1954, when the *Comité directeur* expelled Max Lejeune, chairman of the National Defense Committee of the National Assembly, and suspended sixteen other members. The group had split with party policy by voting against the European Defense Community. On January 19, 1955, the subject was again raised and the *Comité directeur* decided to expel the suspended members from the party. An Extraordinary National Congress was held on February 5 and 6, which confirmed that action of the *Comité*. After receiving a request for reinstatement from the seventeen excluded members, on March 30 the *Comité directeur* agreed to put the matter of reinstatement before the next regular congress.[36] The last act in the drama took place on July 31, 1955, when the Forty-seventh National Congress agreed unanimously "minus one vote," to reinstate all seventeen. In the words of the secretary-general, this action "signified neither a change of party line in regard to foreign affairs, nor the imposition of a disavowal of an action by the *Comité directeur*. It concerned solely an attempt to mend the unity of the party in the face of what could be a difficult election."[37]

While the entire postwar system of discipline in the SFIO was weighted heavily in favor of the militants, not all observers were of the opinion that it remained successful. Writing in *Le socialisme trahi*, André Philip (who not incidentally had been expelled by the *Comité directeur* in March, 1958, for criticizing party policy in a nonparty publication) complained that the entire system collapsed when the Socialists came into power. This was done by propaganda, censorship, and especially by the underuse and misuse of party organs, especially the *Comité directeur*. According to Philip, the *Comité*, whose job it was to control the actions of the secretariat and the parliamentarians' group, was not convened more than once a month; and when it did meet it was confined to minor administrative details and not to matters of policy. When the SFIO was in power in France, the party was completely subordinated to the government and the parliamentarians.[38]

Party Finances

The SFIO was financed by the individual party members. Both ordinary funds and election expenses were met by selling monthly dues stamps to individuals. Dues stamps were sold to the federations in denominations of 32 francs, 55 francs, or 100 francs, set by the National Congress. In 1954 these three categories gave the central treasury 30,948,384 francs, 2,640,715 francs, and 663,200 francs, respectively.[39] Each federation then added the amount it needed to support its own activities. The section purchased the stamps for the sum of the central and federation fees, and, in turn, added its own fees before selling the stamp to the individual member. Inasmuch as the lower party organs had almost complete freedom to fix the amount charged, the prices of dues stamps sometimes varied from one federation to another, and even among the sections of a single federation.[40]

The individual party member was free to choose the category of dues stamp that he felt he could afford. For those who were willing to contribute more, there were supplementary stamps, and there was a special category for parliamentarians. These stamps, plus incidental income from the sale of Socialist publications and so forth, provided party revenue. It was often suggested that apportioning dues according to ability to pay might make for a better financial foundation, but nothing of the sort was done. Resistance to this scheme, interestingly enough, came largely from poorer members who did not want to become classed as "cut-price Socialists."[41]

The SFIO's system of finances tended to provide a steady

income and to give the rank and file members a sense of participation and belonging. Above all, it helped to avoid the evils of undue influence exerted by rich contributors. In addition the freedom to fix the price of dues stamps gave the lower party organs an independence almost unique among French political parties. There was a major drawback to the system, however. Since the representation of a federation in the National Congress was based on the number of paid-up memberships it could account for, there was nothing to prevent a wealthy federation from purchasing additional party cards to increase its power in party councils.

Clientele and Membership

Despite the logic of Socialist philosophy as articulated by the party theoreticians and the strength of the party's organizational structure, the SFIO never became as attractive to Frenchmen as its leaders predicted. Neither did it attract a majority of the French voters, nor come even close; nor did it ever become the single largest party in the French multiparty system. Throughout the Fourth Republic, as before, its appeal remained to a great extent localized as regards both geography and social class.

The SFIO's greatest appeal of all times came in the first post–World War II election of 1945 when it attracted over 4½ million votes, or 23.21 percent of all the votes cast. The SFIO's votes fell in the three succeeding elections—the two in 1946 and the one in 1951—to rise slightly in 1956 and in the first ballot in 1958. It fell again in both ballots of 1962. By 1967 it was a part of the Federation of the Democratic and Socialist Left and thus its exact totals are not available, although it can safely be assumed that it continued to fall. Table 1 gives an overview of Socialist voter strength since World War I.[42]

As the electoral strength of the SFIO fluctuated, so did its membership. Table 2 traces SFIO membership from its beginning in 1905 until 1966, showing how many Frenchmen were willing to pay for a party card and graphically illustrating the year-to-year fortunes of the party.[43]

Before examining the composition of the party and its elite, one should take note of the geographical distribution of the SFIO's votes and of its membership. The 1951 inventory of the party's

Table 1. SFIO Electoral Strength

Election	No. of Socialist Votes	% of Total Votes
1919	1,727,963	21.25
1924	749,647	8.15
1928	1,698,084	17.68
1932	1,964,384	20.05
1936	1,955,306	19.35
1945	4,561,411	23.21
1946 (June)	4,187,818	20.71
1946 (November)	3,431,954	17.54
1951	2,744,924	14.29
1956	2,927,000	15.8
1958 (1st ballot)	3,176,557	15.5
1958 (2nd ballot)	2,574,606	13.8
1962 (1st ballot)	2,319,662	12.6
1962 (2nd ballot)	2,304,330	15.2
1967* (1st ballot)	4,207,166	18.79
1967* (2nd ballot)	4,505,329	24.08

*Total for the Federation

power is provided in Table 3. As Table 3 reveals, of the twenty departments with the largest industrial population, only 7 were on the list of departments with the strongest Socialist vote, and only 8 were included in those with the highest number of SFIO members. (There were 90 departments at the time.) In short, the SFIO was a power to be reckoned with in some areas where there was also a concentration of industrial power, but a disproportionate amount of its strength lay in the South and West.

Four departments tended to dominate the SFIO throughout its history—Nord, Pas-de-Calais, Bouches-du-Rhône, and Seine. In 1945 the largest party federation was Pas-de-Calais, followed by Nord and Seine. As Table 3 shows, by 1951 Pas-de-Calais had fallen to second place and Bouches-du-Rhône had replaced the Seine as third. By the middle 1960s, Bouches-du-Rhône, which was the department of Gaston Defferre, the only person to pose a serious threat to the leadership of Guy Mollet (Pas-de-Calais), had become the largest federation. Second place was taken by Pas-de-Calais, third by Nord, and Seine a poor fourth. As regards the concentration of party power in these departments, Pas-de-Calais,

Table 2. SFIO Membership, 1905-1966

Year	No. of Members	Year	No. of Members
1905	34,688	1933	131,044
1906	40,000	1934	110,000
1907	52,913	1935	120,083
1908	56,963	1936	202,000
1909	57,977	1937	286,604
1910	69,085	1938	275,373
1911	69,578	1939	180,279
1912	72,692	1940-44	(World War II)
1913	75,192	1945	335,705
1914	93,218	1946	354,878
1915	25,393	1947	296,314
1916	25,879	1948	223,495
1917	28,224	1949	157,897
1918	15,827	1950	140,190
1919	133,277	1951	126,858
1920	179,787	1952	116,327
1921	50,449	1953	113,455
1922	49,174	1954	113,699
1923	50,496	1955	116,680
1924	72,659	1956	117,740
1925	111,276	1957	119,597
1926	111,368	1958	114,469
1927	98,034	1959	104,352
1928	109,892	1960	102,644
1929	119,519	1961-62	191,339
1930	125,563	1963-64	178,834
1931	130,864	1965-66	174,056
1932	137,684		

Nord, and Seine accounted for one-fifth of the votes at the 1945 party congresses. By 1967 the four dominating departments together constituted a majority in party congresses. Not only was the SFIO's power shrinking, but it was being concentrated in fewer departments.[44]

As may be inferred from Table 3, the SFIO was never the working-class party it hoped to be in spite of its philosophy and its

Table 3. Industrial Population and Socialist Strength in French Departments in 1951

Industrial Population		Socialist Vote		Socialist Membership	
Department	Percent	Department	Percent of Total Vote	Department	Members (in thousands)
Nord	60.9	Haute-Vienne	32.1	Nord	10.2
Pas-de-Calais	55.9	Landes	31.5	Pas-de-Calais	9.4
Belfort	54.3	Aude	30.4	Bouches-du-Rhône	7.5
Meurthe-et-Moselle	53.7	Ariège	29.9	Seine	6.2
Seine-et-Oise	51.6	Basse-Alpes	27.8	Haute-Vienne	3.1
Loire	51.4	Var	25.2	Seine-et-Oise	2.6
Rhône	50.2	Pas-de-Calais	25.1	Haute-Garonne	2.2
Moselle	49.3	Nord	23.6	Gard	2.0
Seine	48.7	Ardennes	23.2	Gironde	2.0
Haut-Rhin	47.2	Haute-Garonne	22.7	Aude	1.8
Seine-Maritime	47.2	Creuse	22.0	Hérault	1.7
Bouches-du-Rhône	46.0	Gironde	21.8	Dordogne	1.5
Oise	45.9	Somme	21.6	Somme	1.5
Ardennes	45.4	Cantal	21.5	Var	1.4
Vosges	44.9	Côte-d'Or	20.7	Haut-Rhin	1.1
Doubs	42.7	Aveyron	20.6	Pyrénées-Orientales	1.1
Aude	41.6	Deux-Sèvres	20.3	Landes	.9
Seine-et-Marne	40.0	Bouches-du-Rhône	20.2	Oran	.9
Somme	39.6	Gard	20.1	Côtes-du-Nord	.8
Bas-Rhin	38.7	Doubs	20.0	Ariège	.8

declarations. Nevertheless, it did reflect fairly well the composition of the French electorate as a whole.

For comparison, the French voter and the SFIO voters have been analyzed according to sex, age, and education. The male SFIO voter outnumbered the female in 1962 by 58 percent to 42 percent. The voting population in 1962, however, was composed of 52 percent women and only 48 percent men. As regards age, on the other hand, the SFIO voter was closer to the national average. In 1963, for instance, 26 percent of the SFIO voters were 21 to 34 years of age, 32 percent from 35 to 49, 27 percent from 50 to 64, and 15 percent 65 or older. For the same age groups, the voting population was 31 percent, 26 percent, and 17 percent, respectively. In education, too, the SFIO voter was fairly close to the national norm. Eighty percent had a primary education, 17 percent secondary and technical or commercial, whereas only 3 percent had gone to college or university. The percentages for the electorate as a whole were, respectively, 70, 26, and 4.

Even more telling is a comparison of Socialist voters and SFIO members according to occupation. A public opinion poll taken in 1951 by *Sondages* found the Socialist voters employed as follows:[45]

Workers	21%
Government employees	13%
Retired	10%
Artisans, tradesmen, and professional	10%
Farmers	8%
Agricultural workers	6%
Clerks (nongovernmental white collar)	6%
Without profession (mostly housewives)	26%

A similar breakdown of the SFIO membership in 1951 shows the following composition:[46]

Government employees	24.9%
Workers	24.3%
Retired	12.8%
Artisans and tradesmen	12.3%
Clerks (nongovernmental white collar)	8.8%
Farmers	7.4%
No profession	6.9%
Professional	2.6%

Using a slightly different classification system, the French Political Science Association came up with similar results for the two groups eleven years later.[47]

The important difference between the two groups is the increased percentage of government employees who were actually members of the SFIO as compared with those who just voted for the Socialist party. "Government employees," it should be noted, includes public school teachers, a group the SFIO pursued assiduously in its recruitment efforts. MacRae has mentioned the affinity of the SFIO for public school teachers, and Simmons quotes the party's annual report of 1959, which notes that "to attempt to recruit workers is an excellent thing, but to recruit a teacher or a professor is no less so, their particular qualifications making them very efficient in the sections."[48]

A 1957 study of the SFIO sections in Lyons, some of the results of which are offered by André Philip in his book *Les Socialistes*, reveals a similar pattern. Out of a total of 475 members, 9 percent were found to be less than thirty years of age, 46 percent from 30 to 50, and 45 percent over 50. Fourteen-and-a-half percent were classified as workers, 13.8 percent as artisans and tradesmen, 21 percent clerks *(employées)*, 24.3 percent minor civil servants, 2.6 percent senior civil servants, 9.9 percent retired, 7.1 percent women without a profession, 3.5 percent professional, and 3.3 percent students. Of those classified as minor civil servants, 23 percent (or 5.4 percent of the total) were police officers. Almost half of these police officers, André Philip points out, became members of the SFIO during the government of Guy Mollet.[49]

An investigation of the party elite is even more enlightening. The following chart tabulating the social composition of the party worker in 1952 was the result of interviews of federation executive committees, candidates for legislative elections of June, 1951, Socialists in the Council of the Republic, the National Assembly, and the *Comité directeur:*[50]

Government employees	37.4%
Workers	11.4%
Retired	7.7%
Artisans and tradesmen	10.6%
Clerks	13.5%
Farmers	6.8%
No profession	2.5%
Professional	10.1%

Especially striking here when compared to the social composition of the electorate and the SFIO membership is the predominance of the government employee (which includes school teachers) and the further decline of worker representation. Interesting also is the increased proportion of professional people in the party elite.

To give a more specific illustration, a 1957 survey of the Lyons party sections showed that the section secretaries included a teacher, a chief inspector of the national railroad, a salesman, an artisan, a worker, an industrial designer, and an economic survey officer *(inspecteur aux enquêtes économiques)*. Likewise there was only one worker on the eleven-man federation executive committee.

While the age of the party worker again did not reveal any important deviation from the ages of the member or the voter— 67.5 percent below the age of 50 and 31.5 percent above—only 12.1 percent were women. Of those in national or federal organs of the party, or representing the party in legislature, only 5.6 percent were women. Although there have been some exceptional women leaders in the SFIO, such as Mme Paule Malroux, onetime secretary-general and treasurer of the Socialist group in the Assembly of the French Union, women were obviously under-represented in the party elite considering their numbers in the Socialist electorate and party rank and file.

Leadership

It is now time to move one more step up the ladder of command to the national *Comité directeur* and the party in parliament. In analyzing the party in parliament, the survey undertaken by Harvey G. Simmons on Socialist deputies for 1956, 1958, 1962, and 1967 is very helpful.[51] First, it shows that a large majority of Socialist deputies had had previous political experience, mostly in the Fourth Republic, before being elected to parliament. In 1956, for instance, out of 93 Socialist deputies, 49 had been mayors; 20, ministers; 21, secretaries or under-secretaries of state; and 9, members of a ministerial cabinet or similar office. In 1962, 46 out of the 64 Socialist deputies were mayors of towns at the time of their election. Twenty-five, it must be noted, were mayors of cities with less than 20,000 inhabitants and 14 from cities with

20,000 to 39,999 inhabitants. Four more had been mayors before election, 5 had been ministers, 4 secretaries or under-secretaries of state, and 3, members of a cabinet or similar office. The composition in 1967 was close to that of 1962. The second revelation is the high degree of education of the Socialist deputies. For the same four years, of those for whom information could be obtained, 78 percent were recipients of university degrees. Law predominated with 23 percent, followed by Letters with 22 percent. An additional 11 percent were graduates of "training colleges."

The third and perhaps most interesting fact revealed by the Simmons survey is the high number of professional people, especially educators, among the Socialist deputies. A total of 33 percent of all deputies for whom information could be obtained for all four years were school teachers (17 percent) and professors (16 percent). The next largest group was doctors and pharmacists with 12 percent, then lawyers with 11 percent. Following in order were minor civil servants with 9 percent, journalists with 6 percent, high government officials with 6 percent, and executives with 5 percent. The worker represented only 4 percent, sharing ninth place with the farmer (also 4 percent). The SFIO was far from being a worker's party as far as representation in parliament was concerned.

Regarding the *Comité directeur*, the controlling organ of the SFIO (especially when the party was not in power), a number of very interesting facts are revealed by the Simmons survey. Looking at the data in the same manner used with the Socialist deputies, the first factor was the high level of political experience that the members brought with them into the *Comité*. Of those for whom information could be obtained, only 23 percent had not served in a political office. Sixty-three percent had attained the high position of deputy. Second, as in the case of the members of parliament, the committee contained a large number of professional people, especially educators. For the period 1945 to 1966, 23 percent began their careers as professors in lycée, college, or university, and 16 percent as school teachers. Next in importance were journalists (13 percent) and lawyers (13 percent). These four professions, then, accounted for 65 percent of the membership of the *Comité directeur*. The worker was not the lowest, but accounted for only 7 percent. Third, the professional background of the *Comité* members, as with the deputies, was reflected in their high level of education. Seventy-five percent of the members for the years 1945 to 1966 had university degrees, 27 percent of them in Law and 24 percent in Letters.

The Simmons survey provides two more important insights into the SFIO's *Comité directeur* regarding age and tenure. The entry of younger people into the governing circles permitted by the reorganization of the party after World War II was reflected in the 43.7 average age of *Comité* members in 1945. From that time on, however, the average age increased steadily. By 1955 it was 51 and by 1965, the last date of the Simmons survey, it was 53.9. As for tenure, it was found that the members of the *Comité directeur* were reelected with regularity. From 1947 to 1967, excluding 1956 when the *Comité* was enlarged from 31 to 45 members, the average rate of reelection was approximately 81 percent. As a result, some were nearly permanent members. Simmons reports that between 1945 and 1966, the average number of years that a member served was close to seven. There were thirty-eight members who had served more than ten years and three who had served for twenty. There was, therefore, a great deal of continuity in the overall direction of the fortunes of the party, at least during the period following World War II.

Guy Mollet

The SFIO had three major leaders during its existence. The first was Jaurès, the dynamic intellectual, humanist, pantheist, writer, and poet who officiated at the birth of the SFIO and who struggled so hard to eliminate internal dissension in order to bring about a truly unified party. From 1905 to his assassination in 1914, Jaurès was the undisputed leader of the SFIO. The second was Léon Blum, the quiet, dignified, scholarly statesman who guided the destiny of the SFIO in the interwar years and presided over the first exercise of power by French Socialists in the Popular Front government of the 1930s. The third, and the one of most importance to us here, was Guy Mollet, who took over the reins of the party in 1946 and relinquished them only when the SFIO gave up its independent existence in 1969.

In contrast to his predecessors, Guy Mollet was a true product of the party he led. Born of a working-class family in Flers, Orne, in the same year that the SFIO was created by Jaurès, Mollet attended the college at Flers and the university at Lille, where he received a bachelor's degree in English. In 1936 Mollet obtained his first teaching position as a professor of English at the college in Arras, Pas-de-Calais, later moving to the lycée in Arras, where he held a professorship until 1944. Guy Mollet joined the party in the early 1920s and in 1939 was elected secretary-general of the Federation of Education, a Socialist teachers' trade union. Mollet was captured by the Germans in 1940, and when he returned to Arras in 1942, he became the principal organizer of the Resistance movement in the Pas-de-Calais region. In 1945 Mollet ran for, and was elected to, the office of mayor of Arras, a position he was held until the time of his death in 1975.

Although Guy Mollet had an excellent reputation in Pas-de-Calais by 1945, he was not too well known outside the region. This fact was quickly changed. Mollet was chosen to represent his region in the two Constituent Assemblies of 1945 and 1946, and in 1946 he was elected deputy to the National Assembly by the Pas-de-Calais department, another post he was to retain throughout the remainder of SFIO's existence. Finally in 1946 Mollet made his bid for the leadership of the SFIO and won.

The year of Mollet's election as secretary-general was a crucial one for the SFIO, as it marked the change from the Resistance party to the first postwar peacetime party. When the war ended in France in 1944, and political parties could once again come out in the open, the *Comité directeur* of the SFIO, which had been organized during the Resistance with Daniel Mayer acting as secretary-general, immediately plunged into the enormous and demanding task of rebuilding the party's machinery.

In the months preceding the 1946 National Congress, when it was decided that elections to the *Comité directeur* would be held, Daniel Mayer took pains to spell out a new party program that he believed would permit the SFIO to ride what many felt was a mounting groundswell of pro-Socialist sentiment. Basically, Mayer asked for a revision of party doctrine along humanitarian lines that would appeal to all good men of the Left and Center who had worked so well together in the Resistance. In other words, many of the sharp edges of Socialist doctrine in the past repugnant to those on both sides of the SFIO would be eliminated or toned down. Léon Blum, after his return to Paris from a Nazi prison camp, gave his whole hearted support to Mayer and his program.

Mayer might have won the day and thus changed the entire future of the SFIO as well as becoming its undisputed leader if it had not been for two major events. The first was the poor health of Léon Blum. When Blum returned he was a national hero, but his health problems severely restricted his party activities. Although he did take over the direction of *Le Populaire* and his writings in that journal were read with respect by the party faithful, he was forced to refuse the place reserved for him on the *Comité directeur*. Blum was not, therefore, in any position to give his protégé Mayer all the support and protection he would otherwise have given. The second event was, of course, the poor showing of the SFIO in the 1946 elections. Far from emerging as the first party of France as it had hoped, the SFIO ran third after the Communists on the left and the MRP on the right. The failure of the party in the 1946 elections naturally reflected on its secretary-general.

By the time the delegates from the federations met in Paris on August 29, 1946, for the National Congress, it was evident that Daniel Mayer was in for a difficult time. A strong traditionalist opposition, which had remained fairly muted up to the elections, came out in the open just prior to the congress. Led by the mayor of Arras, Guy Mollet, the traditionalists attacked both Mayer's leadership and his "revisionism." Not only should Socialist doctrine not be watered down, Mollet said, it should be followed to the letter. The opposition carried its attack to the floor of the congress. Mayer was repeatedly attacked for bad management of the party, for the poor electoral results, and especially for concessions to the bourgeoisie. The SFIO was a working-class party and should remain so. Mayer and Blum attempted to defend Mayer's leadership of the party and the need to revise the doctrines of socialism, but failed.

The opposition, under the skilled leadership of Guy Mollet, made the normally routine acceptance of the secretary-general's report to the congress *(rapport moral)* the deciding issue. All opposed to Mayer's leadership and revisionism were asked to reject it, and Mayer's report was refused by a vote of 2,975 to 1,365 (with 145 abstentions). So massive was the defeat that Mayer and several of his leading officials promptly resigned. The verdict of the congress was reaffirmed in the elections to the *Comité directeur* which followed. The elections favored the traditionalists and their leader. Guy Mollet's leadership of the SFIO was formalized in September when the new *Comité* held its first meeting and elected Mollet its secretary-general. As pointed out by Alfred Grosser, Guy Mollet's strength at the congress was a result of his heading one of the most important federations, as well as his energy and savoir faire. When this was coupled with the support of Augustin Laurent, secretary-general of the Nord federation, there was no doubt who would win.[52]

Guy Mollet's policies in the Fourth Republic and the first part of the Fifth will be the subject of the next four chapters. It is appropriate here to end with a few overall impressions of Mollet as a leader. Almost all observers agree that Mollet was a dynamic and master tactician. One scholar calls Mollet's speaking style "earnest" and "forceful, incisive and lucid."[53] Another describes Mollet as an "extraordinary strategist" and points out that "not even his enemies denied his consummate abilities as parliamentarian and his uncanny sense of what party members would or would not tolerate."[54] Williams states that Mollet was "uncannily sensitive" to public opinion, and Grosser notes Mollet's "capacity to maneuver" and his unfailing "understanding of the psychology of the militants."[55]

Notes

1. Williams, *Crisis and Compromise*, p. 71.
2. *Règlement du Parti* (Paris: SFIO, 1946), Arts. 3-7.
3. Ibid., Arts. 4 and 8.
4. Charles A. Micaud, *Communism and the French Left* (New York: Praeger, 1963), p. 200.
5. *Règlement du Parti*, Arts. 9-11 and 14.
6. Ibid., Art. 20.
7. Ibid., Arts. 31-34.
8. Williams, *Crisis and Compromise*, pp. 63, 66, 370-71.

9. *Règlement du Parti*, Arts. 21-27.

10. See *Bulletin intérieur*, no. 78 (May 1955), pp. 117-18, 129.

11. Ibid., pp. 141-42.

12. *Règlement du Parti*, Art. 29.

13. Ibid., Art. 41.

14. See *Bulletin intérieur*, no. 78 (May 1955), pp. 147-70.

15. *Règlement du Parti*, Arts. 29-46 and 69.

16. Williams, *Crisis and Compromise*, p. 100.

17. André Philip, *Le socialisme trahi* (Paris: Plon, 1957), p. 200.

18. *Règlement du Parti*, Art. 26.

19. Ibid., Arts. 42-46.

20. Ibid., Annex, "Rapports entre le Comité directeur et le Groupe parlementaire," May 1952.

21. Micaud, *Communism and the French Left*, p. 201.

22. Ibid., p. 202.

23. Ibid.

24. This material on the SFIO's auxiliary organs is taken primarily from the excellent account contained in Harvey G. Simmons, *French Socialists in Search of a Role: 1956-1967* (Ithaca, N.Y.: Cornell University Press, 1970), pp. 181-200.

25. Ibid., p. 192.

26. Ibid., p. 197.

27. Daniel Ligou, *Histoire de socialisme en France 1871-1961* (Paris: Presses Universitaires de France, 1962), p. 594.

28. Blum, *For All Mankind*, pp. 103-104.

29. *Règlement du Parti*, Arts. 49-56 and 61.

30. Ibid., Arts. 50-58.

31. *Bulletin intérieur*, no. 66 (June 1953), p. 117.

32. *Règlement du Parti*, Arts. 63-68, and *Bulletin intérieur*, no. 53 (April 1951), pp. 19, 172.

33. *Règlement du Parti*, Art. 13.

34. Duverger, *Les partis politiques*, p. 191.

35. *Règlement du Parti*, Arts. 60-61.

36. *Bulletin intérieur*, no. 78 (May 1955), pp. 165, 177-78.

37. *Le Figaro*, July 1, 1955, p. 11.

38. Philip, *Le socialisme trahi*, pp. 200-201.

39. *Bulletin intérieur*, no. 78 (May 1955), pp. 13-21.

40. Duverger, *Les partis politiques*, pp. 79-80.

41. Ibid., p. 97.

42. Pierre Rimbert, "L'avenir du Parti socialiste," *La Revue Socialiste*, no. 54 (February 1952), p. 127; *New York Times*, January 4, 1956, pp. 1-2.

43. Figures for 1905 to 1952 are from Duverger, *Les partis politiques*, pp. 88-89. Figures for 1953 and 1954 were supplied by the Bureau of the SFIO.

44. See Simmons, *French Socialists*, pp. 171 and 238-39; and Graham, pp. 87-88.

45. *Sondages*, no. 3 (1952), as quoted in Rimbert, "L'avenir du Parti socialiste," p. 203.

46. Pierre Rimbert, "Le Parti socialiste, SFIO," in Association Française de Science Politique, *Partis politiques et classes sociales en France* (Paris: A. Colin, 1955), p. 197. The figures for the social composition of the membership of the SFIO are the result of an inquiry undertaken by the French Political Science Association in 1951. The 14,518 members of the SFIO interviewed represented approximately 13% of the total members in France proper, and came from 400 sections in 81 out of 90 French departments. As pointed out in the survey, this sample does not permit complete accuracy but does give an indication. Ibid., p. 195.

47. Simmons, *French Socialists*, p. 275.

48. Ibid., p. 189. See also MacRae, *Parliament, Parties and Society*, p. 53.

49. Philip, *Les socialistes* (Paris: Editions du Seuil, 1967), p. 176.

50. Rimbert, "Le Parti socialiste," p. 197.

51. For the information that follows on the *Comité directeur* of the SFIO and the Socialist deputies, the authors are deeply indebted to the extensive survey work done by Harvey G. Simmons presented in his book *French Socialists in Search of a Role: 1956-1967*, pp. 284-91.

52. Alfred Grosser, *La IVe République et sa politique extérieure* (Paris: A. Colin, 1961), p. 114.

53. See B. D. Graham, *The French Socialists and Tripartisme, 1944-1947* (Toronto: University of Toronto Press, 1965), p. 96.

54. Simmons, *French Socialists*, p. 208.

55. See Williams, *Crisis and Compromise*, p. 109, and Grosser, *La IVe République*, p. 115.

Part 2
The SFIO in and out
of Government

4
The SFIO and Domestic Issues in the Fourth Republic

In the study of any political party, it is difficult to assess precisely its impact on domestic public policy. Legislative proposals often have obscure origins, and policy processes tend to follow their own momentum. Furthermore, for any political party, programmatic preferences are interwoven with ideological constraints and tactical calculations. However, it is possible to determine several areas of particular concern for the SFIO after the liberation of France and, indeed, throughout the Fourth Republic: (1) rebuilding the country's shattered economy, securing an equitable distribution of resources, and involving the public authorities actively in both endeavors; (2) enlarging the scope of laic education at the expense of parochial education; (3) restoring the republican system of government, preferably in such a way that the predominance of parliament over the executive established during the Third Republic would be perpetuated; (4) insuring that the SFIO would participate effectively in government; and (5) maintaining the party's revolutionary mystique in the face of competition from rival leftist or "progressive" forces.

The SFIO and the New Postwar Regime

The first problem confronting the SFIO was the form of the postwar political system. General de Gaulle, the wartime leader of the Free French, who in 1944 had become the provisional prime minister of a broadly-based coalition cabinet, favored the continuation of the constitution of 1875, in consonance with his view that the Third Republic had not come to an end with the Occupation and that he, in his person, embodied its continuity. De Gaulle thought that if a new constitution were to be written, it would have to be approved in a popular referendum. The Radicals, too, favored the old constitution, probably less because of historic legitimacy than nostalgia for the important position the party had occupied during the Third Republic. The SFIO, together with the MRP and the PCF, favored an affirmative vote on a referendum, to be put before the people simultaneously with the parliamentary election, on the question of whether the new parliament should be a constituent assembly; the Socialists agreed with the MRP that, if a constituent assembly came into being, it should have a time limit of seven months for its work.

Unlike the PCF, the SFIO had no constitutional text of its own, but its ideas, which it largely shared with the Communists, reflected the position taken at its thirty-seventh Congress in favor of a unicameral legislature, a weak presidency, an independent judiciary, an electoral system based on proportional representation, and an absolute separation of church and state, particularly in the field of education. As we have seen, the first draft constitution based on these principles was rejected in a referendum held in May, 1946. According to one source,[1] the rejection of the draft, by little over a million votes, was due in part to the negative votes cast by many Socialists who had feared that the proposed constitutional arrangements would unduly enhance the power of the PCF.

The parliamentary elections which took place in June, 1946, resulted in a considerable loss for the Socialists (21 seats), a smaller loss for the PCF (8 seats), and a net gain for the MRP (19 seats). The new constitutional draft that emerged from the Constituent Assembly, and was subsequently adopted by the French people in October, 1946, by the hardly overwhelming majority of 9 million to 7.8 million, reflected, to some extent, the ideas of the SFIO, moderated by those of the MRP. The Socialists' preference for a British-type system emerged in two areas: the National Assembly would be the major legislative body, with the new Council of the Republic in a largely consultative role; the prime minister would be the true executive, with the new president in a purely decorative role. The SFIO and the

Communists favored some kind of "functional representative" body in the form of a small technical chamber in which interest groups—in particular trade unions—would be represented. This chamber, essentially an advisory one, would help the parliament formulate economic plans and would strive to secure the adherence of the affected economic sectors to the plan. The MRP, however, preferred a larger, and more active, sectoral representative body structured in accordance with Catholic social doctrine along more "corporative" lines. The result was a compromise: the establishment of the Social and Economic Council, an advisory body composed of some 200 members. Many Socialists had also agreed with the Communists in preferring a weak prime minister, subject to systematic control by parliament. But in order to prevent excessive irresponsibility of the legislature, and in order to safeguard the cabinet against too many censure motions, the SFIO agreed with the MRP in proposing the automatic dissolution of the Assembly if two cabinets were ousted in a five-year period. Moreover, the SFIO and the MRP were in accord in suggesting that constitutional amendments proposed by the Assembly should be ratified by popular referenda. These last two ideas were not to be embodied in the new constitution; as a consequence, the SFIO was never completely satisfied with that document. Although the draft constitution, with its extensive bill of rights, mirrored many of the progressive programmatic references of the SFIO and the PCF, it failed to incorporate a socialist-proposed provision that "the right to hold property shall not be exercised contrary to social utility."[2] In any case, with the popular endorsement of the constitution and the inauguration of the Fourth Republic, the SFIO became one of the most consistent defenders of that regime in the conviction that it provided a perfectly adequate framework for the promotion of the party's social and economic goals.

The SFIO was conscious of its strategic position between the PCF and the MRP and of the strength and independence that position provided for democratic socialism. The SFIO asserted its readiness to work with either party after de Gaulle left the government early in 1946 by agreeing to serve in the cabinet with the PCF, but only if the MRP were included as well. In this way the SFIO would remain the indispensable connecting link between the extreme anticlerical Left and the (then) moderately leftist Catholic republicans. The SFIO probably did not know at that time whether it was more profitable to align itself clearly with the MRP or the PCF. In the first Constituent Assembly, the PCF had been the most numerous party and had taken away enough working-class votes that the SFIO felt it had better collaborate with the Communists or lose even more support. But in the second Constituent Assembly (1946), the MRP had ousted the PCF from first place: was the MRP, then, the wave of the future? The SFIO was cognizant of the fact that the MRP was sufficiently republican and leftist to permit collaboration; but the MRP's clericalism was too pronounced, and the SFIO could afford to turn a blind eye neither to the taunts of the PCF for whom MRP meant *mensonge, réaction,* and *Pétainisme,* nor to its own militants, who dreamed of a revival of the Popular Front. There was, moreover, confusion within the ranks of the SFIO on the amount of stress that should be placed on traditional Marxist doctrine to attain a practical reformism that suddenly seemed promising in the context of the tripartite coalition of reform-oriented parties.

This confusion was manifested in the struggle over the party's leadership. Daniel Mayer, a protégé of Léon Blum, was replaced as secretary-general of the SFIO by Guy Mollet at the Thirty-seventh National Congress of August, 1945. This was clearly a victory of the ideological hardliners against those who adhered to Léon Blum's notions of socialist humanism. In order to head off criticism from militants of his own party, in order to outflank (or outshout) the Communists, and hence in order to solidify his own position, Mollet asserted the need for doctrinal purity, reiterated the party's Marxism, and stressed that the party, although committed to democratic processes, must not place exclusive reliance on parliamentary activity in promoting its goals. This was Mollet's own interpretation of the program of the thirty-seventh congress, which had reaffirmed the traditional principles of Marxism: historical materialism, the labor theory of value, the class struggle, and the inevitability of revolution. At the same time the congress had stressed the indissoluble connection between socialism and democracy and had provided for the option of defining the revolution as a restructuring of society and economy, while also accepting Blum's view of socialism as a vehicle for "the liberation of the human person." The proof that the SFIO could hold a hard line and remain—perhaps primarily—committed to practical reform, was demonstrated when the thirty-seventh congress also endorsed the party's manifesto of November, 1944, which had called for the safeguarding of individual liberties and the protection of property as well as for the nationalization of the dominant branches of the economy: energy, primary resources, heavy industries, transport, insurance, and credit.

Nationalization and Economic Planning

Throughout the Fourth Republic the domestic programs of the SFIO remained consistent: there was a close relationship between the positions enunciated at National Congresses and those reflected in the legislative behavior of Socialist deputies.

This harmony was particularly apparent with respect to nationalization policy. In September, 1944, the cabinet began the process of nationalization, often by means of decrees initiated by Socialist and Communist ministers jointly. Since both the SFIO and the PCF were committed to nationalization, it is difficult to determine precisely which party was the chief initiator of these bills. Proposals to nationalize the coal mines were introduced by a Communist minister; measures to nationalize the Bank of France and three other large banks, as well as thirty-two insurance companies (out of nearly a thousand), were prepared by Socialist André Philip. Most Socialist deputies voted for nationalization bills of whatever origin, although they had to overcome the lukewarm and occasionally hostile attitudes of certain individual party leaders, such as Christian Pineau, who was unenthusiastic, or Paul Ramadier, who had fought unsuccessfully against a joint SFIO-PCF bill to nationalize gas and electricity.[3]

There is reason to believe that Ramadier's opposition was inspired by political prescience and by tactical considerations. Under the etatist formula of nationalization (adopted for *Régie Renault*, for example), management of an industry was put directly under the control of the government, while under the syndicalist formula, which was chosen for gas and electricity (as well as the coal mines), the enterprise was put under a tripartite management board, composed of representatives of the national office (in effect the responsible ministry), the trade unions, and the consumers.[4] After 1947 the Communist-oriented CGT maintained a membership double that of the Force ouvrière (FO), and union representation in nationalized industries clearly implied Communist domination of them. In addition, Ramadier's minister of industrial production, Marcel Paul, was a Communist who used his position to appoint fellow party members as representatives of the consumers. It was feared that the PCF would utilize its presence in nationalized industries to foment strikes.

After the breakdown of the triparty coalition in 1947, the enthusiasm of the PCF for the existing structure of nationalized industries waned, while that of the SFIO, which was more inclined to utilize the public economic sector for etatist (i.e., republic-saving) purposes, waxed. After a Socialist (Robert Lacoste) had become minister of industry, a decree was promulgated providing for greater ministerial (as opposed to union) control over the appointment of board members, a reduction of the terms of office of representatives of unions and consumers, and frequent rotation of the board members. In general Socialist control over nationalized industries made it more difficult for the Communist unions to disrupt the economic life of the Republic and impede economic planning.

The SFIO National Congresses continued to produce resolutions favoring nationalization. In fact, when Jules Moch made a speech at the National Congress of 1951 opposing the nationalization of the steel industry (and favoring expenditure on armaments rather than social investments), he was the object of such furor from the militants that he had to resign from the *Comité directeur*.[5] However, Socialist deputies did little to advance nationalization policies in parliament. Such hesitancy was probably realistic, since the Socialist voters were clearly divided on the issue, and since the majority of the supporters of the SFIO's left-of-center parliamentary allies clearly opposed nationalization.[6]

By and large the SFIO supported the idea of the French-style indicative planning, but Socialist leaders were not of one mind about it. The most skeptical was Ramadier, who, according to

André Philip, was a Neo-Socialist reintegrated into the SFIO but retaining "a Radical temperament." "He believed more in the free play of the laws of nature than in the power of men to surmount them."[7] Léon Blum (who before World War II had not been a *planiste*) and many other leaders of the SFIO supported the Monnet Plan, which was inaugurated in 1946, despite its capitalist orientation—in part because it was to be based on nationalized industries. Most Socialists, while accepting the idea of a comprehensive plan, were critical of the structures and processes of the Monnet Plan, in particular the relative absence of parliamentary involvement in the choice of economic options. They criticized the insufficiently "social" content of the plan, arguing that workers' demands for guaranteed wages, housing, and social benefits took a back seat to the quest for increased industrial investments and productivity. That is why the SFIO agreed with the FO in making the advancement of workers' benefits as independent of the plan as possible by advocating (1) the expansion of collective contracts determining salaries *and* conditions of work that would be extended by government fiat to cover an entire category of workers; (2) an automatic sliding scale for wages that would be independent of the plan; and (3) a "social plan" to be enacted by parliament alongside the economic plan.[8]

In order to make "industrial democracy" more meaningful at the factory level, the SFIO not only supported de Gaulle's proposal to create worker-management committees *(comités d'entreprise)* in large private industrial firms, but successfully amended the government bill so as to strengthen their powers and extend them to all medium-sized enterprises, to the public service sector, and to agriculture. (De Gaulle favored such committees because he saw them as instruments to weaken the class struggle, while the SFIO viewed them as a means to foster industrial democracy, despite the fact that their work fell far short of genuine "codetermination" [*cogestion*].) It should be noted that on occasion the SFIO had to sacrifice its antiliberal economic principles on the altar of expediency. Blum's partial conversion to a liberal economic policy in the spring of 1946 was undoubtedly related to his successful attempt to secure large loans and outright grants from the United States, as well as the annulment of French World War II debts.

Such adaptability, which was due as much to realism as to the SFIO's desire to remain faithful to the wartime Resistance coalition, provoked frequent criticism by the rank and file, which accused the party leadership (especially Daniel Mayer) of an excessively conciliatory attitude toward the MRP and other bourgeois parties and of unnecessary submissiveness to de Gaulle's ideas.[9]

The SFIO and Agriculture

Like all Marxist-inspired parties, the SFIO originally had devoted less attention to the agricultural than to the industrial sector. But by the beginning of the Fourth Republic it had become clear that industrial workers had been drawn more consistently to the PCF. Moreover, after Liberation the agricultural sector still accounted for nearly a third of the French labor force, and the farmers and their dependents were seen as possessing significant electoral potential. Indeed, despite its proletarian mystique, the SFIO, throughout the Fourth Republic, drew most of its support from rural communes.[10] In 1952, for example, 42 percent of Socialist votes came from localities of fewer than 2,000 inhabitants. But since only 7.4 percent of farmers were members of the SFIO in 1951, and since there were political parties much more traditionally attuned to agricultural interests, the SFIO did not have specifically agricultural political machines. Farmers were represented in the party's Central Agricultural Committee, a body that concerned itself with propagandizing the farmer and formulating farm policy. But not all party federations had agricultural committees; the party's organizational implantation in rural communes was rudimentary; and its monthly farm journal, *Forces paysannes,* had a small circulation.

Since two-thirds of agriculture during the Fourth Republic was in the hands of small- and middle-scale family farmers, "no political party dared not to pose as the defender of private peasant property."[11] So although the SFIO remained committed to the nationalization of various economic sectors, despite its preference (in principle) for the cooperative organization of the agricultural sector, the party conveniently recalled the distinction once made by Marx between the private farmer who uses his own labor and the farmer who exploits the labor of others.[12]

It is nevertheless possible to speak about a uniquely socialist farm policy. Under the Popular Front government of Léon Blum, such a policy had been expressed in the creation of a National Wheat Office, through which the government helped to market agricultural produce at fair prices for the farmer. During the period of tripartism, the SFIO had the opportunity to provide its imprint while M. Tanguy-Prigent, a Socialist, functioned as minister of agriculture; even after the SFIO had ceased to be a partner in government coalitions, many progressive agricultural policies originated with Socialist deputies. However the SFIO was unclear about whether the state should be a decision maker or a mediator on agricultural problems—whether the state should be as *dirigiste* on agriculture as on industry, or whether it should intervene only in case of disagreements between the family farm producer and the consumer in the matter of prices. Hence the policies promoted by the SFIO reflected both approaches.

Tanguy-Prigent, the party's chief agricultural expert in the early years of the Fourth Republic, has been described as both a technocrat and as a "rigidly sectarian" Socialist.[13] On the one hand, as a prominent Resistance politician, he clearly opposed the corporativistic agricultural structure of the Pétain regime; on the other hand, he had little faith in the ability of farmers to modernize agriculture without the active involvement of the government. Hence he favored an integrationist approach, i.e., the establishment of a unified agricultural association legitimated by the government. Tanguy-Prigent was probably the wrong man to preside over such integration. As a Socialist, he was atypical of the French farming community in general; the Confédération générale de l'agriculture (CGA) that he had helped to form in 1944 was too leftist in orientation. Subsequently the importance of the CGA—and the influence of Tanguy-Prigent— began to decline when the Fédération nationale des syndicats d'exploitants agricoles (FNSEA), a major component of the CGA, showed itself to be clearly dominated by Catholics, conservatives, and believers in the organizational autonomy of the farmers.

Nevertheless, it was through the efforts of the SFIO that the comprehensive Farm Law of 1946 was passed. This law provided that sharecroppers had the right to renew their options at the expiration of their leaseholds and that the owner could repossess the land only if he undertook to work it himself, or if his children worked it. Sharecroppers could acquire ownership at low interest rates, and those who were forced to leave the land obtained compensation for the improvements they made on the land. The sharecroppers had the right to join a marketing cooperative and their conflicts with owners were to be resolved by arbitration tribunals *(tribunaux paritaires)* to which both sides elected an equal number of representatives. In 1953 the SFIO introduced bills in parliament to establish a fund to compensate losses due to natural disasters and to set up a guarantee fund for buying up surplus products so as to stabilize prices. The party remained consistently interested in improving the livelihood of farmers by extending social security coverage to them and by facilitating the farmers' acquisitions of the land they worked—without, however, transforming them into capitalists.

Education and *Laïcité*

The SFIO was equally consistent throughout the Fourth Republic in pursuing a policy of *laïcité* in education. In view of the fact that of 31 elementary school teachers in the Assembly in 1951, two-thirds were Socialists; that of the 84 educators at all levels elected, almost half belonged to the SFIO; and that more than a third of all Socialist deputies in the Fourth Republic had at one time or another been educators,[14] it was not surprising that the National Federation of Teachers (FEN), though nominally nonpartisan. was ideologically close to the SFIO. The SFIO's legislative proposals on education clearly reflected the minimum program of the FEN, which included the enlargement of government appropriations for public elementary and secondary schools and the corresponding dismantling of public support for parochial schools. In the early years of the Fourth Republic, the SFIO was instrumental in securing appropriations for 1,000 additional state elementary school teachers and in bringing in bills to extend the national laic school system to kindergarten and nursery school levels.[15]

In its legislative endeavors, the SFIO worked closely with a number of progressive and laic clubs in a *Commission nationale de défense laïque* and in parliament Socialist deputies collaborated with Communist and Radical deputies in a *Cartel d'action laïque* (although the PCF had tried unsuccessfully to exclude Socialists from that cartel). The SFIO could not, however, eliminate the competitive, nonlaic educational sector—perhaps because it did not try hard enough. Although the SFIO maintained the verbal onslaughts against clerics that had been characteristic of the Third Republic, the party's political position was not without realism. The SFIO favored a gradualist approach of not totally suppressing the parochial schools, but rather eventually integrating them into the state system of education.[16] In any case Socialist deputies, together with Communists and Radicals, voted against the Barangé Law, which provided for governmental subsidies of children attending parochial schools. After that bill's adoption in 1951, the Socialists, now in the opposition, annually introduced unsuccessful bills to rescind the law. It should, however, be noted that the Barangé Law was a watered-down version of the Marie bill, which had provided for direct governmental grants to Catholic schools, and which the SFIO, with the help of the anticlericals from other parties, was able to prevent from passing.

The SFIO's national leadership made a point of elevating *laïcité* to one of the chief features distinguishing Socialism from other parties, e.g., the Radicals and the Union démocratique et socialiste de la Résistance (UDSR), some of whose members had opted out of the parliamentary fight against the Barangé Law. This position was not uniformly held within the SFIO. The Defferrist wing continued to insist that there should be no rigid national position regarding *laïcité* and that each regional federation ought to arrive at its own conclusions on the issue. This lack of unanimity was, for example, reflected at the party's Forty-first National Congress in 1949, when a resolution to abolish parochial schools altogether was adopted by a relatively slim majority (2,582 against 2,065). Later Defferre accused Mollet—who was not averse to attracting Catholics to the SFIO—of making no effort to abrogate the Barangé Law when he was premier.[17] For the SFIO, national unity was above its fight for anticlericalism: "in a spirit of conciliation, and owing to special circumstance," the party acquiesced in the status quo in Alsace,

where there had been a long tradition of governmental
subvention of the Catholic school system.[18]

The SFIO and the Working Class

There is no doubt that historically the SFIO's credentials of
leftist traditionalism were genuine enough to enable Léon Blum
to insist, in the late 1940s, that the working class belonged to the
SFIO,[19] and the SFIO consistently supported trade unions to
improve the condition of the working man. Unfortunately, in
France the autonomous bargaining tradition, a characteristic of
Anglo-Saxon democracies, was still underdeveloped; the ideological fragmentation and relative insolvency of trade unions
made it difficult for them to force employers to adhere to
agreements made and existing laws did not grant unions the right
to organize in the factories.

The SFIO, in turn, was often prevented from pursuing goals
favored by organized labor. Many militant unionists tended to
distrust the SFIO because of its commitment to social and
economic change by parliamentary means. Parliament was
traditionally distrusted by the workers because it was looked upon
as too much given to immobilism, or worse, to transpartisan
pragmatic deals aimed at preserving the system of social and
economic privileges. It was recognized that local notables and
other bourgeois leaders had come to dominate the SFIO's
parliamentary group as much as they dominated other parliamentary groups (except for the Communist one). Hence the
working class frequently saw a solution to its problems by
extrainstitutional means: either by the intervention of a charismatic (and sometimes antirepublican) leader or else by unmedi-
ated and anomic mass action led by militant trade unionists.

In several industrial democracies, socialist parties have
succeeded in securing working-class support by pretending to
absorb the revolutionary mythology of trade unions, or by
establishing rapport with them through the co-optation of union
leaders into the party. Unfortunately, the linkages between the
SFIO and trade unionism were tenuous throughout the Fourth
Republic. The largest trade union was the CGT, and its relations
with the PCF were so close that the union was widely regarded as

the Communist party's "transmission belt." The FO, which was
established in 1947, was ideologically close to the SFIO in the
sense that it was committed to republican institutions and
liberties and, therefore, shared its anticommunism, but there were
more Socialists in the CGT than in the FO.[20] This fact may well
explain why the SFIO, despite its penchant for law and order,
refused in the summer and fall of 1947 to go along with the
Radicals and the UDSR in supporting the government's attempts
at controlling numerous strikes (especially in electricity and gas
and other nationalized industries) that had been ordered by the
CGT.[21] The FO was too small in terms of membership, and its
relationship to the SFIO too uncertain, for use by the Socialists
either as a transmission belt or as a vehicle for generating mass
electoral support among workers. Ten years after the founding of
the FO the number of Socialist workers belonging to the CGT
must have been sufficiently worrisome for the National Council
of the SFIO to adopt a motion stating that membership in the
CGT was incompatible with membership in the SFIO.[22] The
SFIO continued to demand the autonomy of the union vis-à-vis
the party (unlike the PCF, which considered the CGT subordinate to it). This may have been less a matter of principle than an
attempt by the SFIO to make the best of a bad situation. However,
the SFIO would have liked to collaborate with—and perhaps
control—the FO. In 1949 the SFIO complained that its activities
relating to the implantation of its ideas on socialism in the
comités d'entreprise were impeded by the FO's insistence on
defending the independence of trade unions.[23] As a consequence
of such insistence, the union element was feebly—if at all—
represented in any institutionalized fashion at national echelons
of the SFIO. In the mid-1940s, only one member of the *Comité
directeur* was a prominent trade union figure—in stark contrast to
the close liaison between the PCF and the CGT in France, and to
the interchange of personnel between trade unions and social
democratic parties in Sweden, West Germany, and Austria. To be
sure, the National Congresses of the SFIO elected, and heard
reports from, national labor commissions *(commissions nation-
ales ouvrières)*, but these were not clearly the mouthpieces of trade
unions and existed, moreover, alongside many other topical
commissions (e.g., on youth, women, agriculture, education,

veterans, artisans, and shopkeepers). Nevertheless, there *were* large areas of agreement between the SFIO and the FO not only on general social and economy policy, but also on collective bargaining. Although, as we have seen, the SFIO favored parliamentary solutions to the problems of workers, the party agreed with the unions on the importance of collective bargaining, on the extension of specific labor-industry contracts by ministerial decree to cover the entire industry, and on opposition to the compulsory arbitration of labor disputes.[24]

During the decade following the Liberation, and particularly during the period of tripartism, the proworker orientation of the SFIO's parliamentary members had been greatly inspired by its competition with Communist deputies, although even then such orientation remained somewhat forced.

After the collapse of tripartism, and under the Third Force coalition (composed of SFIO, Radicals, MRP, and Conservatives) that replaced it, the SFIO had to make certain tactical adaptations in order to justify its continued participation in government. On one such occasion the SFIO even supported an antilabor piece of legislation. In the autumn of 1947 MRP deputy Teitgen introduced a bill permitting the government to outlaw any strike that threatened the Republic, or threatened other workers' right to work. Initially only the MRP and the Radicals supported the bill, while the SFIO, together with the PCF, opposed it, since both Left parties recognized the bill as repressive. But during the parliamentary debates, the PCF's opposition was so fierce, and there were so many insulting remarks made about the SFIO—and especially about Jules Moch, who had just become minister of the interior—that many SFIO deputies finally voted for the bill. The SFIO argued that the bill could have been worse, and that the law would be a dead letter in any case because Moch, as the responsible minister, would not enforce it.[25] But the SFIO was put on the defensive because, regardless of its position on the bill, a militant Socialist, Edouard Depreux, as Moch's predecessor in the interior ministry, had helped break up a general strike against the Truman Doctrine and the Marshall Plan.[26] Therefore, the PCF appeared to many to be the only reliable defender of the worker.

The SFIO had by no means lost interest in the worker, but it had become more concerned with the preservation of the Republic, which it saw under attack from the extreme Left and the extreme Right. At a party congress in Lyons in the summer of 1947, the bulk of the delegates accepted a report from the SFIO's left wing critical of Ramadier's excessive conservatism on social and economic issues, yet a majority also endorsed the position of the *Comité directeur* that "one must simultaneously resist Gaullism and communism."[27] The pragmatism (or opportunism) of the SFIO was manifested during the municipal elections of November, 1947, when individual Socialist candidates made all kinds of alliances: sometimes with Radicals, MRP, PCF and even members of the Gaullist RPF.

But SFIO's concern with power was not absolute. In view of the increasingly conservative economic position of the MRP and the ideological divisions among Radical politicians, and in view of the inclusion of Conservatives in most cabinets between 1947 and 1951, progressive legislation emanating from the government must of necessity be attributed to the Socialist coalition partners. Moreover, after 1948, the SFIO could not head governments mainly because it did not agree with Radicals, the MRP, and the Moderates on economic issues. In 1949 the coalition that included the Socialists collapsed because they opposed government policy on wages. For instance, Daniel Mayer used his position as minister of labor to "thaw" the wages of some workers, in contravention of the policy of wage restraint embraced by the Queuille government. In February, 1950, the Bidault government weakened when the Socialist ministers resigned over its unwillingness to grant the salary increases for workers demanded by the SFIO. In June of the same year, the Socialist deputies helped defeat the Bidault government in response to its refusal to raise the pay of civil service workers. In large measure Jules Moch's failure to be endorsed as premier in October, 1949, was due to his projected policies in parliament: he had announced that he was in favor of greater salary increases for the workers, the control of prices, the reform of the tax system, and the elimination of tax fraud, as well as greater investment in social projects (he was invested, but did not keep his office more than a few days).[28] Moch was in any case not an ideal spokesman for the SFIO. In a lengthy discourse which he delivered at the National Congress in 1950, he not only reaffirmed his criticism of the PCF but also suggested that the

Marxism within his own party had become irrelevant in the face of a new socioeconomic reality created by modern methods of production and by the *embourgeoisement* of the working class.[29] His position was echoed by André Philip, who distinguished between the "pure" capitalism of the small enterprises and the "managerial" capitalism that James Burnham had discussed— the one reactionary, and the other progressive—and he suggested that social progress can sometimes be achieved in collaboration with progressive bourgeois parties.

In any event, in 1951 the SFIO decided to join the opposition. This decision was by no means unanimous. On the one hand, the local militants, who dominated the federations and the party congresses, opposed any participation in a coalition that was too conservative for them and that might risk the wrath of the SFIO's working-class supporters. On the other hand, there were the Socialist *ministrables* in parliament who favored continued participation. Many of the members of the SFIO parliamentary group were conservative enough to find little difficulty in collaborating with Radicals and centrists. Most of the deputies— among whom it was often difficult to tell where SFIO ideology ended and Radical ideology began[30]—tried to perform a balancing act between the ideological militants and the pragmatic "participationists," but they failed to secure the necessary authorization from the party's congress and the *Comité directeur* to join the government, or even to support it. The position of Guy Mollet was neither clear nor consistent. At a November, 1949, meeting of the National Council of the party, he asserted that "history has shown that the defense of the social conquests of the working class can also be accomplished in opposition."[31] Mollet proved to be the decisive factor in keeping the SFIO out of the government, although in 1950 he was to be (again) personally favorable to the idea of Socialists joining in a coalition headed—and dominated—by non-Socialists.[32] However, at the forty-fourth congress in April, 1952, Mollet, bowing to the adamant oppositionist pressure emanating from the federations, said:

> The existence in the Assembly and in the government of a strong "liberal" minority, while it forbids the party to stand surety for conservative measures by means of participation in it, calls upon

the party to recover its vigilance and to resume its activity in the fight against poverty.[33]

The SFIO continued as before to work in favor of improving the lot of the underprivileged. From 1951 to 1954 Socialist deputies sponsored bills to raise old age pensions and family subsidies, to secure greater benefits for the blind, war invalids and veterans, and to establish a sliding-scale system for increases in minimum wages for workers.[34]

The programmatic outlook of Socialist deputies was determined not only by the leftist ideological commitments that emerged from the party congresses but also by certain pragmatic considerations. The remark attributed to a left-wing Catholic about the MRP—that its behavior was "to sit in the Center in order to promote policies of the Left with the help of the Right"[35]—can be applied, with some modification, to the SFIO as well. Its policy (or tactic) was to promote progressive legislation with the help of both the Center-Left and the extreme Left, or more precisely, to balance the revolutionary and oppositionist rhetoric imposed upon the party by tradition, by its own militants, and by its competition with the PCF, against its desire to participate in government, to preserve the Republic, and to promote social reform. Some of the party's legislative proposals, such as those relating to *laïcité* and the reduction of military credits, did not entail great political risk, since such a position was clearly consistent with the party's ideology and was supported by the Radicals, the Communists, *and* the working class, but the proposals had only a minor indirect effect on the Socialist goal of redistributing income.

Although the National Congress made resolutions annually about the need to make the tax system more progressive and to raise the number of tax inspectors—and certain Socialist deputies introduced the appropriate bills—the Socialist parliamentary group did not pursue the matter too strenuously; in 1954, while Pineau and several other deputies faithfully reflected the *Comité directeur*'s ideas on tax reform, the parliamentary group as a whole, "profiting from discussions of government bills [on tax matters], has each time opposed our own solutions," that is, voted for the more conservative government measures.[36]

The Socialist deputies' somewhat evasive stand on tax reform was a consequence of the changing—and more diverse— composition of the party's electorate.[37] In a study undertaken in 1956, Micaud found that only one-fourth of the metal workers interviewed mentioned the SFIO as the party most interested in workers. The majority cited the PCF, although more workers expressed confidence in Mollet (or Mendès-France) than in any particular Communist leaders.[38] In the early 1950s only 7 percent of Socialist candidates in elections were workers, as contrasted with 26 percent of Communist candidates, and only 3 Socialist deputies in the 1951 parliament were workers, in contrast to 39 among the Communist deputies.[39]

By the time SFIO returned to the government and Guy Mollet assumed the premiership (in February, 1956), the party had become as conservative as was possible for one with Marxist traditions and revolutionary rhetoric. As Maurice Duverger put it:

> There is no doubt that the SFIO has become *embourgeoisé*... that some of its leaders are corrupt or incompetent, that it no longer has either doctrine or program, that its influence has declined, that it can no longer refurbish its cadres and that its young electorate is turning away from it.[40]

This judgment was undoubtedly too harsh, although it was later to be echoed by André Philip and other Socialist leaders. Mollet's abandonment of oppositionism, after years of political starvation on the national level, was understandable, and his quest for power did not mean that the party had become reactionary. Indeed, the SFIO's congresses continued to reflect the militancy of certain federations and activists in their resolutions. At the same time, the party's working-class orientation was becoming highly intel- lectualized, expressing itself in preoccupations of relatively little import to the ordinary working man: resolutions about pacifism, aid to underdeveloped countries, relations with French colonies, repression in Tunisia and Morocco, the imprisonment of trade union leaders in North Africa, and the international solidarity of the working class.[41] The Socialist parliamentary party, despite its inclination to pragmatism, continued faithfully to promote *laïcité,* and to support progressive social and economic programs—or at least to make speeches about the desirability of such programs, an activity viewed by many Socialists as a substitute for voting on these programs or for strenuously promoting them.[42]

Among French intellectuals there has always been an imbalance or dichotomy between ideas and actions, with one often functionally autonomous of the other. Fauvet once said that among French intellectuals the belief was widespread that "thinking about a problem is tantamount to its solution."[43] This *déformation intellectualiste* was especially pronounced within the SFIO. It is probably true that the middle-class members of the SFIO—in and out of parliament—were the most doctrinaire of all the Socialists.[44] But that stemmed not so much from their middle-class status as from the fact that many were professionally concerned with ideas rather than action (or the exercise of power). It was said that "there are in France 10,000 school teachers who look exactly like Guy Mollet."[45] Nineteen of the 28 school teachers in the Assembly of 1951-55 belonged to the SFIO, and 13 of the 28 professors; in the Assembly elected in 1956, 16 of the 34 school teachers belonged to the SFIO, and 15 of the 46 professors.[46]

Preserving the Republic

As the teachers reinforced the intellectualizing predilections of the party, so the growing numbers of civil servants in the SFIO increased its etatism. The SFIO had, of course, always been in favor of preserving the Fourth Republic—as demonstrated by its policies of streamlining institutions, preserving French territorial patrimony, and balancing the budget—but the party became more obviously preoccupied with preservation after it broke with the PCF, and after the Gaullist and Poujadist strength increased in the Assembly.

In particular the SFIO was concerned with the maintenance of a credible defense structure, although the party's position was not without ambiguity. In 1945—after the SFIO had entered the government—Socialist deputies, agreeing with their Communist allies that resources were too limited to justify both socio-economic and defense expenditures, had announced their refusal to vote for "wasteful" military credits, and André Philip's proposal for a 20 percent reduction of military appropriations was approved by parliament without much difficulty.[47] The same parsimony applied to a bill (also introduced by Philip) to grant draft exemptions to conscientious objectors. In 1948—after the SFIO had broken with the Communists—Socialist deputies adhered to a directive of the *Comité directeur* to "fight against inflation" mainly by advocating a 25 percent reduction in military expenditures, i.e., a savings amounting to 12 billion francs.[48] When Premier Schuman proposed a smaller reduction, making his proposal a matter of confidence, Socialist deputies voted against him and caused his government (in which Moch served as a minister of the interior) to fall. But two years later, when Moch was defense minister under Pleven, the Socialists acquiesced in the raising of military expenditure to make possible a reinforcement of French troop levels in Germany. This measure had been demanded by the United States as a quid pro quo for American economic aid to France.[49] Similarly, in 1951, the SFIO parliamentary group "anxious to assure the security of the country against all aggression," supported the bill of a Radical government to strengthen armaments. The SFIO, as a party with a decidedly pacifist orientation, constantly emphasized the dangers of nuclear warfare. Nonetheless Mollet was not averse to France's pursuing a nuclear armaments program, which of necessity entailed considerable expenditure—though in 1956, as premier, he promised that France would not explode her first atomic bomb before January, 1961.[50] Like many other nationalistic Frenchmen, he did not wish to see his country caught unprepared in the event of West Germany's acquisition of nuclear weapons.

A similar concern for preserving the Republic—a concern frequently equated with undermining the position of the Communists—determined the SFIO's stand on immigrants. In conformity with its humanitarianism, the SFIO was very active in behalf of immigrants and refugees. It spoke for them in parliament, in government commissions, in the *comités d'entreprise*, and elsewhere throughout the Fourth Republic. The party was helpful in getting working and residence permits and finding jobs and housing for these people. It also aided in getting deportation orders cancelled and frequently facilitated the naturalization process by intervening with prefects and with the Ministry of the Interior. There were, however, occasional inconsistencies. When in 1947 the government provisionally withdrew a bill facilitating immigration, especially from Eastern European countries, citing "public order" as its reason, the SFIO found this withdrawal justified, "due to the behavior of certain foreigners during recent strikes."[51] Perhaps too many foreign workers had joined the CGT—or even worse, the PCF.

In 1951 the National Congress of the SFIO complained about the obstructionist tactics used by the antirepublican forces and adopted a resolution demanding that "working methods of parliament should be revised so as to put an end to the organized sabotage by the enemies of the regime, and so as to obtain a better system of legislative activity." Despite its earlier commitment to a strong Assembly government, the congress now asked that parliament should henceforth devote itself primarily to general principles by enacting framework laws *(lois cadres)* and leave to the executive the task of filling in the details by means of regulatory measures.[52]

In subsequent years the SFIO's interest in streamlining parliament continued. One of the better ideas frequently expressed by SFIO militants—and quoted with approval by the party leadership in the spring of 1955—was the notion that there were too many aspirants for cabinet posts, too many parliamentary assemblies, and too many deputies, whose number ought to be reduced drastically, " because the machine at Palais Bourbon has become too heavy, too slow, [so that] it is virtually impossible to work in it in a serious fashion."[53] A motion presented by the SFIO bureau for consideration by the Forty-seventh National Congress, held in July, 1955, recommended, inter alia: the obligatory attendance of deputies at parliamentary sessions; the resignation of deputies with too many absences; a ban on the pursuit of any other profession by deputies during their term of office; the raising of deputies' salaries to make them more immune to external pressures; and the abolition of absentee voting.

After the fall of the Mendès-France government—which the SFIO had supported but had not joined—the party returned to opposition but continued to be preoccupied with the functioning of the regime.[54] In November, 1955, in an attempt to weaken the two extremist parties that provided the greatest threat to the Republic—and incidentally in order to enhance its own electoral fortunes—Socialist parliamentarians introduced a bill to establish a new electoral system. The newly proposed single-member district system with a run-off ballot *(scrutin d'arrondissement majoritaire à deux tours)*, which was really a revival of the system that had existed at various times during the Third Republic, would have made it difficult for Gaullists and Communists to make alliances with more centrally-situated parties, and would therefore hopefully reduce the parliamentary representation of those parties. The bill was beaten down by a bare majority composed of the PCF and the Gaullists,[55] as well as the MRP (which was worried about the greater risks of anticlerical electoral deals). It should, however, be noted that the SFIO's electoral opportunism was not unlimited. In the elections of January, 1956, the SFIO decided to combine *(s'apparenter)* with the Mendèsists under the existing system of proportional representation, thereby voluntarily losing twenty or thirty parliamentary seats.[56]

When Mollet became prime minister in February, 1956, he was supported by most of the republican parties; that is, he was joined by Mendèsist Radicals and even by Gaullist deputies, many of whom had begun to feel themselves part of the regime; and he was also supported (though not joined) by the PCF, the MRP, and the Conservatives. He was opposed only by the Poujadists, who doubtlessly owed their election to many Gaullists who remained steadfastly against the Fourth Republic. The eclecticism of Mollet's original coalition reflected the ambiguity of his policies. As prime minister he continued to promote progressive legislation. Much of this legislative activity concentrated on such neutral matters as the preservation of *laïcité* and the extension of civil liberties; but the SFIO also attempted, in many cases successfully, to promote the resolutions of its forty-seventh congress. Thus the Socialists managed (often with the help of the Communists) to extend paid vacations, old age benefits, veterans' payments, and the tax obligations of the wealthy. This took a certain amount of courage. Although Mollet was "master of the legislature," and although the votes of the 100 Socialist deputies were crucial on most legislative proposals,[57] Mollet's continuation in the premiership depended upon his ability to play off the leftism of the SFIO's federation militants against the petit-bourgeois, small-town radicalism of many Socialist voters. Such radicalism was reflected in statistics indicating that there were many more Frenchmen who preferred Mendès-France to Mollet as premier.[58]

Despite the fact that the SFIO firmly believed in greater public expenditures—especially for social matters and public works— Mollet, during a parliamentary debate, in reply to a charge by a moderate that he had increased public outlays, said that the only such increase he had been responsible for concerned old-age pensions![59] Although still committed to parliamentary supremacy, Mollet—after the ideas of Edgar Faure, who had been premier in 1951—had his cabinet adopt an "organic decree" by means of which he put before the Assembly a unified budget bill that did not allow for amendments aimed at reducing revenues or increasing expenditures. (Mollet also infringed on civil liberties in Algeria by means of special decree laws.) Yet although he took care not to offend the centrists and moderates, the conservatives defected from Mollet's government on the issue of economic policy, which they considered too spendthrift despite Mollet's disclaimers. And although he remained *laïciste*, and generally agreed with the PCF on domestic policy, the latter, too, withdrew its support, both because Mollet had hardened his position on Algeria and because—adhering to guidelines of the National Congress—he remained opposed to a united front. At the same time, Mollet hardened his socialist rhetoric in order to soften opposition to his leadership, which was being voiced with growing frequency in the party's National Council. One of his critics, André Philip, had gone as far as to publish a broadside against Mollet *(Le socialisme trahi)* for which he was expelled from the party at the end of 1957.

The party's image suffered especially from its continued hard-line position on the Algerian issue, which threatened to divide the SFIO and to produce a civil war in France. As late as February, 1958, many Socialists did not yet perceive a *crise de régime,* and felt that the Republic could be saved and a military takeover averted by an opportune reshuffling of the coalition. There was, however, disagreement on the kind of coalition. Mitterrand favored a leftist coalition based on the Socialists and the UDSR; while Mollet appeared to favor, at least publicly, a return to opposition, no doubt echoing the feeling of a majority of members on the National Council. But in fact Mollet continued to support the new government of Radical Félix Gaillard and later served in the MRP-dominated government of Pflimlin, who succeeded Gaillard.

By May, 1958, the question of the preservation of the Republic had taken precedence over both doctrine and domestic program. The SFIO's annual report for 1957-58, while mentioning as a matter of course the party's continued preoccupation with progressive social and economic legislation, seemed to put even more stress on institutional matters. In summarizing the SFIO's parliamentary activity, the annual report mentioned the fact that Socialist deputies had introduced some thirty bills and argued for, or asked questions about, many others. But on these matters there must have been considerable disagreement among the deputies, as contrasted with the virtual unanimity within the parliamentary faction, about "all the *important* decisions (questions of confidence, electoral reform, constitutional revision, reform of local finances . . .)."[60]

In view of the growing attacks on the parliamentary regime, the report stated, "Our party must be the essential pillar of the Republic."[61] At the same time Socialist deputies' involvement in parliamentary activities was somewhat less than sustained. From October 1, 1957, to March 31, 1958, the absentee rate for Socialist deputies was very high (exceeded only by that of the Radicals). This fact was indicative both of internal institutional decay and of the SFIO's declining faith in the Fourth Republic parliamentary government.

Notes

1. Williams, *Crisis and Compromise*, p. 24.
2. Roger Quilliot, *La SFIO et l'exercice du pouvoir* (Paris: Fayard, 1972), p. 82.

3. Ibid., p. 120. On the SFIO's position regarding nationalization, see the text of its "Charte de Combat" in *Le Populaire*, April 2, 1946.

4. Mario Einaudi, Maurice Byé, Ernesto Rossi, *Nationalization in France and Italy* (Ithaca, N.Y.: Cornell University Press, 1955), pp. 96-101.

5. Quilliot, *La SFIO*, p. 369.

6. In a public opinion poll conducted in August, 1953, 37% of Socialist voters indicated that they thought the nationalization of large enterprises a good solution, while 36% felt it was a bad one (and 27% did not answer the question)—as against 70% of Communist voters and only 14% of Radical voters answering in the affirmative. *Sondages*, no. 1 (1954).

7. Philip, *Les socialistes*, p. 132.

8. *Bulletin intérieur*, no. 80 (June 1955), pp. 3-9; and no. 92 (June 1957), p. 8.

9. Quilliot, *La SFIO*, p. 172. See also *Bulletin intérieur* (August, 1946).

10. Paul Fabra, "La SFIO," in Jacques Fauvet and Henri Mendras, eds., *Les paysans et la politique*, Cahiers de la Fondation Nationale des Sciences Politiques, no. 94 (Paris: A. Colin, 1958), pp. 85ff.

11. Ibid, p. 87.

12. In 1945 Tanguy-Prigent, the minister of agriculture, established a rural land office whose function it was to acquire the (excess) lands of collaborators and to lease them to peasants—the cost of acquisition to be borne by the National Treasury.

13. Gordon Wright, *Rural Revolution in France* (Stanford, Calif.: Stanford University Press, 1964), pp. 95-104.

14. James M. Clark, *Teachers and Politics in France: A Pressure Group Study of the Fédération de l'Education Nationale* (Syracuse, N.Y.: Syracuse University Press, 1967), p. 102.

15. *Bulletin intérieur*, no. 42 (1949), pp. 126f.

16. Jacques Malterre and Paul Benoist, *Les partis politiques français* (Paris: Bibliothèque de l'Homme d'Action, 1957), pp. 63-64.

17. Simmons, *French Socialists*, p. 158.

18. *Bulletin intérieur*, no. 69 (April 1952), p. 137.

19. Ligou, *Histoire du socialisme*, pp. 566-67.

20. Micaud, *Communism and the French Left*, pp. 86, 183.

21. The SFIO as a party was in this case clearly at odds with Premier Ramadier, Interior Minister Moch, and even President Auriol—all of them Socialists. In June, 1947, Auriol refused to accede to a demand by the CGT to intervene in the government decision to break up the strike against the nationalized railroads. Evidently neither Ramadier nor Auriol wanted to aid the CGT gratuitously, and, *a fortiori*, the Communists. See Vincent Auriol, *Journal du septennat*, vol. 1 (Paris: A. Colin, 1970), pp. lviii, 264-65.

22. "Parti Socialiste, 50e Congrès National," *Bulletin intérieur*, no. 102 (May 1958), p. 171.

23. *Bulletin intérieur*, no. 42 (1949), p. 45.

24. *Bulletin intérieur*, no. 80 (June 1955), pp. 3-9, and no. 84 (1956), p. 165.

25. Despite Moch's reputation as a strikebreaker and as one who believed the PCF to be perfectly capable of plotting against, the state, he wanted to help reduce tendencies within the SFIO toward a repressive anticommunism that might only serve to inflame the passions of the Communists. See Vincent Auriol, *Journal de septennat*, vol. 2 (Paris: A. Colin, 1974), p. 541.

26. Jacques Fauvet, *Histoire du parti communiste français*, vol. 2 (Paris: Fayard, 1965), p. 206.

27. Ligou, *Histoire de socialisme*, pp. 553-54.

28. Quilliot, *La SFIO*, pp. 333-34.

29. Ligou, *Histoire de socialisme*, p. 602.

30. MacRae, *Parliament, Parties and Society*, p. 43.

31. Jacques Fauvet, *Les forces politiques en France* (Paris: Editions Le Monde, 1951), p. 69.

32. MacRae, *Parliament, Parties and Society*, p. 70.

33. "Parti Socialiste, 44e Congrès National," *Bulletin intérieur*, no. 60 (April 1952), p. 6.

34. *Bulletin intérieur*, nos. 53, 60, 72 (1951, 1952, 1954).

35. Cited in Philip, *Les socialistes*, p. 111.

36. "Parti Socialiste, 46e Congrès National," *Bulletin intérieur*, no. 72 (July 1954), p. 83.

37. Ligou, *Histoire de socialisme*, pp. 596-97. According to Mattei Dogan (in S. M. Lipset and S. Rokkan, eds., *Party Systems*

and Voter Alignments [New York: Free Press, 1967], p. 152), in 1956 about 23% of SFIO voters belonged to the salaried petite bourgeoisie and 13% to the independent bourgeoisie.

38. Micaud, *Communism and the French Left*, p. 140. The same study revealed that 90% of the metal workers were indifferent to politics and maintained that "political parties are all the same," p. 141.

39. Pierre Rimbaud, "Le parti socialiste SFIO," in Association Francaise de Science Politique, *Partis politiques*, p. 20.

40. Maurice Duverger, "SFIO: mort ou transfiguration?," *Temps Modernes* (special issue on "La Gauche"), vol. 10, no. 112 (1955), 1863-1885.

41. "Parti Socialiste, 47e Congrès National," *Bulletin intérieur*, no. 78 (May 1955), especially pp. 189-201.

42. On the progressive bills introduced by SFIO deputies, see *Bulletin intérieur*, no. 42 (July 1949), pp. 126ff.

43. Fauvet, *Forces politiques*, p. 66, and Jacques Fauvet, *La France déchirée* (Paris: Fayard, 1957), p. 38.

44. Williams, *Crisis and Compromise*, p. 96.

45. Ligou, *Histoire de socialisme*, p. 567.

46. Fauvet, *France déchirée*, p. 66.

47. Ligou, *Histoire de socialisme*, p. 535.

48. *Bulletin intérieur*, no. 42 (1949), p. 119.

49. *Bulletin intérieur*, no. 53 (1951), pp. 85-87.

50. Edgar S. Furniss, *France: Troubled Ally* (New York: Praeger, 1960), p. 265.

51. *Bulletin intérieur*, no. 42 (1949), pp. 43-44.

52. Motion of André Laurent, adopted by the Forty-third National Congress. See *Bulletin intérieur*, no. 60 (May 1951), p. 136.

53. *Bulletin intérieur*, no. 78 (May 1955), pp. 11-12.

54. Ibid., p. 77.

55. *Bulletin intérieur*, no. 84 (May 1956), pp. 74, 79.

56. Malterre and Benoist, *Les partis politiques français*, pp. 59-60.

57. Williams, *Crisis and Compromise*, p. 53.

58. In a poll conducted during the campaign of 1955, 27% preferred Mendès-France as against 2% who preferred Mollet.

Williams, *Crisis and Compromise,* p. 54n.

59. Nathan Leites, *On the Game of Politics in France* (Stanford, Calif.: Stanford University Press, 1959), p. 46.

60. *Bulletin intérieur,* no. 102 (May 1958), p. 77.

61. Ibid.

5

The SFIO and International Policies in the Fourth Republic

The internationalist theme, which was dominant in the writings of so many of the party's philosophers, had a dual foundation. First, the basic economic theories of Marx, which the Socialists accepted at least in their broad outlines, were considered to be universally valid. "The party," reads the 1946 Declaration of Principles, "is essentially international because economic laws have become universal."[1] Second, the Jaurèsian humanitarism in the socialist philosophy taught that the proletariat of all of the countries of the world had just as much right as the French to enjoy the privileges of living under a socialist regime. Consequently Socialists had two major duties. The first was to propagate the faith in all corners of the world, as well as in their own land. The second was to work to eliminate those conditions throughout the world which militated against its acceptance and its achievement. Ideally the French Socialist would have liked to see a peaceful world devoid of political, economic, or social barriers: a worldwide brotherhood embracing the socialist faith.

This chapter will explore the tactics adopted by the SFIO during the Fourth Republic, both in and out of the government, to achieve these goals and to respond to certain important international events. Although the French Socialists might have been able to adhere fairly closely to their avowed aims in some matters of domestic concern, in the international arena major discrepancies between the ideal and the real tended to occur with distressing regularity.

Parts of this chapter have appeared in *ORBIS* 4, no. 4 (Winter 1961):478-491.

The Socialist International

The Socialist International was the vehicle chosen by the SFIO for the propagation of the socialist philosophy throughout the world, and no national party tried harder to keep that body alive and active. The name of the SFIO itself—the French Section of the Worker's International—attested to this preoccupation.

True to its calling, the SFIO helped spearhead the drive to reactivate the Second International after World War II. French Socialists were among the exiles who met in London during the war under the auspices of the British Labour Party to keep the socialist spirit alive and, as soon as it became clear that Hitler was going to be defeated, began to push for the reestablishment of a formal organization. The importance of this task to the SFIO was affirmed by the caliber of men it sent to the meetings. In a meeting held in March, 1945, for instance, the SFIO was represented by such important party leaders as Vincent Auriol, Charles Dumas, Salomon Grumbach, Louis Lévy, Jules Moch, and André Philip.[2] Nonetheless the early efforts to revivify the International were not successful.

While most parties were willing to discuss issues of mutual importance, they felt that there were more important tasks than the reactivation of the Socialist International. In order to prepare for that eventuality, a series of steps were taken to provide a framework for discussion and a base for Socialist propaganda. In May, 1946, a Socialist Information and Liaison Office was established in London, attached to the Secretariat of the British Labour party, and six months later the Consultative Committee of the International Socialist Conference was added to provide information and to plan for future congresses.

No real progress in the reinstatement of the Socialist International was made until 1947. In July of that year, at a meeting called by the Socialist Information and Liaison Office, Guy Mollet of the SFIO, and a Belgian colleague presented a lengthy and reasoned argument in favor of the immediate reestablishment of the International. Confronted by opposition from several of the parties represented, especially from the delegates of the British Labour party, it was decided not to act on the suggestions made by Mollet and his colleague. It was agreed, however, to establish a commission of study and to transform the Consultative Committee (or COMISCO as it was dubbed by the popular press). COMISCO held a number of conferences in 1948 and 1949 at which the SFIO pressed for the establishment of a true Socialist International. At a conference in London in December, 1949, COMISCO elected a secretary, Julius Braunthal, and at a conference in Copenhagen in June, 1950, a Committee of Nine, headed by Guy Mollet, was created to prepare a Common Declaration of Principles for a reactivated International. In Frankfurt am Main, in July, 1951, the draft declaration prepared by the Committee of Nine was adopted, and the delegates voted to designate the meeting then in progress the First Congress of the new International.[3]

Organizationally the new International was quite similar to earlier Internationals. Its organs included a congress which met every two years in which each of the constituent parties had one vote. The congress was the supreme organ of the International with power to proclaim the principles of the organization, to revise the fundamental statute and to admit new members by a two-thirds majority vote. The next organ in the hierarchy was the council, made up of two delegates from each member party, four from the Socialist Union of Central-Eastern Europe, one from the International Council of Social Democratic Women, and one from the International Union of Socialist Youth. The council met at least once a year, and its job was to formulate policy on current political issues, convene congresses, examine applications for membership, elect the International's chairman and vice-chairmen, examine the secretary's annual report, approve the annual buget and membership fees, elect the secretary and decide on the locality for the seat of the organization.

The International also had a bureau of delegates from eleven member countries to supervise the day-to-day activities of the organization, such as convening council meetings and establishing its agenda. At the center was the Secretariat, headed by a secretary who was elected by the council and responsible to the bureau. The Secretariat's duties included the preparation of official organs for conferences and meetings, the exchange of information among member parties, and the publication of the official organ, *Socialist International Information*. Because of the size of the British Labour party, its previous successes in British elections, and predictions of successes to come, as well as the fact that the provisional bodies had been headquartered there, London was made the headquarters of the International and Morgan Philips, secretary of the British Labour party, was elected its first chairman.[4]

As regards policy, the work of the Socialist International was spelled out in broad terms by the Frankfurt meeting in a document entitled "Aims and Tasks of Democratic Socialism." In general, this document, which is divided into four parts, is not too different from statements of principle of any of the West European socialist parties. The first part, entitled "Political Democracy," states that the socialist parties involved intend to work through the democratic process. The second part, "Economic Democracy," states the need for overall state planning of production in order to meet the immediate needs of "full employment, higher production, a rising standard of life, social security and a fair distribution of income and property."[5] This planning must be achieved in a democratic manner and does not presume public ownership of all the means of production. The exact formula would depend on the needs and desires of the particular country involved. The section on "Social Democracy and Cultural Progress" devotes itself to outlining a code of individual economic and social rights, such as the right to work, the right to leisure, the right of adequate housing, and various other human rights the Socialists deemed necessary to the maximum development of human personality. The fourth and final section of the document deals with "International Democracy." Democratic socialism is international, according to this section, "because it aims at liberating all men from every form of economic, spiritual and political bondage" and "because it recognizes that no nation can solve all its economic and social problems in isolation."[6] Although "absolute" national sovereignty must be transcended, the aims the Socialists profess can only be achieved through voluntary cooperation between nations. This section of the basic document also attests to the socialist desire for world peace and the need to eliminate all vestiges of colonialism. All in all, this document, which was the work of a number of men from a number of national socialist parties, could have been written without difficulty by a member of the moderate faction of the SFIO.

The Socialist International was an instant success, at least on paper. Within four years supporters were claiming 42 affiliated parties with a membership of 10,405,639 and an estimated voting strength of 66,133,360.[7] As would be expected, European socialist parties provided the overwhelming portion of the membership, with the British Labour party alone accounting for 6,498,027 members and 12,405,246 voters. The SFIO in fact was quite far down the list in both membership and voting strength. Outside Europe, the Socialist International claimed the membership of socialist parties in Argentina, Canada, Japan, Israel, New Zealand, Uruguay, and Jamaica. The 42 parties also included consultative members such as the Indian Praja Socialist party, the U.S. Socialist party, the U.S. Social Democratic Federation, and the Vietnam Socialist party.[8]

By 1955 the organization of the Socialist International had taken on a fairly definitive form. Its major organs were meeting regularly, and it had helped create four important affiliated organizations, the International Union of Socialist Youth (IUSY), the Asian Socialist Conference, the Socialist Union of Central-Eastern Europe and the International Union of Social Democratic Teachers. Conferences and meetings were held on a variety of matters dear to the hearts and minds of the Socialists, such as the socialist press, European unity, and almost every other matter of conceivable importance. In the period October, 1951, to November, 1955, for instance, conferences were held on problems of underdeveloped countries, election and propaganda techniques, socialism and religion, problems of population and migration, sports and cultural organizations, broadcasting and film propaganda techniques, problems of socialist municipal administration, and techniques of government economic planning. These activities resulted in major policy statements by the International on such subjects as policy for the underdeveloped areas of the world, colonialism, socialism and religion, the proposed Special United Nations Fund for Economic Development (SUNFED), population and migration, the United Nations, and the "international situation."[9]

While the SFIO was proud of its efforts to reactivate the

International, to a certain extent it retained an ambivalent attitude toward its child. In a way, it was almost forced by its ideology to give the International its active and enthusiastic support. Certainly nothing in the SFIO's tradition would have permitted them even to think of joining the Communist International. Its support for the International included the participation of high-ranking French Socialists in its hierarchy, as well as regular representation at conferences and meetings and a willingness to meet its financial obligations. The French, for instance, were given one of the two vice-chairman posts. Louis Lévy, one of the SFIO's more important international theoreticians, was selected to occupy that position in 1951 and was succeeded the following year by Guy Mollet.

The SFIO was never quite satisfied, however, with the slowness with which the International achieved its aims. This was due at least in part to a certain amount of jealousy. While the SFIO did not have the numbers, many felt that they could do a better job than the British in policy matters. Many also felt that the larger labor parties were not as international in viewpoint as they ought to be in order for the International to be a true moving force in Europe and in the world. This situation prompted André Philip, when he was still a member in good standing, to state that "the advance of Socialism . . . in Britain and Scandinavia has been wholly linked with national policies and institutions. Thus, Socialism in practice has tended to become purely national in character, and, as a result, to divide rather than unite the workers."[10]

In any case, the SFIO was such an integral part of the International that it is necessary to know one in order to know the other. Many of the declarations and actions of the International were the reflections of the dynamism of the most active, if not the largest, of its member parties. Yet the SFIO could not help but be influenced by the decisions of conferences and meetings that brought together the representatives of the most important Socialist parties in the world. In any consideration of the SFIO it is also imperative to keep in mind that, as a member of an international group, the SFIO had more potential influence in international affairs than could a purely national political party. Above all, it should be remembered that the socialist movement, of which the SFIO was a part, was international in character and purpose. The revived International was a reflection of this fact.

International Cooperation and Disarmament

A firm supporter of the United Nations, as it had been of the League of Nations, the SFIO believed that international organization could be the answer to maintaining peace between nation states and aiding the countries of the world in their quest for the elimination of political, economic, and social bondage.[11] French Socialists felt, however, that many changes would have to be made in the UN before it could effectively carry out these ambitious tasks. Their proposals varied from simple to complex, from short term to long range. The long range goal of the SFIO was to transform the UN into a world government. In the view of the Socialists, the UN should become a true world legislature with the power to make decisions binding on all nations. All nations, including France, should be willing to give up some of their sovereignty to make this possible. In order to put force into the UN's decisions, the term "aggressor" should be defined as any nation that refused to submit an international dispute to arbitration. All states should keep military forces in readiness to participate in various measures of collective security action against any country named an aggressor by the United Nations. Eventually an international police force *(gendarmerie international)* should be formed, larger than the forces at the disposal of any member nation, which would become the UN's permanent security force.[12]

Convinced that a workable system of collective security could only be achieved after a general reduction in armaments, the SFIO gave its complete support to the UN in its quest for a workable disarmament plan. Not only did the SFIO have an influence in establishing disarmament as one of the primary tasks of the UN, but, until the French under de Gaulle withdrew from active participation in disarmament talks in and outside of the UN, the French Socialist Jules Moch proved to be one of the most dynamic spokesmen for disarmament that the UN had. In general the SFIO championed a compromise approach to the problem in an attempt to bridge the gap between the Russian and American positions. In fact Moch's formula, "neither control without disarmament, nor disarmament without control," saved the disarmament discussions more than once. Writing in 1957, Mollet stated that the socialist position on disarmament consists of three inseparable parts, "general, simultaneous, and rigorously inspected."[13] It must be general in that it must include all types of weapons, because with any type of weapon there is always the risk of aggression, and it was not the aim of the Socialists to "humanize" war but to eliminate it altogether. Disarmament must be simultaneous in order to eliminate any "zones of insecurity." Finally, it is essential that disarmament be rigorously inspected in order to prevent any of the partners from surprising the others. This inspection should take all possible forms, including inspection from the air and on land, inspection of communication centers, inspection of military manpower and expenditures for the military. The SFIO condemned the decision by de Gaulle to withdraw France from disarmament negotiations and continued right up to the end to press for her return to the disarmament bargaining table.

The SFIO was not unaware of the problems involved in disarmament. In a report to the SFIO in May, 1955, Jules Moch stated that although there were no technical reasons why a disarmament treaty could not be drafted, and though prospects at that time for a treaty were brighter than ever, he warned that such a treaty "can never be signed before the solution of the great existing political problems."[14] In order to hasten the solution of the fundamental international problems that stood in the way of collective security and disarmament, the SFIO backed every effort to advance a rapprochement between Russia and the United States. In 1950 the Forty-second National Congress of the SFIO supported Trygve Lie's journey to various capitals to promote new negotiations between the East and the West. At the Forty-fifth National Congress in July, 1953, a resolution was passed calling on France to take the initiative in bringing about "negotiations, including a four- or five-power conference, for the purpose of achieving either a general international settlement, or, as a first step, limited but precise agreements, which would make real progress and improve the international atmosphere."[15] The SFIO, according to Guy Mollet, was favorable to negotiations between Russia and the United States "under any circumstances providing that the parties are serious."[16] Along this same line, the SFIO backed the various confidence-building proposals made by the two major powers, such as the Antarctic Treaty of 1959, the partial nuclear test ban treaty of 1963, and the 1966 treaty on the peaceful uses of outer space. The SFIO also was a supporter of plans to halt nuclear proliferation.[17]

There were also a number of immediate steps that could be taken to make the United Nations more effective in peacekeeping while awaiting the long term achievements of world government and universal disarmament. At various times the SFIO put itself on record as supporting plans to make the UN completely universal, including the admission of Communist China, to eliminate the veto in the Security Council, and to arrange for better coordination between the UN and the specialized agencies. Among the complaints aired by French Socialists were the failure of members to live up to their obligations under the charter, the failure of the UN to be impartial in its decisions, and its inability to enforce them. In this regard it is interesting to note that Guy Mollet at one point complained that while France, Great Britain, and Israel carried out the UN's resolutions after the Suez crisis of 1956, the UN condemnation of Russia for its aggression in Hungary remained purely academic as did the UN directives to Nassar concerning the security and use of the Suez Canal.[18]

Always a good friend to the newer countries of Africa and Asia, the SFIO was in the vanguard of those who wished to put into operation the ideals of self-determination of peoples set forth in Article 1 of the United Nations' Charter. This attitude was inherent in the concept of liberation of man from political bondage contained in the SFIO's 1946 Declaration of Principles, and the Socialists were quick to join the anticolonial bandwagon at least insofar as it did not apply to Algeria. The SFIO adhered to, and to a great extent was responsible for, the declaration adopted at the Stockholm congress of the Socialist International in 1953 calling for the abolition of colonialism in all of its forms.[19] And as the new nations began to appear in the international society, the SFIO was one of the first to express the need for massive developmental aid through UN auspices. The SFIO not only supported all of the UN technical assistance and development programs—such as SUNFED, the aborted plan to divert billions of dollars from armaments to development[20]—but also constantly called for increased spending in these areas.

European Union: Toward a Third Force

While achievement of world peace and universal government remained the basic overall objective of Socialist international policies, many of the concrete issues that faced the party during the Fourth Republic demanded a more practical approach. One of the most important of these issues was determining the role that Europe should play in an imperfect world and what Europe should do to help prepare the world for the millennium. As it turned out, the French Socialists found that under the severe pressures of post–World War II European politics, it was necessary to abandon a major part of its international doctrinal stance. The result was a rather curious mixture of the idealistic and the pragmatic, neither of which were truly served.

The offer of economic aid to Europe, in what has become known as the Marshall Plan, was the first test the SFIO was forced to undergo. France was in desperate need of help to restore her war-damaged economy. It was not surprising, therefore, that the great majority of the SFIO welcomed aid from the capitalist United States with open arms. Party leaders, however, took pains to place it in a broader perspective. Blum saw the Marshall Plan as a catalyst for European unity because it provided for close economic cooperation between the participating states. According to André Philip, it gave Europe a four year period to become economically independent of the rest of the world.[21] Similar sentiments were expressed in a resolution passed unanimously at the 1948 Socialist National Congress. In this resolution the SFIO voiced sincere appreciation for the American aid that had permitted Europe "to avoid an imminent catastrophe." However, it also went on to make the point that foreign aid was acceptable only when it permitted Europeans to choose their own forms of economic and social institutions, and aid was effective only when it could be used to create a greater production of essential goods and to build new industries for a continental market.[22]

The Council of Europe, when it came into being in early 1949, was considered by the Socialists to be an excellent foundation for the building of a united Europe, and plans were made to achieve that purpose. The council, or any other organization for that matter, should be furnished with a democratic central organ to which would be given the power to plan production of all essential goods, to fix prices, and to control investments. Through unity, and only through unity, would Europe hope to increase its riches to the point necessary and possible in a modern world. A united Europe would not be just another autarchy nor a mere branch of the economy of one of the world's two major power blocs. It would become the prime mover in lowering all of the world's economic barriers and a participant in all efforts toward international economic cooperation. In the beginning at least, any such system should embrace all free nations, including Great Britain and Scandinavia. Ultimately, of course, it would be open to all nations, continental or otherwise, that adhered to its principles.[23]

Socialists took pains to point out that such a united Europe would be neither neutralist nor oriented toward the Soviet Union. As Guy Mollet stated in an article in *Foreign Affairs* in 1954, neutralism had negligible support in France, and the SFIO in particular opposed neutralism in all of its forms. Furthermore, the secretary-general of the SFIO insisted that "no Socialist has ever been or will ever become the accomplice either of those who hate America or of the Bolsheviks. . . . We know," continued Mollet, "how much democracy . . . owes to the courageous American interventions in the two world wars. Nor do we forget that we owe a large part of the material recovery of Europe to the spirit of solidarity shown by the American Government and the American people."[24]

However, a united Europe must be permitted to guide its own destiny. If Europe was to become wholly dependent upon the United States, the free nations would be no more than satellites, or at most junior partners, unable to conduct even their domestic affairs according to their own interests and aspirations. Such a Europe could never be considered a trustworthy ally of the West. Moreover, according to the leader of the SFIO, it would never be in a position to use its good offices to help bring about a solution of the conflict between the United States and the USSR.

When the Council of Europe did not grow as desired by the SFIO, it turned its efforts to the creation of a smaller economic unit.[25] The French Socialists, for instance, found the Schuman Plan for a European Coal and Steel Community a practical application of many of the principles for which they had fought. It provided an inroad into the principle of unlimited national sovereignty, a beginning to the functional integration of Europe, and a first step toward international economic planning. It had the additional benefit of eliminating an area of conflict between France and Germany and thus provided a basis for a rapprochement between those two traditional enemies. Similar arguments were offered in favor of Euratom and the European Economic Community (EEC). Though the SFIO supported the Schuman Plan, the Rome Treaty creating the EEC (also known as the Common Market) was negotiated by the Mollet government, and bills providing for it and Euratom were passed by the French parliament under the ministry of Bourgès-Maunoury, a protégé of Mollet.

True to their tradition, however, the French Socialists considered these plans only a step in the right direction and expended a great deal of energy attempting to bring them closer to the SFIO's ideal. First, an effort was made to gain the adherence of other European powers, especially Great Britain and the Scandinavian countries. Second, efforts were made to give the Coal and Steel Community and the Common Market a democratically elected governing body with all the powers necessary to impose its decisions, powers considered essential to workable international planning. Third, the SFIO insisted that all governing bodies were to be kept completely clear of any conflict of interest. No individual of authority in the Coal and Steel Community administration, for example, would be allowed to have any financial interests whatsoever in private coal and steel companies. Fourth, an effort was made to tie the communities politically to the Council of Europe. This objective, according to the SFIO, would have a double advantage. It would ensure democratic control over all major policy decisions and at the same time strengthen the council.[26]

European military cooperation provided a different test of socialist principles. The first such test came when France was invited to join NATO. In view of its emphasis on "third forceism" in matters of economic cooperation, the SFIO could have been expected to have some major reservations. The SFIO however, did not hesitate to give its support to NATO. If Europe was in any danger—and the Socialists felt it was—that danger came from the East not the West. Europe could not stand alone in the face of Soviet aggression, therefore it had to ally itself with the United States. Although NATO was considered to be a stopgap measure until a more powerful united Europe could take over its own defense, it did have elements that appealed strongly to the SFIO. First, NATO was broadly conceived. For the first time the United States was committed to a peacetime alliance with Western Europe, and the future of Great Britain and certain of the Scandinavian countries was tied to that of their continental neighbors. Second, the NATO treaty contained provisions for possible future cooperation among the member powers on economic and social matters.

As it happened, it was a European military issue that divided the Socialists in a manner equaled only by the Algerian crisis of 1958. The issue was the European Defense Community. When the EDC was originally proposed, the SFIO hoped it would become the military arm of the Council of Europe to be used in accordance with decisions made by common agreement. It would also provide for the strict supervision of the rearmament of Germany.

When it became apparent that EDC had no chance of becoming the military arm of the Council of Europe and that Great Britain and the Scandinavian countries were reluctant to enter the agreement, the enthusiasm of many Socialists for the scheme began to cool. On ideological grounds it was argued that without Great Britain and Scandinavia it would be but another con-firmation of "little Europe." The SFIO was committed to unity on a much larger scale. A more down to earth ground was a fear of Germany. Marcel-Edmond Naegelen, writing in *La Revue Socialiste* in 1953, stated that in his opinion France would be incapable of providing the fourteen divisions required of it because of her commitments to the French Union, while Germany was easily capable of providing twelve divisions on the continent, thus assuring a predominance of German power in EDC. Furthermore, according to Naegelen, no one could be certain that the Germans would not join the Russians if and when an invasion of France should take place, just as Germany joined Russia in 1939.[27] Whatever one thinks of the logic of the argument, the fear of a rearmed Germany had strong roots in France. Another reason for opposing EDC, one that was given much less publicity in SFIO organs, was a fear of Catholic domination of EDC councils. Christian Democratic parties were in power in both Germany and Italy, and there were strong Catholic parties in France and Belgium. Without the British and Scandinavians, it was feared that the Catholics would use the EDC for their own purposes.[28] Criddle also lays a great deal of emphasis on a basic French nationalism, citing speeches of SFIO leaders accusing the proponents of EDC of threatening to destroy the French army.[29]

In order to placate the hesitaters, the SFIO drew up a set of three conditions for Socialist support of EDC:

1. The creation of a political authority capable of exercising control over EDC
2. Britain's full association with the community
3. An American guarantee of full support, including the maintenance of troops on the continent and treaty arrangements obligating the United States to oppose either the withdrawal of any member from EDC or any attempt by a member to regain its military autonomy in violation of the EDC treaty

Only if these conditions were fulfilled would the SFIO endorse France's entry into the European Defense Community.[30]

When the ratification of the treaty finally came before the National Assembly in May, 1954, the SFIO held an Extraordinary National Congress to decide on the Socialist stand. Although the arguments against EDC were eloquently made, the Mollet leadership decided that it was the SFIO's duty to give its support. The delegates to the congress were told that continued French hesitation to ratify the EDC treaty might inspire an "agonizing reappraisal" of United States policy in Europe and that such an appraisal might well result in an American plan to rearm Germany independently. After arguing that the three conditions had been met "in a sufficient measure," the SFIO's leadership first had to beat down a motion to adjourn by a vote of 2,035 to 1,013 (with 91 abstentions and 17 federations representing 315 votes absent). On the matter of substance, whether to support the EDC treaty, ratification was approved by a vote of 1,969 to 1,215, with 265 abstentions. To this motion, it should be noted, was added a clause calling for the speedy conclusion of a nonaggression pact between the West and the USSR.[31]

The party leadership, fearful perhaps that the SFIO parliamentarians might be even less convinced of the need for EDC than the delegates to the congress, decided to invoke party discipline. Consequently, a motion was introduced "impressing on the parliamentary representatives of the Party, the absolute necessity of a united vote, in the Assembly and in the commissions, on the basis of the decision taken by this Congress, and that in the event of indiscipline the *Comité directeur* shall be entitled under Article 60 of the statute of the Party to take all necessary measures to ensure unity and discipline."[32] After a great deal of acrimonious debate, the measure passed by 2,414 votes to 972 with 60 abstentions.[33]

As it turned out, over half of the SFIO parliamentarians voted for the procedural motion by which the Assembly refused to consider ratification of the EDC treaty. As mentioned earlier, this action brought disciplinary action to seventeen Socialist parliamentarians, including all of the major leaders of the anti-EDC group.[34]

The Socialists also supported the strengthening of the Brussels Pact (Western European Union—WEU) when this less potent substitute for EDC was proposed. The resolution of the Extraordinary National Congress directing Socialists to back WEU pointed out that "a new refusal by Parliament would result in a tragic vacuum" leaving France isolated in the face of unlimited and uncontrolled German rearmament. The WEU agreements would help maintain the principle of European and Atlantic solidarity, would furnish a contractual guarantee of British presence, and could provide a basis for a Franco-German reconciliation. However, continued the resolution, the SFIO in accepting WEU must work for certain principles, most importantly:

1. Integration of military forces in a manner that would eliminate the possibility of a rebirth of a German General Staff and German militarism
2. Reinforcement of armament control powers and the establishment of an agency with powers of sanction
3. Creation of an organ charged with the administration and equipment of military forces and the distribution of outside military aid
4. Creation of a Democratic Assembly, with limited but real powers, to which the other organs would be responsible[35]

In accepting WEU, the SFIO made it clear that it did not abandon its stand that durable peace could be obtained only by a universal collective security arrangement and general disarmament. Furthermore, the SFIO would not abandon its efforts to create a united Europe or to find the means of eliminating the areas of conflict between the East and the West.

The attitude of the SFIO toward the various plans for Western and European rearmament was summarized by Jules Isaac: "Bastards perhaps, but of a Russian father."[36]

The Dissolution of the French Empire and the Algerian Disaster

Few if any governments were able to foresee that World War II would mark the end of the old colonial system, and just as few were able to provide for the orderly and peaceful dismantling of their empires when it did at last become inevitable. France was no exception. Of the important non-Communist parties in France, the SFIO was almost alone in having a doctrine that if followed could have guided France well in this endeavor. It did, in effect, help the Socialists to remain ahead of the game while the SFIO was an opposition party, but failed miserably when the party came to power and the colony in question was Algeria.

In the early postwar years the SFIO supported an enlightened colonialist policy well within the confines of the doctrine laid down by the Socialist International. In general the SFIO insisted that all of the provisions of the constitution of the Fourth Republic dealing with French possessions should be faithfully carried out. These provisions, incidentally, were largely the work of a Socialist minister, Marius Moutet. Specifically, the SFIO demanded real powers for the Assembly of the French Union, greater participation of French territories in French parliamentary bodies, social reforms, more participation of natives in territorial governments, and a fundamental reorganization of territorial economies. The latter would have included efforts at industrialization, modernization of agriculture, a comprehensive plan for investments, regulation of exchange problems, and in general the progressive elimination of all practices tending to subordinate local economies to metropolitan France. It should also be noted that the SFIO was in agreement with the general aim of the French Union concept, which was ultimately to establish a free association of independent states somewhat along the lines of the British Commonwealth.[37]

To the SFIO the Indochina affair was a clear-cut issue between right and wrong. A colonial people, inspired by nationalism, were fighting for independence. It was France's duty from the beginning to grant independence to all three constituent states and bring them within the French Union. In the case of Vietnam, the only true native leader was Ho Chi Minh, with whom the French had to negotiate. Although Ho was a Communist, he was first of all a Vietnamese nationalist who had the support of his people. Throughout the war, which began in earnest in the winter of 1949, the SFIO continued to demand an immediate armistice and negotiations with Ho, even if under the auspices of the United Nations.[38]

As the conflict went on, the SFIO continued to press for a negotiated solution including "free elections under international control, freedom for the Vietnam government to choose its international orientation and to negotiate its ties with France, gradual withdrawal of French troops, guarantees against reprisals, and an offer of economic and social assistance.[39] Traditionally pacifist, the SFIO seemed convinced that if peace were only offered, the enemy would gladly accept it. As Odette Merlat stated in an article in *La Revue Socialiste* for November, 1953: "We are still told that it is not certain whether Vietminh wants peace, but how can we be certain when no serious approach has been tried? A people who have fought for seven years must want peace."[40]

In support of its stand the SFIO requested in 1953 that its group in parliament abstain from voting on the question of military credits for the Indochinese war so long as the government continued to avoid entering the negotiations. The SFIO also voiced its disapproval of the American aid offer.

The SFIO supported the convening of the Geneva Conference in 1954, which in effect ended the French military involvement in Indochina. It called for the strict observance of the Geneva agreements and for a rapid withdrawal of all French troops. As an interesting footnote to the Socialist stand on the Indochinese affair, the National Congress resolved in July, 1955, that France should never renounce her "economic and cultural presence" in Indochina.[41]

The SFIO also befriended the nationalist movements in Tunisia and Morocco. In the beginning, however, the SFIO, as was the case with other moderate parties, did not call for immediate independence. It did, however, call for more rapid and far-reaching reforms in the two countries than did the other centrist parties. These included:

1. Fixing specific dates for the end of the protectorates and for successive stages of development toward independent statehood
2. Determination, by common accord, of political, economic, and social reforms that would permit the establishment of democratic institutions. Such reforms should include labor legislation to protect the rights of rural and industrial workers and intellectuals against "feudal" institutions or "capitalistic exploitations"
3. Simultaneous conclusions of treaties of association between the territories and France on military, diplomatic, economic, and cultural matters[42]

As events progressed, the SFIO line turned more and more toward approval of immediate independence. When Mendès-France reached an accord with the Moroccan leaders to bring an end to the rebellion in 1955, he was praised lavishly in the Socialist press and urged to carry out the details of the agreement leading to independence for Morocco with all possible haste. In the case of Tunisia, one of the first major acts of the Mollet government was to sign a protocol proclaiming that country to be an independent state.

If the leaders of the SFIO were able in time to recognize the logic of the situation in Morocco and Tunisia, they failed completely when it came to Algeria. As for learning from experience, the nationalist rebellions in Indochina, Morocco, and Tunisia might as well not have happened. At no time did complete independence for Algeria become a part of Socialist policy. The Socialist attitude toward Algerian independence was best described by a resolution passed at the Forty-third National Congress in 1951, denouncing in blunt terms the "rigid and retrogressive nationalism as well as Stalinist-sanctioned separatism"[43] in Algeria. The Socialists were not alone in their self-deception, however. No other party in France was to adopt the cause of the Algerian rebels as their own, except the Communists. And, as everyone knew, the contrariness of the Communists was only a matter of form and not one of substance. Even General de Gaulle, at least before the fall of Mollet from power over the worsened Algerian situation, was on the side of the majority of Frenchmen. After all, there was the clear statement of intent on the part of the general in his speech in Algiers of October 12, 1947: "Any policy which, on the fallacious pretext of an evolution in reverse, has the effect of reducing the rights and duties of France here, or of discouraging the inhabitants of French origin, who were and remain the pervading influence of Algeria; or finally, any policy that leads French Muslims to believe that they can separate their destiny from that of France, actually only opens the doors to decadence."[44]

Among the reasons generally given for treating Algeria differently from other parts of the empire, three were given a great deal of publicity in the popular press at the time. First, a large number of Frenchmen had made Algeria their home. Out of some 9 million inhabitants, it was claimed that more than a million were settlers who had migrated from France proper. Second, Algeria's economy and political structure had been integrated with that of metropolitan France over a long period of time. And third, since Algeria had had no genuine cultural heritage prior to the arrival of France in North Africa it had subsequently become

French in this most important aspect of its character. Whether real or specious, arguments of this kind led the Socialists and their countrymen to consider Algeria to be essentially French.

Be that as it may, the Algerian nationalists had reason to suspect that the coming to power of Mollet in 1956 might augur well for their cause, better anyway than had it been any other party, except perhaps the Communists. SFIO doctrine did emphasize self-determination, and the Socialists had fought for complete independence for both Morocco and Tunisia. There was also more concrete evidence. For instance, the electoral campaign waged by the left had used Guy Mollet's own slogan: "An idiotic war, with no way out." Further, in his statement to Parliament before leaving for Algeria in February—although he did make a point of the necessity of strengthening "the indissoluble union between Algeria and metropolitan France"—Mollet did emphasize the need to respect the "Algerian personality," to achieve complete equality for all the inhabitants of Algeria, and to organize free elections as soon as possible.[45] Finally there was Mollet's choice of General Catroux, the man who had negotiated the return of the sultan of Morocco, as his resident minister for Algeria.

Many have written of the shocked reaction of Mollet to the screaming, tomato-throwing crowds of European settlers who met him when he arrived in Algiers in February 6, 1956, his quick return to the mainland, the replacement of General Catroux with Roger Lacoste, and the decision that "pacification" of the Muslim nationalist rebels was the first and foremost task of the government. Historians and political analysts have also written of the failure of the Mollet government to consider any alternative to this policy and the tragic results of this inflexibility, which were reversed only when the nation finally handed all power over to General de Gaulle.[46]

In retrospect it is easy to criticize the actions of Guy Mollet in the Algerian crisis. As a man he has been criticized as being aloof and rigid. As a leader he has been criticized for his failure to inform himself of the situation in Algeria before his trip, for his failure of leadership, and for his failure to act as a conciliator between the settlers and the Muslims.[47] Just as seriously perhaps, at least for the doctrine he espoused, Mollet was criticized for being less than a true Socialist. One observer, admittedly prejudiced, hinted that the Mollet government's attitude toward the Algerian affair smacked strongly of racism. Although they outnumbered the European inhabitants nine to one, the Muslims were treated as second-class citizens. Mollet was also called an uninformed colonialist. An even more telling criticism was directed at the Mollet government's failure to do anything, even speak out in public, against the inhuman treatment of captured Muslims by the army and police.[48] None of Mollet's actions, of course, conformed to the teachings of the great philosophers of the SFIO.

Despite the criticisms leveled against Mollet, one thing was certain: his actions did reflect the desires of his constituents, leaders and masses alike. Of the important political parties, only the Communists attacked his formula of repression first and discussions second. Among the prominent political leaders of the day, only Mendès-France was consistent in his demands for at least some liberalization of policy. Even more important was the support from the Frenchman in the street. A series of polls taken in 1956 by *Sondages* revealed that if one eliminated the Communists, a good strong majority was in agreement that repression of the rebellion by military means had priority over negotiation and that almost all believed that Algeria should remain a *département* of metropolitan France. Only well into 1958 did French public opinion concede that Algeria would have to be given her independence sooner or later.[49]

Even if the imperatives of the situation in Algeria were such that Mollet could not have changed the course of events there even if he had wanted to, this certainly was not the case in the Suez war of 1956. In view of the secrecy and immediacy of the operation, there was no time for popular pressure to build up nor was there large scale agitation for action within the leadership of the SFIO or among the leadership of other parties. The decision was, in essence, Mollet's own. As it turned out, Mollet joined forces with the British and the Israelis without hesitation. He chose the path of force, rather than the path of peace—and against a developing country, a former colony. In Julliard's view, by taking this action Guy Mollet became the indispensable man for those in France who believed in the politics of force; he had supported an activity that even the extreme right wing would have feared to voice.[50]

Writing in 1968, Jacques Julliard enumerated five possible reasons that led Guy Mollet to join so willingly in the attack on Egypt. First, Mollet believed that Israel was about to be attacked and thus wanted to aid Israel against the possible aggression. Second, he wanted to guarantee free use of the Suez Canal. Third, he intended to pay back the canal company's shareholders for the losses they had incurred in the nationalization of the canal. Fourth, he wished to retaliate for Egyptian interference in the Algerian war and in so doing dry up the rebellion at its source. And fifth, he intended to put an end to Nasser's dictatorship and the danger he felt it posed to peace.[51] Other reasons given were that the action was forced upon Mollet by the Jews in the SFIO, that it was an attempt to give the French military an easy victory after so many losses and thus to give the average Frenchman a little *gloire.*

The most persistent reason given for Mollet's Suez venture was the fourth one offered by Julliard. Just previous to the attack on Suez, Lacoste is quoted as stating that France "has everything to gain in Algeria by embarking on the military expedition with Great Britain" and "a French division in Egypt is worth four divisions in North Africa."[52] In any case this was the thrust of the official propaganda of the time and could very well be the real one.

If it could be considered any compensation for the abuse that the French and the British subsequently took from many of their friends and a vast majority of the United Nations, the French people approved of the action. In a poll taken in November, 1956, 44 percent of the people polled approved of the invasion, 37 percent were against, and 19 percent had no opinion. Only the Communists, and for some still unexplained reason the Poujadists, disapproved.[53] The National Assembly approved Mollet's actions by 368 votes to 182; in the Senate, a governmental declaration on the subject read by François Mitterrand was overwhelmingly accepted by 298 votes to 19.[54]

As subsequent events have proven, the "non-socialist" foreign policies of Mollet regarding the Suez expedition and the Algerian situation were both complete failures.

Notes

1. "Déclaration de principes," in Mollet, *Bilan et Perspectives*, p. 109.
2. *Bulletin intérieur*, no. 60 (April 1952), p. 82.
3. Ibid., pp. 82-85.
4. Information concerning the structure of the Socialist International comes primarily from Julius Braunthal, ed., *Yearbook of the International Socialist Labour Movement, 1956-1957* (London: Lincolns-Praeger Yearbook, 1956).
5. Ibid., p. 42.
6. Ibid., p. 44.
7. Ibid., pp. 18 and 19.
8. Also included in the forty-two total were affiliated parties of questionable importance to the organization such as Bulgarian, Czechoslovakian, Estonian, Hungarian, Latvian, Lithuanian, Polish, Spanish, and Yugoslav socialist parties in exile.
9. Ibid., pp. 61-64.
10. *Socialist International Information* 3, no. 42 (17 October 1953):755.
11. *Bulletin intérieur*, no. 66 (June 1953), p. 189, and Léon Blum, *Peace and Disarmament*, trans. Alexander Werth (London: Jonathan Cape, 1932).
12. *Bulletin intérieur*, no. 66 (June 1953), pp. 189-90. See also Oreste Rosenfeld, "Les lignes générales de la politique internationale du socialisme," *La Revue Socialiste*, no. 76 (April 1954), pp. 362-67.
13. Mollet, *Bilan et Perspectives*, p. 26.
14. Jules Moch, "Communication de Jules Moch sur les travaux du Comité du disarmement," *La Documentation socialiste*, no. 10 (11-18 June 1955), p. 115.
15. *Bulletin intérieur*, no. 53 (April 1951), p. 149, and no. 72 (May 1954), p. 144.
16. Mollet, *Bilan et Perspectives*, p. 36.
17. See Jules Moch, "Non-dissémination des armes nucléaires et sécurité européene," *La Revue Socialiste*, no. 192 (April 1966), pp. 389-412.
18. Mollet, *Bilan et Perspectives*, p. 29.

19. See *Bulletin intérieur,* no. 72 (May 1954), p. 182-83. The translated text reads in part as follows:

The Congress,
Reaffirms that the abolition of colonialism in all its forms is an essential objective of Democratic Socialism, and conscious of the urgent necessity of economic, social and political development of colonial territories,
Considers that a durable world peace cannot be achieved until all the peoples of the world are free and equal,
Ascertains with satisfaction the appearance of a national consciousness among the peoples of colonial territories under foreign tutelage throughout the world, and
Declares that the Socialist International will lend them all of its assistance and power to obtain independence and the right to govern themselves democratically.

20. See, for instance, *Bulletin intérieur,* no. 110 (May 1959), pp. 162-63. For a similar declaration by the Socialist International, see *Yearbook of the International Socialist Labour Movement,* pp. 52-54.

21. See the excellent discussion in Byron Criddle, *Socialists and European Integration,* pp. 31-38.

22. See *Bulletin intérieur,* no. 42 (May 1949), p. 204.

23. See, for instance, *Bulletin intérieur,* no. 48 (April 1950), pp. 139-42; no. 53 (April 1951), p. 150; no. 60 (April 1952), pp. 80-81; and no. 66 (June 1953), pp. 191-94, 226.

24. Guy Mollet, "France and the Defense of Europe," *Foreign Affairs* 32, no. 3 (April 1954):364-68.

25. Byron Criddle finds some hesitation among the Socialists and blames it on the party's "anticlericalism." There is no reason whatsoever to doubt this interpretation, but in any case it did not deny SFIO support to the various schemes that stemmed from the original Schuman Plan. As will be seen, however, it did seriously affect Socialist acceptance of the EDC. See Criddle, *Socialists and European Integration,* pp. 52-57.

26. See, for instance, *Bulletin intérieur,* no. 53 (April 1951), pp. 182, 185-88, and no. 66 (June 1953), p. 191.

27. Marcel-Edmond Naegelen, "Il faut partir d'autres bases," *La Revue Socialiste,* no. 68 (June 1953), pp. 12-25.

28. For more on the "anticlericalism" issue, see Criddle, *Socialists and European Integration*, pp. 52-55.

29. Ibid.

30. See *Bulletin intérieur*, no. 66 (June 1953), pp. 142, 221, and no. 72 (May 1954), p. 145.

31. *Bulletin intérieur*, no. 78 (May 1955), pp. 148-51.

32. As quoted in Criddle, *Socialists and European Integration*, p. 70.

33. See *Bulletin intérieur*, no. 78 (May 1955), pp. 151-53.

34. See *Bulletin intérieur*, no. 78 (May 1955), p. 197, and Pierre Rimbert, "Mendès-France à pied d'oeuvre," *La Revue Socialiste*, no. 81 (November 1954), pp. 356-60.

35. *Bulletin intérieur*, no. 78 (May 1955), pp. 154-58.

36. Jules Isaac, "Guerre atomique ou coéxistence," *La Revue Socialiste*, no. 79 (July 1954), p. 125.

37. *Bulletin intérieur*, no. 42 (May 1949), pp. 197-204; no. 60 (April 1952), pp. 140-44,; and no. 81 (July 1955), pp. 12-13. See also, "Intervention de Jean Silvande sur la révision du titre VII de la Constitution relatif à l'Union française," *Les cahiers du propagandiste socialiste*, supplement to *Documentation socialiste*, no. 10 (4-11 June 1955), pp. 9-12, and Edouard Marquis, "Essai de définition de l'Union française," *La Revue Socialiste*, no. 89 (July 1955), pp. 167-78.

38. *Bulletin intérieur*, no. 42 (May 1949), pp. 226-28, and no. 66 (June 1953), pp. 158-60.

39. Odette Merlat, "On ne fait pas la Paix, qu'avec ceux à qui on fait la guerre," *La Revue Socialiste*, no. 72 (December 1953), p. 365.

40. Ibid.

41. *Bulletin intérieur*, no. 78 (May 1955), p. 199.

42. *Bulletin intérieur*, no. 66 (June 1953), pp. 167-68.

43. *Bulletin intérieur*, no. 60 (April 1952), pp. 142-43.

44. As quoted in Guy de Carmoy, *The Foreign Policies of France, 1944-1968* (Chicago: University of Chicago Press, 1970), p. 152.

45. Ibid., p. 157.

46. See, for instance, William G. Andrews, *French Politics and Algeria* (New York: Appleton-Century-Crofts, 1962).

47. See, for instance, Micaud, *Communism and the French*

In and out of Government

Left, pp. 236-37, and Jacques Julliard, *La IVe République, 1947-1958* (Paris: Calmann-Lévy, 1968), pp. 201-13.

48. See Philip, *Le socialisme trahi,* pp. 172-76, and Philip, *Les Socialistes,* pp. 161-63.

49. See Pierre Fougeyrollas, *La conscience politique dans la France contemporaine* (Paris: Denoël, 1963), pp. 78, 107, 42-43, and 147.

50. Julliard, *La IVe République,* p. 204.

51. Ibid., p. 203. Julliard points out that so many reasons have been offered for Mollet's action in Suez that even in 1968 it was difficult to decide on which were the correct ones.

52. De Carmoy, *Foreign Policies of France,* p. 159, and Grosser, *La IVe République,* p. 370.

53. See Fougeyrollas, *La conscience politique,* pp. 164-65.

54. See Julliard, *La IVe République,* p. 204.

6

The SFIO and the New Republic

The reentry of General de Gaulle into the political arena at the end of the 1950s caught the SFIO off guard. In the first place, modern economic and social developments were putting in question the traditional assumptions of socialism. Second, as a cadre-led party the SFIO was quite unprepared to react with equanimity to a charismatic figure who represented a substitute for political parties and wished to make them wither. Third, the new regime about to be inaugurated promised to degrade that institution—parliament—which had been the traditional forum of Socialist influence. As the regime unfolded, the SFIO was torn by conflicting aims and expectations, which are set out below in chronological and analytic fashion. Should the SFIO support the General, and in so doing, prevent a greater evil coming from the extreme Right or Left? Could one hope that progressive policies could be promoted in the context of a reactionary institutional setting? What was to be the nature of the SFIO's support of, or opposition to, de Gaulle? More specifically, how could the SFIO oppose the General without allies from the Left who threatened to engulf the party, or without risking the loss of the SFIO's long-time supporters who were becoming enchanted by the politics of symbolism and nationalism? Conversely, how could the SFIO support a Gaullist regime without losing its ideological credibility?

The Fall of the Fourth Republic and the Accession of de Gaulle

Confusion reigned in the ranks of the SFIO from the moment of the first demonstrations and public demands, in mid-May, 1958, for the return of de Gaulle. The initial response of Socialist parliamentarians had been to try to maintain the Fourth Republic and, to this end, to accept the help of the PCF. But when the public demonstrations continued, the SFIO began to waver in this collaboration, fearing the outbreak of a civil war from which the PCF might emerge as the chief beneficiary.

On May 16, Mollet, as secretary-general of the party, addressed three questions to de Gaulle about the conditions under which he was willing to assume leadership. Would the General accept the legitimacy of the present government? Would he disavow the rebellious Committee on Public Safety in Algeria? If asked to form a government, would he present himself to the Assembly and, failing to be invested by that body, would he withdraw his candidacy for the premiership?[1] The General furnished no direct answers but the leadership of the SFIO—at least Mollet and those close to him—chose to interpret de Gaulle's willingness to "assume the powers of the Republic" as an implicit endorsement of republicanism, simply because there was little choice. Corsica had meanwhile fallen to the rebels, and the existing powers of the Republic—in which the Socialists had a part—had been helpless to do anything about it.

The SFIO continued to be apprehensive. On May 25 Mollet sent another letter to de Gaulle in which he did not question the General's motives but expressed the fear that his assumption of power—no matter how temporary—might be interpreted as an authoritarian venture and might therefore strengthen the PCF, the party that would be most likely to react strongly against such a venture. De Gaulle chose to consider this as a veiled gesture of support by Mollet; and the next day, after receiving endorsements from Socialist Vincent Auriol, a former president, and Premier Pierre Pflimlin, de Gaulle announced that he was ready to take steps toward a republican government of national unity.

But on May 27 the Socialist deputies in the Assembly issued a manifesto, by a vote of 112 to 3, in support of the "legally constituted government," and announced that "under no conditions" would they support de Gaulle's investiture. Mollet abstained from that vote.[2] The Socialist deputies also voted to join the PCF in a mass demonstration in support of the Fourth Republic.

The *Comité directeur* opposed this joint endeavor with the PCF. However, some Socialists did join the demonstration, in part because many members of the UDSR and the Radical party had decided to do so, and in part because they feared that a noticeable Socialist abstention from this gesture might drive many working-class supporters of the SFIO prematurely into the arms of the PCF. The demonstration proved futile because the same day Pflimlin resigned as prime minister, and René Coty, too, threatened to resign as president unless de Gaulle were given the premiership. Some Socialists, notably former premier Ramadier, had briefly prevailed upon Pflimlin to stay in office, but in the end Auriol and Mollet, Pflimlin's vice-premier, persuaded him to offer his resignation.

On May 31, when it appeared that de Gaulle could not be stopped, Mollet agreed to participate in the new government. In view of the hostility—or at least division of opinion—within the *Comité directeur* regarding de Gaulle, Mollet dutifully offered to resign as secretary-general, but that offer was, for the time being, rejected. On June 1 de Gaulle was invested by the National Assembly. A bare majority of the Socialist deputies voted against his investiture, but this did not prevent Mollet and two other Socialists from joining the cabinet—ostensibly in their personal capacities rather than as representatives of their party.

De Gaulle's assumption of the reins of government, and Mollet's participation in it, produced the greatest internal crisis for the SFIO since 1933 (when it had been faced with the question of how to react to the fascist menace coming from Germany), and Mollet reached the nadir of his popularity within the party he led.

In his support of de Gaulle's return to power, Mollet was essentially the executor of the will of the SFIO, the party which alone might have been able to prevent the General's investiture—at least if we are to believe Maurice Duverger, who wrote as late as May 9, 1958: "The role of the SFIO is determinant. The Socialist party is the arbiter of the legislature; nothing can be done without it; nothing can be done against it."[3] But the SFIO was too deeply divided to give proper direction to its secretary-general. While some leaders, such as Depreux, Philip, Mayer, Verdier, and Savary, were ready to leave the SFIO in September and to join the newly established Parti socialiste autonome (PSA), others, such as Auriol and Defferre, supported collaboration with the Gaullists.

The "Gaullist wave" could not be resisted by the majority of Socialist deputies, whose anti-Gaullism was whittled down within a few days. The following recapitulation should serve as an illustration:

> May 27: Vote by SFIO parliamentary caucus *against* investiture of de Gaulle: 112 for; 3 against.
>
> May 29: Vote by SFIO parliamentary group approving a letter by Auriol to de Gaulle, asking de Gaulle to "dissociate himself from his enemies of yesterday" (i.e., the generals and the ultra-conservatives): 62 for; 29 against.
>
> May 31: Vote by SFIO parliamentary caucus on investiture *(vote indicatif)*: 77 for; 74 against.
>
> June 1: Vote by SFIO in Assembly plenum on investiture: 42 for; 49 against;
>
> June 1: Vote by SFIO in Assembly plenum on granting special powers: 46 for; 3 against; 45 abstentions.

At a party press conference early in July, 1958, the SFIO tried to minimize the divisions prevailing within the party by insisting that these were honest differences of opinion between the ideological purists and the realists. It was in fact not easy to tell the difference between the two. By mid-1958, most SFIO leaders had recognized that their party must face new realities, must reform itself, or perhaps make novel alliances. On July 2, a new liaison organization, the Centre de la réforme républicaine, was established under the auspices of the SFIO, which called for a regrouping of the entire non-Communist Left, including the Radicals and the MRP, presumably in order to oppose de Gaulle more effectively.

The SFIO and the New Constitution

In the same month, however, Mollet and two Socialists selected by him decided to join the ministerial committee in charge of writing a new constitution. After the appearance of the text Mollet's involvement was criticized as a particularly objectionable example of "Molletism" by several members of the *Comité directeur,* which only a short time earlier had produced a vote of confidence "in all members of the bureau until the next National Congress." It turned out that Mollet's influence on the draft of the Fifth Republic constitution had been considerable. He had supported the provisions strengthening the power of the president, in particular with respect to the exercise of emergency powers.[4]

The new constitution was to be submitted to the people in September. But even before the popular referendum, Mollet's somewhat premature Gaullism manifested itself in his advocating the endorsement of that constitution by the SFIO. Apart from the fact that Mollet had participated in the drafting of the document, he was probably convinced that it contained enough of the traditional features of republicanism—a dual executive, a bicameral legislature, separation of church and state, a nonconfidence provision, welfare-state clauses, and a reference (in the preamble) to human rights—to be acceptable to most Frenchmen.

Considerable hostility to the constitution (and to Mollet's leadership) was expressed at a meeting of the *Comité directeur* in July, and again at the Fiftieth National Congress at Issy-les-Moulineaux in mid-September. Many delegates, led by Georges Brutelle, the deputy secretary, and Albert Gazier, a member of the *Comité directeur,* were worried about the possibility that the new constitution would "imperil individual liberties and the ideals of socialism."[5] Particularly strong opposition was expressed to Article 16, the provision granting exceptional powers to the president during emergencies. Mollet however was convinced that liberties would be preserved, and another supporter of the new constitution, Augustin Laurent, even felt that the establishment of socialism would be feasible under the constitution. It proved impossible to persuade most of the opponents, notably Gazier, Pineau, Naegelen, Mayer, and Leenhardt; but Defferre (who was convinced that only de Gaulle could, and would, solve the Algerian problem) switched to the support of Mollet, a step which contributed to the endorsement of the constitution by the National Congress (2,886 to 1,176). Mollet had prevailed again, but several prominent Socialists then left the party and joined the PSA. These included Daniel Mayer, Mollet's predecessor as secretary-general; Edouard Depreux (who had begun to mount a sharp attack on Mollet in the newly established *Tribune de Socialisme)*; and Alain Savary (who was later to head the SFIO's successor party).

Mollet found himself isolated and criticized within the party leadership, and yet he maintained his position. This was due not so much to the fact that he controlled a large segment of the party press (there were competing Socialist journals); or that he controlled a powerful federation (there were federations more powerful than Nord); or that the party was hopelessly divided; but rather to the fact that in his stand in favor of the new constitution and of collaboration with de Gaulle generally he was perhaps more representative of rank-and-file Socialist opinion than many of his colleagues on the *Comité directeur*. According to a public opinion poll conducted in August, 1958,[6] 58 percent of the Socialist respondents felt that under the Fourth Republic the government did not have enough power; 50 percent, that the Fourth Republic's president did not have any real power; and 36 percent, that parliament had had too much power.

The outcome of the referendum on the new constitution was in all likelihood a foregone conclusion for Mollet. He may have reasoned, realistically, that de Gaulle should have his own instrument to solve the Algerian crisis, and that it was better to be in rather than out of government. Such an attitude is not necessarily to be equated with a *sauve qui peut* philosophy. Just as Mollet had prevailed upon de Gaulle in mid-June to abandon the idea of adding Jacques Soustelle (a hawk on Algeria) to the cabinet by threatening to resign, the Socialist leader probably felt that it would be possible for him to continue to influence de Gaulle's domestic policies toward greater progressivism. For many Socialists, it was not a foregone conclusion that de Gaulle's domestic policies would be reactionary. According to a poll conducted in September, only 6 percent of the Socialist respondents felt that republican liberties would be endangered by de Gaulle himself, while 53 percent perceived such a danger as coming from elsewhere (extreme Left, 16 percent; extreme Right, 22 percent; the army, 3 percent; or de Gaulle's entourage, 12 percent).[7]

The approval of the new constitution by 80 percent of the electorate could be interpreted as the endorsement of the man whose instrument it was destined to be, but it was as yet uncertain whether such approval also signified an explicit repudiation of those parties—notably the SFIO—with which the Fourth Republic and its failures had been identified.

The SFIO remained divided during the campaign for the parliamentary election to take place at the end of November. All Socialists hoped that the SFIO would gain seats or at least hold them, but there was disagreement about how the party would best do this and about what the party's position would be after the election. Many Socialists, meeting at a congress in October, had expressed themselves in favor of an electoral alliance with the PCF for the second ballot; Mollet, however, while appealing for the support of Catholics and other miscellaneous nonlaics, would brook "no compromise with the believers in bolshevism."[8] And as Mollet was insisting that the SFIO should, in the future parliament, fight for national renewal and stand in support of de Gaulle, Gazier campaigned for a "resolute and vigorous opposition." If it was true, as one observer has said, that the SFIO was "a compromise between the dogmatism of a museum and the expediency of empirical politics,"[9] it was difficult to tell during the campaign who were the dogmatists and who the empiricists.

The election results were a disaster for the SFIO. Although the party's share of the total vote increased slightly, from 14.8 percent in 1956 to 15.5 percent in 1958 on the second ballot, its parliamentary representation was reduced from 91 to 40. The Gaullist party, now relabeled Union pour la nouvelle République (UNR), had increased its share of the popular vote from 4.4 percent (under the old label of RPF) to 17.6 percent, and obtained 188 seats, while the PCF, which saw its popular vote diminish from 25.7 percent to 18.9 percent, was left with only 10 seats in the Assembly.

The results obviously constituted a defeat for most of those who had opposed de Gaulle's assumption of power and the new constitution. The most vigorous anti-Gaullists among the Socialists—including such members or former members of the *Comité directeur* as Lacoste, Pinard, Le Troquer, Gazier, and even Defferre and Ramadier—failed to be returned to parliament. To be sure, distribution of seats was heavily influenced by the inequalities inherent in the new single-member electoral system initiated in 1958, which made it more difficult for the PCF to benefit from an *apparentement*, or alliance, with more moderate candidates. Nonetheless, it was clear that Mollet's hope of leading a constructive, or loyal, opposition with the help of sufficient parliamentary supporters was being frustrated. It was the end of a long sequence of Socialist perplexities.

Qualified Participation or Constructive Opposition?

The SFIO was now confronted with a number of options, or rather, dilemmas: if it were to fight Gaullism, it needed help; to make an alliance with the PCF would be to court the danger of being smothered by a disciplined and impressively organized party with a (more or less) constant social base; to make common cause with the MRP might lead to ideological corruption and a weakening of the principles of laicism. To support Gaullism might spell the end of socialism and alienate whatever remained of the traditional base of the SFIO. To support de Gaulle but not his entourage—an attempt that Mollet had vainly made a few weeks earlier—rested on the desperate assumption that de Gaulle could be transformed into a progressive leader. In view of the General's background and the orientation of many of his supporters during the Fourth Republic, this assumption had been questionable to begin with, and, considering the insignificance of Socialist representation in the new parliament, was now totally bereft of realism. As if to emphasize this point, it soon appeared that Gaullist domestic policy was objectionable both in form and in substance to Socialists. During the month of December, 1958, a number of anti-Socialist measures were promulgated by decree, providing for the reduction of price supports for staple foods, of health insurance benefits, and of veterans' payments. On December 27, Mollet resigned as minister of state in de Gaulle's cabinet, together with Eugène Thomas, another Socialist, who had been minister of posts and telecommunications.

The resignations had been unavoidable in view of the vocal criticism by most of Mollet's Socialist colleagues in the Assembly and elsewhere,[10] and in view of the PCF's call for vigorous opposition to de Gaulle's domestic policy from all "socialist workers." Still, Mollet withheld the announcement of his resignation until January 8, the day on which de Gaulle would relinquish the premiership to assume the presidency, and Michel Debré, who had been minister of justice, would become the new prime minister. In the first week of January, de Gaulle reportedly made a last try to persuade Mollet to participate in the new government.[11] Mollet may therefore still have clung to the hope that if de Gaulle would not reconsider the nomination of Debré he might at least desire to pursue a policy that was not completely "Gaullist."

While the Algerian crisis persisted, however, Mollet was not ready to make a clean break with Gaullism. Throughout most of 1959 he remained in readiness to rejoin the government should de Gaulle show a willingness to "evolve" with respect to his attitudes to domestic policies.[12] Until such evolution, he wished the SFIO to be a *contreproposant*, a role designed to enable the party to keep one foot in the door to respectability, responsibility, and, ultimately, power, and to let de Gaulle know that there were alternatives to a government headed by Debré. Mollet was not completely alone. Leenhardt, who was the spokesman of the SFIO in the new Assembly, also tried to dissociate de Gaulle from Debré when he attacked government policy.

At a National Council meeting on January 10-11, the SFIO repreated its criticism of de Gaulle's economic policy and, while it listened to the denunciations by Gazier of Mollet's leadership, implicitly supported Mollet's position (including his anti-bolshevism). It called for the formation (around the SFIO) of an alliance of "all republicans and democrats . . . in order to check totalitarian tendencies of the Right or the so-called Left."[13]

The "Mollet thesis" appeared to be vindicated by the results of the municipal elections of March 8 and 15. Many of the Socialist candidates who had spurned an appeal by the PCF for a Popular Front made second-ballot alliances with Radical or even MRP candidates—Mollet himself owed his reelection in Arras to MRP support—and the SFIO even improved its position slightly. And Gaston Defferre, the Socialist leader who had consistently spoken for the anti-Communist elements in his party, secured an increase of over 50 percent in Socialist representation in the Marseilles municipal council, and a month later he entered the Senate.

Early in April, 1959, Mollet accorded an interview to *L'Aurore,* a conservative newspaper, in which he outlined his ideas on opposition:

> I think that the government and the loyal and constructive opposition can, without compromise on one side or another, maintain contact, as is done in Great Britain. The SFIO represents a political force large enough to deserve being kept informed in certain areas, especially in international affairs. . . . Because of totalitarian dangers which appear on the Right and on the Left, and because of a dislike in certain quarters for the great republican principles, the SFIO would like to bring about a political realignment solely on the basis of a common attachment to democracy.[14]

These curious remarks were not only in conflict with the ideas of a resolute opposition, demanded by Gazier, to which most of the *Comité directeur* was now committed, but they also still indicated a confusion of the politics of principle with the politics of opportunism. In the first place, Mollet's admiration of British governmental patterns was inconsistent with his steadfast support of the presidential decision making implied in the Fifth Republic constitution, or at least in de Gaulle's interpretation of that constitution. This presidentialism meant above all de Gaulle's arrogation of exclusive responsibility for foreign affairs—e.g., the solution of the Algerian problem. It is difficult to see how anyone could expect the General to consult with the political parties in parliament, let alone an opposition party. Secondly, the interview shows that Mollet still insisted on a distinction between de Gaulle and the UNR in disregard of the fact that UNR candidates had to take a loyalty oath to de Gaulle and of the fact that the UNR had integrated into its ranks a considerable number of antirepublican elements of the Right. Thirdly, if republican principles included laicism, why did Mollet actively seek the support of the MRP as he had done in his own constituency during the recent municipal elections?

In conformity with his republican realism, Mollet began discussions in the spring of 1959 with Félix Gaillard, the leader of the moderate wing of the Radical Party. These discussions were aimed at the establishment of a broad republican front that was to be anti-Gaullist as well as anti-Communist.

However, the obverse of Mollet's "thesis" was also soon manifested when, early in May, several hundred SFIO militants from various federations gathered at Puteaux for a series of Socialist doctrinal study sessions. While Jules Moch called for an adaptation of Socialist philosophy to contemporary socio-economic realities and suggested the establishment of a short-term legislative program *à l'anglaise,* Mollet argued for the retention of a Marxist ideological approach. In attributing Mollet's reversion to a doctrinaire position to pragmatic motives, one may cite the fact that he had perceived the militants to be a majority at the sessions or the fact that he did not wish to be outflanked on the Left by the PCF, which had made important gains in the municipal elections.

By mid-1959, disenchantment with the new government was widespread within the SFIO, and most Socialists had broken with Gaullism. Mollet still continued to defend his endorsement of the new constitution, but he—as well as André Chandernagor, a member of the *Comité directeur*—aimed his criticism at Debré rather than de Gaulle for violating it. Moreover, Mollet still hoped that if the SFIO obtained a parliamentary majority in the near future, it would be able to work under the Gaullist system to promote progressive policies. For others, however, among them Gazier, Pineau, and Moch, the possibility of a left-wing Gaullism had become an illusion or a contradiction in terms, and one could no longer reasonably attack Debré without also implicating the General.[15]

These disagreements were fully reflected at the Fifty-first National Congress of the SFIO, which took place at Issy-les-Moulineaux on July 9-12. Mollet and his allies—notably Augustin Laurent—criticized Debré but remained steadfast in their support of de Gaulle (1) because under his leadership the basic individual freedoms were being maintained; (2) because Mollet was convinced that de Gaulle would solve the Algerian problem; and (3) because he hoped that the General would eventually conduct "a policy close to our own from a human and liberal point of view."[16] Despite widespread criticism of Mollet's stewardship (led by Moch and Pineau), several motions hostile to Mollet that had been introduced at the congress were not adopted, and despite the approval of resolutions criticizing the government far beyond the scope intended by Mollet, he was reelected to the *Comité directeur* by a vote of 2,518 to 1,134 and reappointed as a secretary-general. The reasons for this apparent inconsistency are varied. First, it could not be proved that Mollet's leadership had been detrimental to the SFIO: since September, 1958, fewer than 5 percent of the members of the party had defected. Secondly, Mollet continued to control one of the three or four most powerful federations of the party; and thirdly, the opposition within the party (led by Gazier and, somewhat less wholeheartedly, Defferre) was divided and unable to produce an alternative to Mollet.

What appeared to vindicate Mollet's faith in de Gaulle was a declaration by the General on September 6 that the Algerians would be given a free choice between independence and continued association with France and a promise, ten days later, of Algerian self-determination. But on September 8, Michel Debré, de Gaulle's premier, declared before the Assembly's foreign affairs committee that there would be no negotiations with "rebels." The SFIO sent congratulations to de Gaulle; and Tanguy-Prigent, a member of the *Comité directeur* and a severe critic of the Fifth Republic, wrote an article calling upon Socialists to support the General against his premier.[17] But while Tanguy-Prigent seemed to agree for once with Mollet's distinction between the president and his premier, he soon became disenchanted with the SFIO. In October he and many other Socialists, including ten former deputies, resigned from the party and joined the Parti socialiste autonome (now led by ex-Socialist Depreux and ex-Radical Mendès-France), because the SFIO had abandoned "the road to socialism."[18]

The SFIO still supported de Gaulle on Algeria; indeed, on October 15, the Socialists (together with the MRP, the Center-Left, and most of the UNR) voted in favor of an Assembly resolution supporting the General's publicly proclaimed stand in favor of Algerian independence. At the same time disenchantment with Gaullist domestic policy, fed by rising prices and the generally reactionary economic measures of Finance Minister Pinay, had become so widespread that the Left was gradually regaining its popularity. According to one source,[19] the Gaullist deputy of La Nièvre, Mitterrand's old constituency, was reported to have said that if new elections were held, the leader of the UDSR would regain his seat. Mollet was still wedded to his *idée fixe* and attempted to rally behind de Gaulle "that part of the working class which he has alienated because of his retrogressive social policy," so that the president would succeed with his "democratic solution to the Algerian problem."[20] But the government did not make Mollet's position easy: it added to Socialist dissatisfaction by renewing discussions on educational reform, with the apparent aim of putting through an antilaic school measure.

When the SFIO's National Council met in November, Mollet congratulated himself for his stewardship, under which the party had recently lost "only" 10 percent of its members. But most of the council members had become so critical of government policy (except, of course, on Algeria) that they demanded an end to all collaboration with the regime. Jules Moch was criticized for having consented to be a government representative at the UN Disarmament Commission, while another Socialist, Pierre-Olivier Lapie, was expelled from the party because he had agreed to preside over the Assembly's *commission d'étude*, which was to examine the feasibility of public support for confessional schools.[21]

During the same month the SFIO (together with the Radicals, to whom the Socialists were drawing closer) introduced a censure motion in the Assembly. The motion failed to get the requisite majority, with only the SFIO, PCF, and Radicals (and a few MRP deputies) voting for it. The same combination of the Left (but excluding the antilaic MRP) was equally unsuccessful in preventing the passage on December 31 of the *loi scolaire*, which permitted the government to grant subsidies to parochial schools under contract to the Ministry of Education. This bill (which came to be known as the Debré Law) was in effect a compromise between the total integration of the parochial schools into the system of public education and their complete freedom with respect to the state. It was realistic in view of the fact that a large proportion of French children were attending Catholic schools and that, according to a public opinion poll taken in 1959, more than half of the non-Communist Left *opposed* the abolition of subsidies to such schools.[22]

According to the same poll, a third of the extreme (i.e., Communist) Left was equally opposed to the suppression of state aid. Still the relationship between the SFIO and the PCF was embittered by the fact that the minister of education, under whose auspices the bill had been prepared, was a Socialist, André Boulloche. The earlier expulsion of Lapie from the SFIO for collaboration on the school issue apparently did not furnish a precedent, for the party had not seen fit to expel Boulloche. The SFIO leaders claimed that Boulloche, although perhaps still a Socialist, was no longer a member of the SFIO, or at least that he no longer represented the SFIO in the cabinet. Nonetheless, when the SFIO took the step of formally expelling him, the PCF suggested that he had merely been put on a "vacation" from the party. On December 23, Boulloche—who had opposed the *loi scolaire* throughout—resigned as minister of education.[23]

At the beginning of 1960 it looked as if unity within the Socialist ranks was being restored when the party, under the leadership of Mollet, appeared finally to have returned to an opposition status. Still, there were Socialists (led by Gazier) who were not entirely convinced that Mollet would for long resist the temptation again "to play the game of the Elysée,"[24] either in order to participate in government personally or in order to aid those Gaullists who hoped for an opening to the Left. Mollet may have been encouraged by the dismissal in January 1960 of the conservative Antoine Pinay as finance minister. He may also have been heartened by the fact that de Gaulle seemed determined to resist the right-wing militarists when he reaffirmed his more liberal position on Algeria, dismissed General Massu from his command, and took steps to crush the mutiny of the officers in Algeria. Although a few months earlier Mollet had agreed with some of his party colleagues that the Gaullist regime was monarchical, it still represented—in the face of the threat by the military—the "republican order," and he therefore indicated his readiness "to sacrifice even the style of democracy in order to pay off the Algerian mortgage."[25] The SFIO endorsed his position when it joined the UNR, the MRP, and most of the Independents, both in the Assembly and the Senate, in voting special powers to the president under Article 38. On January 31 the SFIO established a liaison committee with the UNR "for the support of

General de Gaulle," (in whom both Mollet and Defferre continued to express confidence). This continuation of "constructive opposition" was, however, not fated to last long.

In March the SFIO demanded that the parliament be convened for a special session to deal with the agricultural and other domestic problems. When, despite the 296 signatures (i.e., more than the requisite majority) de Gaulle refused to convoke the special session, in violation of Article 29 of the constitution, most of the Socialists felt that the idea of the General's representing republican legitimacy had become untenable. Even Mollet was now forced to admit publicly that de Gaulle was mocking his own constitution, and he now called for a "union of all the democrats" to oppose the General.

The SFIO in Opposition

The turn toward systematic opposition on the part of Mollet and the SFIO as a whole was due not only to the unconstitutional behavior of de Gaulle but also to other circumstances. First, there were some doubts about the extent to which de Gaulle's commitments on Algeria could be trusted, for during a voyage to Algeria in March he had told his officers that "the Algerian problem will take a long time to settle, and not until after a victory by French arms."[26] Secondly, a new leftist party—which took the name of the old Parti socialiste unifié (PSU)— had been created in April, 1960, from the PSA and other dissident Socialists and Communists, with the possibility of additional defections to this new party. Thirdly, the Radical party and even the MRP were becoming more leftist.

As if to prove his good republican faith and to justify his current opposition to Gaullism, Mollet presented to the Assembly some sections of the *procès-verbaux* of the Constitutional Committee (in which he had participated) tending to show that de Gaulle and Debré were violating the spirit of their own constitution. Almost at the same time Vincent Auriol resigned from the Constitutional Council where, as former president of the Republic, he had served ex-officio. He felt that the council had not been properly consulted on important constitutional matters, such as the *loi scolaire*, the revision of the status of the colonial

French Community, and the nonconvocation of parliament. Although Auriol's resignation had been on his own behalf and had taken place shortly after he had resigned from the SFIO, the gesture could not but add to the respectability of opposition to Gaullism, particularly since, as will be recalled, the former president of the Fourth Republic had been instrumental in bringing about the General's return to power.

The definitive break with Gaullism occurred at the Fifty-second National Congress of the SFIO in early July, 1960. The congress, following the lead of the *Comité directeur*, the Jeunesses Socialistes, and other ancillary organizations, denounced the government's domestic policy, especially its footdragging on the forty-hour week; insufficient attention to social security; inadequate investments in public works; inadequate price supports for small farmers; and its inability to solve the housing shortage.[27] A large number of delegates, led by Albert Gazier, demanded a complete severance from de Gaulle and a disengagement from his "paternalistic monarchy," questioned the need for continued party discipline, criticized Mollet's leadership, and suggested that the SFIO as a party was no longer cognizant of "the great movements that are transforming the world."[28] While Mollet defended his own republicanism (he had, after all, recently made an Assembly speech critical of de Gaulle's monarchical tendencies) and progressivism (he referred to the SFIO's continued critique of capitalism in Africa!), he still insisted that the General was the "best man" under the circumstances, and he still rejected the demand of some of his colleagues for collaboration with the Communists. The differences within the SFIO were again papered over when Mollet was reelected to the *Comité directeur* and his position was supported by a weak majority of the delegates. The *Comité directeur* reelected Mollet as secretary-general; this action was facilitated by the absence from that body of several opponents of Mollet (e.g., Fuzier, Pineau, and Weill-Reynal) who had refused to take their seats in protest against certain machinations by the secretary-general.[29]

By September, 1960, even Mollet had been brought around to clear opposition. This belated conversion was due to the fact that Mollet's support within the party appeared to be declining, to de Gaulle's negative attitude toward the United Nations, NATO, and European unity, and to the General's "antiquated national-ism," which the *Comité directeur* attacked with increasing frequency. Although the SFIO's opposition to Gaullism was now sufficiently unambiguous to convince several recalcitrant party members to end their boycott of the *Comité directeur,* unity within the party was by no means fully restored. While Mollet agreed with most of his party in its opposition to the nuclear *force de frappe ("c'est de la folie,"* he had said), and led the party in its vote for a censure motion on the government's European policy, he disagreed with many of his colleagues when in November the General announced that a referendum to open negotiations on Algeria would take place in December. Mollet reacted very favorably to the new policy (while at the same time criticizing de Gaulle for his disregard of parliament); Defferre was skeptical about it because the fighting in Algeria would continue; Gazier opposed the referendum because of his opposition to the regime as a whole; and Max Lejeune opposed it because he favored an *Algérie française.* Mollet's position was finally upheld in the *Comité directeur,* largely because Defferre swung—as he had done two years earlier—to the support of the secretary-general.

If it was difficult to determine what the position of the SFIO should have been with regard to the merits of the referendum, it was equally difficult to show what conclusions were to be drawn from the 55 percent "yes" vote on the referendum on January 9, 1961. Perhaps the referendum would have failed if the SFIO opposition had been very clearcut—and the General might have been forced to leave the political scene. Perhaps de Gaulle's popularity was still so great that nothing the Socialists might have done would have altered the result of the referendum; moreover, an exaggerated Socialist negativism might even have served to alienate the SFIO further from the electorate. While the SFIO did not publicly regret having given its support, it made its position clear that the referendum should by no means be construed as Socialist support for the idea of the "indispensable man." In the words of Christian Pineau, "the confidence that [the referendum] has given to de Gaulle is not blind; it has a precise object . . . and cannot be renewed if he does not fulfill the task the people have explicitly given him."[30]

The SFIO wished, however, to give its endorsement of the

referendum a proper leftist character in order to compete with the Communist party. For that reason the SFIO signed a manifesto on January 19 calling for negotiations with the Algerian nationalists, which was also being endorsed by the FO, the Confédération française des travailleurs chrétiens (CFTC), the FEN, the Jeunes Agriculteurs, the Radicals, and even the left-wing Gaullists (the Union démocratique de travail [UDT]).

To maintain its leftist character remained as difficult for the SFIO in 1961 as it had been on earlier occasions. In competition with the PCF, the "super-Left" (i.e., the somewhat illegal collaborators of the FLN), and those forces of the Left that were united behind Mitterrand in their opposition to the Fifth Republic, the "respectable" Left of Mollet could assert itself convincingly only so long as Algeria was still a problem and de Gaulle appeared to be the man capable of solving it. However, the SFIO also had to broaden the "progressive" base of its actions. Thus when de Gaulle, in April 1961, invoked Article 16 in order to deal with the revolt of the parachutists, the SFIO endorsed the resort to this emergency provision (against the opposition of the PCF) with the help of the FO, CFTC, FEN, UNEF (Union nationale des étudiants de France), the Federation of Veterans, the Independent Socialists, the Radicals, and (less wholeheartedly) the PSU, in order to fight against "fascist aggression."[31] By virtue of its support of several trade unions that threatened general strikes, the SFIO could even claim some credit for having mobilized the working class to "save the Republic from the generals."[32] In all likelihood Mollet personally retained his doubts about the efficacy of spontaneous public street action for political ends, not only because he had committed himself in his long political career to public order and to normal parliamentary methods of protest and change, but also because he feared that the PCF would always try to exploit such actions for their own purposes. In fact, while the PCF accused Mollet of taking public order more seriously than socialism, the Communists themselves considered it expedient to maintain the Gaullist system. During the episode of the terrorist *plastiqueurs*, the CGT, the Communists' "transmission belt," organized a "popular militia" at Régie Renault to help save the Fifth Republic and was even granted the use of vehicles for its activities by Renault's director.[33]

The clash between the proponents of public order, led by the secretary-general, and the Socialists led by Gazier and Pineau was reflected in the disagreements at the Fifty-third National Congress of the SFIO in May 1961. Many leaders of the SFIO remained opposed to the use of Article 16; Gazier was convinced that France was slipping irremediably into a regime of personalism, and even Jules Moch had become so hostile to the General that he was less adamant in his opposition to the Communists; but Mollet still justified the use of Article 16 as legitimate and insisted that France was still a democracy. Defferre again came to the rescue of the secretary-general by favoring the use of Article 16 in the present instance. Mollet retained his majority, but it was not strong enough to put through the congress any fundamental program, except a call upon de Gaulle to undertake "speedy negotiations" on Algeria (which were about to begin in any case in Evian).[34]

By the fall of 1961 the SFIO had regained much of its internal unity, since even Guy Mollet, it seemed, had become overtly committed to opposition to de Gaulle. To determine the precise reasons for this conversion is difficult. Certainly one factor was the relatively poor performance of the SFIO in the municipal elections in June, in which many Socialist candidates had won on the second ballot (i.e., the run-off vote) only with the help of the PCF; another was the systematic disregard of parliament by the General and his government. Early in September Mollet had initiated an unsuccessful censure motion against the Debré government for its failure to maintain an adequate price structure for agriculture. In the same month the *Comité directeur* convoked a special meeting of the National Council to discuss, and criticize, the political institutions of the Fifth Republic, in particular such provisions as Article 16. This discussion had been preceded by Mollet's personal critique of the studious disregard by de Gaulle of the political parties, the parliament, and the "free trade unions," and his attempt to insulate "the sanest part of the nation" from political decisions.[35]

At the same time, Mollet tried to organize a *cartel républicain* together with the Radicals. The secretary-general's opposition to de Gaulle had now developed to such a pitch that when there was an assassination attempt on the General, Mollet was not too indignant: he agreed with Georges Bidault that an *attentat* against a people was far more serious than one against a man.[36] At the SFIO's headquarters, politicians (Mollet now doubtlessly among them) were so convinced that the new opposition stance would facilitate a "republican union" presided over by Mollet and comprising the Socialists, the Radicals, the MRP, and perhaps even the PSU—a union that would achieve the dual purpose of isolating the PCF and toppling the Gaullist regime— that there was increasing talk about _après-Gaullisme._[37] The republican union did not, however, materialize, in large part because the PSU continued to insist on its own formula—a Popular Front. This was rejected by the SFIO not only because it was to include the PCF, but also because it was to be headed by Mendès-France. At the same time, Mollet's all-out fight against Article 16, belated though it was, had become academic almost as soon as it was heralded: the General outmaneuvered the democratic forces by announcing in September that the application of the controversial article would be ended for the time being.

Mollet had definitely abandoned his belief that without de Gaulle there would be chaos, and in this respect he was now in agreement with most of the leadership of the SFIO. For all practical purposes Mollet had come around to accepting the existence of the Fifth Republic and saw the task of the SFIO as one of safeguarding France's democratic institutions in that context. Henceforward, Mollet promised, he would campaign "for the defense of parliament" and the restoration of its authority—a commitment that produced a semblance of rapprochement between Mollet and Gazier. A resolution adopted unanimously by the National Council condemning both the government and its domestic policies was an anticlimatic ratification of Mollet's (more or less final) conversion to anti-Gaullism.[38]

Notes

1. _Bulletin intérieur,_ no. 105 (July 1958), p. 5; and _Année politique 1958,_ p. 59 (hereafter _AP_).

2. Edgar S. Furniss, _France, Troubled Ally,_ p. 342. See also

Jean Poperen, *La gauche française: le nouvel âge, 1958-65* (Paris: Fayard, 1972), pp. 51-61.

3. Quoted in Annie Douël, "L'accession du Général de Gaulle au pouvoir et la SFIO," mimeographed (Paris: Fondation Nationale des Sciences Politiques, April 22, 1960).

4. François G. Dreyfus, *Histoire des gauches en France, 1940-1974* (Paris: Grasset, 1975), p. 203.

5. *AP 1958*, p. 113; and Jean-André Faucher, *La gauche française sous de Gaulle* (Paris: John Didier, 1969), p. 11.

6. Institut français d'opinion publique poll, August 1958, cited in Fougeyrollas, *La conscience politique*, p. 59.

7. Ibid., p. 63.

8. *AP 1958*, pp. 130-31, 149.

9. Jacques Droz, *Le socialisme démocratique, 1864-1960* (Paris: A. Colin, 1966), p. 312.

10. In mid-December Auriol had resigned from his federation (Haute-Vienne) of the SFIO in protest against Mollet's leadership. The resignation was not made public for two months. *AP 1959*, p. 21.

11. *AP 1959*, p. 41.

12. Faucher, *La gauche française*, p. 30.

13. *AP 1959*, p. 8. See also Pierre Avril, *Le régime politique de la Ve République* (Paris: Librairie Générale de Droit et de Jurisprudence, 1967), p. 292.

14. *AP 1959*, p. 42.

15. Faucher, *La gauche française*, pp. 22-24; and Furniss, *France, Troubled Ally*, pp. 396-97.

16. *AP 1959*, pp. 81-82; and Faucher, *La gauche francaise*, p. 24.

17. "Aider de Gaulle," *Le Monde*, September 13, 1959.

18. *AP 1959*, pp. 111-12.

19. Faucher, *La gauche française*, p. 27.

20. *AP 1959*, p. 248.

21. *AP 1959*, pp. 130-31.

22. Dreyfus, *Histoire des gauches*, p. 222. The figure cited for Catholic school attendance, 43%, is probably an exaggeration.

23. *AP 1959*, pp. 144-45, 153; Jacques Chapsal, *La vie politique en France depuis 1960* (Paris: Presses Universitaires de France, 1966), p. 405; and "Loi d'aide à l'enseignement privé," *Journal officiel*, January 2, 1960.

24. Faucher, *La gauche française,* p. 36.

25. Ibid., pp. 30, 37.

26. *AP 1960,* p. 27; and Faucher, *La gauche française,* p. 39.

27. *Bulletin interiéur,* no. 114 (May 1960), pp. 21-23.

28. *AP 1960,* p. 73.

29. Mollet had allegedly prevented the election of a M. Dardel to the *Comité directeur* because the latter had been elected a regional councillor with the help of the PCF. *AP 1960,* p. 74.

30. *AP 1961,* p. 9.

31. *AP 1961,* pp. 42, 54-56.

32. *AP 1961,* p. 58.

33. Faucher, *La gauche française,* pp. 50, 69.

34. *AP 1961,* p. 68.

35. *Le Populaire,* September 8, 1961.

36. Faucher, *La gauche française,* p. 77.

37. Ibid., pp. 77-78. Cf. *AP 1961,* pp. 125, 131.

38. *AP 1961,* pp. 120-21.

Part 3
Toward Revitalization

7
In Quest of Realignment and Redefinition

The task of safeguarding the democratic nature of French institutions, while infusing a more progressive content into French policies, was one which the SFIO lacked the power to promote alone. But the SFIO's switch to steadfast opposition proved easier than the creation of an acceptable working relationship between the SFIO and the other opposition forces, without whose help there could be no meaningful anti-Gaullist alliance.

Looking for Allies

Many Socialists persisted in their distrust of a Popular Front involving collaboration with the Communist party. An understanding with the PSU was an alternative method of achieving a credible leftism; but the PSU, although anti-Communist, not only refused to join the SFIO without the Communists, but also published a joint communiqué with the PCF accusing the Socialists of attempting to create an anti–Popular Front. The Socialists' *Comité directeur* reacted by suspending all discussion with the PSU, but this did not prevent Socialists in some districts from establishing liaison committees "for the defense of republican liberties" with both the PSU and the PCF.[1]

The Socialists remained uncertain about the method of pursuing their anti-Gaullism. At the end of 1961 various trade unions (CFTC, CGT, UNEF, FEN) organized a symbolic work stoppage in protest against the Organisation armée secrète (OAS). The FO did not wish to participate in the strike (although individual members of that union supported the idea), largely because its sponsoring party, the SFIO, was afraid that the demonstration would be exploited by the PCF. When the MRP expressed its support for the action, however, the SFIO was compelled to do likewise. Although forbidden by the Paris police prefecture, the demonstration took place anyway; the police intervened, and the *Comité directeur* denounced the police's "savagery."[2]

The opposition to de Gaulle that had developed by early 1962, embracing most non-Gaullist parties and most economic associations, had become significant enough to induce the SFIO's leaders to believe that de Gaulle would soon have to leave the scene. On January 16 Mollet had dinner with a wide assortment of personalities: Pinay (Independent); Maurice Faure (Radical); André Colin (MRP); and leaders of the FO, CFTC, and the Jeunes Agriculteurs. On that occasion it was decided to discuss the establishment of a center-left coalition (reminiscent of the coalition of 1956) to succeed de Gaulle. The PCF was left out, and so was the PSU, which referred to the dinner meeting as an "exercise in Fourth Republic nostalgia."[3]

One immediate result was the establishment of a "National Action Committee against the OAS and for a Negotiated Peace" composed of representatives of the SFIO, the Radicals, the Center-Left, and miscellaneous Leftist groups. Since neither the PCF nor the PSU—nor, in fact, the MRP or Independents (Pinay's group)—participated in it, the committee could, in clear conscience, afford to appeal to all "democratic organizations of the Left."

However, the Socialist accord with the democratic forces foundered because of Mollet's doctrinaire position: during the municipal election campaign, Mollet attacked not only the PSU (which had not participated) but also the CFTC, because in fighting against the OAS, it had aligned itself with the CGT. Nonetheless, early in February, the SFIO was forced to march with the PCF and the PSU.

The SFIO was in the opposition, but that opposition was still responsible and constructive. This implied that the Socialists would criticize de Gaulle when they felt that he was acting in an unrepublican or un-Socialist manner and would support him when such support served a good purpose. Thus on March 18, 1962, when de Gaulle announced that a referendum on the Evian talks with Algeria would soon be forthcoming, the SFIO's Permanent Bureau immediately favored a yes vote. The National Council of the party endorsed this position, but Mollet was careful to note that "our 'yes' does not mean approval of . . . the general policy of the government." The SFIO's position was in part opportunistic: it hoped that the Socialists' responsible attitude might convince the General that, if he turned somewhat to the Left—and incidentally brought the Socialists into the government—his regime would be safely maintained.[4] These hopes were dashed in April 1962 when the Debré government fell and de Gaulle, with no overture to the democratic Left, chose Pompidou, a much more conservative figure than his predecessor, as the next premier.

Whatever influence the SFIO had in the cabinet was now gone. The SFIO initiated discussions with the Cercle Tocqueville, the Club Moulin, and other political groups about strategies for a "return to democracy" and also began to reexamine the possibility of an opening toward the PCF. This seemed necessary because a center-left coalition appeared too narrow, and because it was not certain that the Radicals could be relied upon or could resist being bought off by the Gaullists.

This emerging practical collaboration, which, to be sure, fell short of a Popular Front, manifested itself in various ways. From May to September Mollet and other Socialist leaders made many statements referring to a *crise de régime* and expressed their determination to fight against "absolute monarchy."[5] In midsummer the SFIO voted together with the PCF and MRP— though in vain—against the passage of the Pisani bill on agriculture, which reduced farm price support. The SFIO also agreed with the PCF in opposing de Gaulle's new constitutional amendment providing for the direct election of the president of the Republic, and condemned both the method of accomplishing it (i.e., by a referendum in which parliament would be bypassed) and the substance of the amendment, which Gazier characterized as a *"comédie plébiscitaire."*

At a meeting in Puteaux on September 6, 1962, the National Council of the SFIO still rejected any alliance with the

Communists and committed itself to fight against "all totali-
tarians of the Right and the so-called Left."[6] Nevertheless, during
the Senate election campaign, the PCF supported the (successful)
motion to oust Debré that had been introduced by the SFIO and
other democratic parties and defended by Mollet.

During the election campaign that followed the dissolution of
the Assembly, Mollet and Defferre, in an optimistic mood,
announced that "the majority is ready to constitute a republican
government."[7] Presumably such a postelection republican
government would consist of all the anti-Gaullists except for the
PCF. But at least for electoral purposes, Mollet was willing to put
up with, indeed to invite, Communist support. He permitted the
Socialists to vote for anyone but the UNR on the second ballot,
even if the alternative were a PCF candidate, and second-ballot
alliances between PCF and SFIO candidates proliferated (except
in Bouches-du-Rhône, because of Defferre's opposition). Such
alliances favored the SFIO in Nord, which was close to Mollet's
own constituency, and although the PCF got more support from
the SFIO than vice versa,[8] the SFIO emerged as a main beneficiary
of the electoral alliance: it increased its Assembly representation
from 41 to 65 (as against a PCF gain from 10 to 41 seats).[9]

It is uncertain whether Maurice Faure was correct when he said
that the election results were a clear expression of "resistance . . . to
personal power."[10] After all, UNR parliamentary representation
increased from 17.5 percent to 31.9 percent, and the SFIO lost
almost 900,000 votes.

These results also indicated that a marriage of convenience
between Socialists and Communists might have to be continued
after the elections if the Socialists wished to avert electoral disaster
in the future. The SFIO had lost much of the working class and a
significant portion of the young electorate in the preceding four
years through defections to the UNR, the PCF, and the PSU (in
that order). This lesson was not lost on the Socialist leadership. At
a National Council meeting at Puteaux on December 16, many
members, led by Gazier, expressed the desire for a regular Popular
Front; and even Mollet hoped that "some day" such unity could
be achieved. (The PCF, for its part, had said that even such
problems as NATO and *laïcité* would be no insurmountable bar
to a restoration of the unity of the working class.)[11] As if to show

its own readiness for unity, and in order to emphasize its socialist radicalism, the SFIO issued a declaration at the opening of the new parliament on December 10, 1962, in which it called for the abolition of capitalism, reiterated its belief in *laïcité*, and reaffirmed its revolutionary character.[12]

If by the end of 1962 it appeared that the SFIO, and, more particularly, Guy Mollet, had definitely joined the opposition, it was by no means clear that that conversion had been a matter of conviction. For over three years Mollet had attempted to defend de Gaulle and uphold the legitimacy of the Fifth Republic in the vain hope that de Gaulle would be appropriately grateful, turn leftward, and perhaps embrace democratic socialism. As late as the spring of 1963, Mollet (with the aid of Jules Moch) secured a majority in the *Comité directeur* to vote down a motion, introduced by Defferre and Chandernagor for submission to the Fifty-fourth National Congress, to condemn the regime and to create a commission to watch over developments of the "constitutional situation." Mollet's counterproposal, which the *Comité directeur* accepted, merely emphasized opposition to "the present plebiscitarian system" and called for the strengthening of the role of parliament.[13]

When all hope for democratization was clearly frustrated, and the SFIO lost much of what remained of its revolutionary image to the Communists, it attempted to retrieve its voter support by insisting on its republicanism cum socialism, and by demonstrating that it embraced the workers' cause. Thus in March, 1963, Mollet fully supported the miners' strike launched by the CGT, CFTC, and FO in protest against low wages, and together with PCF leader Maurice Thorez, declared his solidarity with the strikers. However, when the miners refused to heed the government's order to return to work, Mollet declared that government authority was being mocked![14] This gesture was probably due less to his conversion to etatism than to the fact that the Socialist party's one reliable element of electoral support came from the civil servants—the *petits fonctionnaires*—who were professionally committed to public law and order. It was also due to Mollet's doubtlessly justified fear that any extended strike would be controlled and politically exploited by the Communists.

This fear of the Communists, which accounted for Mollet's persistent refusal to enter into a Popular Front arrangement with the PCF, had not, as we have seen, prevented the secretary-general from tolerating (if not hoping for) electoral alliances with and support from the Communists. Mollet's preoccupation with tactics was shared by Gazier, according to whose dismal analysis the SFIO and the Left in general were powerless *without* Communist support but *with* such support would become perverted.[15]

Mollet had repeatedly offered the possibility of restructuring an opposition out of the forces of the non-Communist Left, which would have to include the MRP as the only meaningful (and more or less socialist) alternative partner. Indeed, at the MRP congress in May 1963 there was some sentiment in favor of joining with the SFIO in a non-Communist labor alliance. But nothing came of that because Mollet's laicism asserted itself at the last moment: in a speech to his federation (Pas-de-Calais) Mollet accused the MRP of being a hybrid party of bourgeois workers united only by religion.[16] The secretary-general attacked the Radicals, too, as bourgeois opportunists.

Given Mollet's insistence on the retention of the rhetorical trinity of socialism, *laïcité,* and revolution, there seemed to be no alternative to a renewed flirting with the PCF, which had again asked the Socialists to join it in a Popular Front. But that matter had to be handled carefully lest the SFIO leadership be fragmented anew. At the Fifty-fourth National Congress of the SFIO at Issy-les-Moulineaux (May 30 to June 2, 1963), the delegates were at pains to avoid any discussion of Fifth Republic institutions. Earlier a number of members of the *Comité directeur* had proposed the submission of a motion to the forthcoming congress condemning the regime and creating a constitutional watchdog commission. Mollet had been against the proposal and it had failed. Instead Mollet had persuaded the *Comité directeur* to adopt a substitute motion expressing opposition to "the present plebiscitarian system" and favoring an enhanced role for both parliament and the premier.[17]

It was clear that disillusionment with the Gaullist regime was highly qualified and by no means universal among the Socialists and hence that a Popular Front was at least premature. Yet some leaders, notably Gérard Jaquet, did call for the SFIO to seek the support of the PCF; others, like Defferre, favored a rapprochement with the Communists *in principle*, but suggested that the SFIO be in no hurry; and still others, like Boutbien and Leenhardt, opposed any overture at all to the PCF. Finally, there was George Brutelle, the adjoint secretary-general, who had for some time been convinced that a unification of all socialist-inclined parties was absolutely necessary, and that the new socialist force to be constructed ought to comprise all who adhered to some form of *democratic* socialism, including the PSU and the trade unions (the pro-clerical CFTC among them). Brutelle was not convinced that the disagreements among the various groups were primarily of an ideological nature, and he alluded to the factor of personal ambition and to the widespread hostility to Mollet's leadership that existed in many places. Brutelle was generally supported in this assessment by a good many members of the *Comité directeur,* including Defferre. Mollet answered by accusing Brutelle and his supporters of "revisionism" and implied that he was ideologically more comfortable with the Communists than with the motley group of allies envisaged by Brutelle. The secretary-general clearly agreed with some of the positions of the PCF, such as the demand for the nationalization of the banks, but rather than rushing headlong into a Popular Front, he favored a public dialogue with the Communists, and later, perhaps, real contact and collaboration if the PCF's attitudes indicated a partial conversion to the ideas of the SFIO.

The SFIO reelected Mollet as secretary-general and adopted a ten-point platform it felt could be accepted by a variety of Socialists. This platform called, inter alia, for the reform of education, an expansion of social investments, the scrapping of the nuclear deterrent, democratic planning, European integration, and the strengthening of political democracy by reestablishing the powers of parliament.[18]

In the second half of 1963 there were frequent contacts not only between young Socialists and Communists, but also with the PSU (often under the auspices of the Club Jean Moulin) and the Radicals (at the Club des Jacobins). Mollet and his supporters on the *Comité directeur* continued to shy away from any formal alliance with the Communists because of the secretary-general's traditional distrust of that party, because it competed with the SFIO and its (by now increasingly irrelevant) Marxist slogans, and because it was larger than the SFIO and might absorb it in the event of any organizational fusion.[19] Yet he shared with the Communist party an appreciation of the need for an alliance of the Left, and he was aware that an alliance with the centrist anti-Gaullists was not appealing to many obdurate anticlericals.

The Abortive Candidacy of Defferre

The tactical objection of many Socialists to dealing too openly with the centrists was clearly mirrored in Mollet's attitude regarding the presidential candidacy of Gaston Defferre, the Socialist mayor of Marseilles. That candidacy had been actively promoted, under the name of Monsieur X, by Jean-Jacques Servan-Schreiber's *L'Express* and by various clubs at the end of 1963. At a special congress at Clichy early in February 1964, the SFIO officially endorsed Defferre's candidacy, but it did so half-heartedly. Mollet resented Defferre, who had so often supported the secretary-general in the past, for many reasons. Defferre agreed with Mollet in his distrust of the PCF, but Defferre's alternative strategy, an alliance with the MRP and other center forces within the framework of a Social Democratic Federation, was strongly opposed by the secretary-general. The MRP was distrusted because of its clericalism, conservatism, and the opportunistic weakness for compromising with Gaullism (alluded to earlier). there was also the fear that in any new federation, the ideological purity as well as the organizational independence of the SFIO would be diluted.

This fear was not without substance. First of all, the brain trust promoting the candidacy of Defferre was not really socialist, and it had chosen the mayor of Marseilles more for his dynamism than his socialism. Second, the personalities that had been consulted by *L'Express* included economists, political scientists, and even leaders of the Jeunes Patrons, whose identification with socialism was, to say the least, problematic.[20] Third, there was the question of how Defferre's candidacy might affect the leadership position of Mollet himself. One writer[21] states that it constituted "the greatest blow to Mollet's authority" because the secretary-general, who did not wish to be a candidate himself, had committed the tactical error of having done nothing from June to October, 1963, to prevent Defferre (or anyone else, for that matter) from announcing his candidacy without prior approval by the *Comité directeur* or the party congress. There did not even exist any statutory procedure within the SFIO for the selection of a candidate for the presidency.[22] Mollet had clearly not utilized his leadership to institute such a procedure and, in fact, he had been responsible for shelving the debate on institutions at the Fifty-fourth National Congress at Issy.[23] Fourth, there was the matter of Defferre's own interpretation of the president as an arbiter who is above parties and therefore independent of them—an interpretation that threatened to open the SFIO to charges by Communists and others that Defferre was a quasi-Gaullist in that he wanted to resort to a personalism of his own in order to compete with that of de Gaulle. Most important was the fact that the SFIO had been confronted with a fait accompli engineered from the outside.[24]

For Gérard Jaquet, a member of the *Comité directeur,* that last fact was of no great significance: the main point was that Defferre was a good Socialist, an excellent candidate, and that "by his style, by his behavior, he has shown himself capable of favorably impressing those circles with whom he has already been in contact."[25] Moreover, Defferre's centrist inclinations might well make it difficult for the center forces to promote their own candidate and thereby weaken the prospects of a united non-Communist fight against Gaullism. It is not clear whether Mollet was persuaded by Jaquet's reasoning. In any event the SFIO, and Mollet personally, at last endorsed Defferre's candidacy at the special congress at Clichy in February, 1964,[26] largely because the failure to do so might publicly indicate a lack of party unity, and also because there was then no visible alternative to that candidacy. However, the party insisted on two points: (1) that Defferre accept the SFIO's demand that the Fifth Republic constitution be so interpreted as to lead to a weakening of presidential powers and to the restoration of ministerial responsibility to a strengthened parliament, and (2) that there was no need for Defferre himself to define an electoral position on socioeconomic matters because, as it happened, the SFIO already had a program of "socialism."[27]

The SFIO supported Defferre in his provincial campaigns in the first half of 1965, but Mollet insisted that this support be conditional upon Defferre's full adherence to the Socialist position.[28] Soon, however, divergences between Defferre and the leadership of the SFIO became more apparent. The mayor of Marseilles insisted as before that he opposed any alliance with the PCF and that, if elected, he would never permit the inclusion of Communists in his government. Mollet may have shared Defferre's views on that matter, but he probably considered the public articulation of such views to be ill-timed.

In the spring the SFIO, persuaded by the PCF, continued its dialogue in the form of public exchanges of opinion in *Le Populaire* and *L'Humanité*.[29] The PCF repeatedly proclaimed its desire for a rapprochement with the SFIO and frequently supported the main elements of the Socialists' socioeconomic policies. At its congress in May, 1964, the PCF, while reaffirming its adherence to democratic centralism, also stressed the need for internal democracy in the Communist party apparatus. Though many Socialists were convinced that the PCF remained essentially Stalinist, there was an increasing number who were now ready to repudiate the old belief (expressed earlier by Edouard Depreux) that "the Communists are not to the Left, but to the East, of the Socialist party."[30]

Although the SFIO and other forces of the non-Communist Left, including Mitterrand, leader of the Convention des institutions républicaines (CIR), continued to support Defferre's candidacy despite his refusal of any dialogue with the Communists, the position of the mayor of Marseilles was becoming more insecure. A presidential preference poll conducted at the end of May, 1964, indicated that de Gaulle had the support of 42 percent of the electorate; PCF candidate (as yet unnamed), 10 percent; while Defferre's support had slipped from 23 percent to 13 percent in one month.[31] Furthermore, the SFIO was becoming increasingly embarrassed by Defferre's ongoing dialogue with the MRP, which the Communists publicly interpreted as evidence of the SFIO's alliance with clericalism. Yet in the fall of 1964, Mollet continued to support Defferre and still thought an alliance with the non-Communist Left (under the auspices of a *comité des démocrates*) would be feasible without sacrificing socialism. In a speech in October, 1964, Mollet analyzed the party situation as follows: the MRP is divided between "reactionaries and progressives"; among the Radicals are some "whose place will be with us"; there are certain other Socialists—i.e., in the PSU—of whom some "will return to us."[32]

At the same time Mollet's opposition to Gaullism was becoming *"dur et total,"*[33] and he was almost ready to contract any alliances to bring it down. There was also the hope that after the death of Maurice Thorez (which had occurred in July, 1964) the PCF would become more flexible; and finally, if Mollet moved to the Left himself, he could deal with the PCF directly in order to outflank the PSU and deprive *that* party of the pleasure of acting as a matchmaker between the SFIO and PCF.

The logical consequences of these considerations were twofold: at a meeting of the National Council in November, the SFIO decided first to enlarge the dialogue with "the socialist family" to include "republicans who, although quite distant from socialism, are unequivocally opposed to the present regime,"[34] and to make electoral alliances with them, if necessary, to bring down the UNR; and second, to find an alternative to Defferre. For Mollet any alliance with the PCF must have seemed an evil, the recognition of whose ultimate necessity he wished to delay. In mid-1964 he had proposed a federation to the Radicals, but Maurice Faure, their leader, had refused to commit himself because one of the conditions posed to them—to quit their association with the MRP—was unacceptable. The support of the MRP was unwelcome to Mollet not merely because of the clerical issue but also because most SFIO leaders, headed by Claude Fuzier, had become convinced of the need to *replace* the Fifth Republic system, whereas for the MRP it was merely necessary to *modify* it.

For Defferre the continued appeal to the MRP and the Radicals did not signify an abandonment of progressivism or even socialism. The participation of left-wing Catholics at *"colloques socialistes"* throughout 1964 seemed to indicate that not all MRP elements were reactionary. Moreover, Defferre's own "socialist" program—insofar as he had one—could not be faulted because it more or less reflected that of the SFIO. But Defferre did seem to agree with the clubs in wishing to modernize socialism into *travaillisme*, that is, a Labour party type of reformism. Mollet opposed such a direction because of his fear that the SFIO might become *embourgeoisé* and lose its revolutionary dynamism (which had by this time become a matter of pure nostalgia), and that the PSU might enlarge its appeal to many current members of the SFIO (there had been frequent contact between younger SFIO members and the PSU in the Club Jean Moulin and the Club des Jacobins).

Early in January, 1965, the SFIO's Federation of the Seine decided upon an electoral accord with the PCF: a joint communiqué announced a common list for the forthcoming municipal elections for most of the constituencies of the Paris area. Elsewhere interparty accords were of a different nature: in Lille (and even in Arras, Mollet's home town) the SFIO made common lists with the MRP, and at Strasbourg some Socialist candidates even aligned themselves with the UNR![35] In still other districts SFIO candidates rebelled and made alliances with Center candidates. Several national leaders of the SFIO demanded the expulsion of such Socialist candidates—apparently not so much because their behavior constituted an unbearable affront to socialist ideology, but rather because of the Communist party's threat that it would maintain its own second-ballot candidate wherever the SFIO had allied itself with "reactionaries." But Mollet's personal toleration, if not encouragement, of such diverse alliances met with charges of opportunism and inconsistency, to which Mollet replied:

> Immoral and contradictory alliances, say some. . . . Don't commit yourselves to the reactionaries, say others. Don't compromise with the Communists, some respond. And everyone who wants us as an ally reproaches us for our other alliances. Let us assure them all: we consider that we are becoming neither communists nor reactionaries. We do not seek to please; we want merely to defeat the UNR.[36]

The electoral policies of the Socialists and of their allies indicate that remarks occasionally made about the "absolute-value orientation" of French political parties may be somewhat exaggerated, for in this case alignments that were ideologically unpalatable were clearly considered worthwhile or even necessary from a tactical point of view. Though the need for such alliances indicated a certain powerlessness of the SFIO to assert itself alone in elections, even on the municipal level where the party's traditional strength lay, it was still a desirable enough electoral partner to both the PCF and the center-left forces to cause them to compete with each other in obtaining Socialist support.

The first-ballot results of the municipal elections of March 4, 1965, were inconclusive. The SFIO generally did better than the PCF in towns of fewer than 30,000 inhabitants, where they outpolled the Communists by more than two-to-one, but in towns over 30,000 the Communists elected about 20 percent more officials than the SFIO.[37] What these results implied for the future of the SFIO was not clear. Could the SFIO have done better with more clearcut Communist support, or, conversely, in more obvious dissociation from the PCF? Should it rather have made common cause, on a nation-wide basis, with the MRP and other centrist parties? Should the party have stood alone and sacrificed tactical expediency for ideological purity? Could one not also argue that the conditions surrounding the municipal elections were quite different from those applying to future national (i.e., parliamentary or presidential) elections?

Although the SFIO did not answer these questions clearly at an information meeting at Clichy in April 1965, a consensus seemed to emerge that some kind of functional enlargement of anti-Gaullist forces was necessary with the SFIO as the nucleus. It was not surprising that the first concrete proposals were made by Gaston Defferre, the man who, as presidential candidate of the party, had the most to gain from an institutionalized opening to the Center. Just as Defferre's candidacy had been foisted upon the SFIO by outsiders, so his ideas concerning a federation of the Left were generated largely outside the Socialist establishment. In April the CIR approved a suggestion made by the mayor of Marseilles for the establishment of a union of *"forces démo-cratiques à vocation socialiste,"* from which the Communists would be excluded but which would be open to the MRP if the latter became more socialist (and presumably less openly clerical). In May Defferre announced that in the forthcoming congress he would propose the creation of a leftist federation that would be "capable of being majoritarian."[38] Defferre's idea was duly submitted to the secretariat of the SFIO in the form of a motion to be introduced at the forthcoming National Congress.

The SFIO and the Federation of the Left

The Fifty-fifth National Congress of the SFIO, which met in Clichy early in June 1965, was dominated by the discussion of Defferre's proposal of a *fédération démocratique-socialiste,* as it was now called, which was to be open to all progressives from the Socialists to the MRP. Since the proposal had been signed by an impressive number of members of the *Comité directeur*[39] and was favorably regarded by several clubs,[40] it could not be dismissed as merely the tactical handmaiden to the political ambitions of the mayor of Marseilles.

There was uncertainty in the camp of the SFIO. The party leadership knew that it could not succeed in national elections without help from other parties. Yet Defferre's idea of a non-Communist federation was deemed unfeasible for a variety of reasons. By excluding the PCF and substituting the MRP, the SFIO was in danger of losing its revolutionary, laic image. Moreover, the MRP was far from enthusiastic, for fear that it might become a mere satellite of the SFIO. Mollet preferred a federation extending from the PSU to the Radicals. While he agreed with Defferre on the exclusion of the PCF—at least on the organizational level—he disagreed on the need to include the MRP. However, the PSU would not enter the proposed federation without the Communists, and the laic Radicals had reservations about entering without the clerical MRP![41] (The latter phenomenon cannot be rationally explained on the basis of traditional ideological cleavage; perhaps the Radicals realized that despite the torrent of rhetoric to the contrary, the issue of clericalism had become, after all, quite unimportant.)

Another argument related to the nature and structure of the federation. Mollet saw in Defferre's scheme the danger of *travaillisme* (i.e., a sacrifice of the principles of classic socialism); more important, he disagreed with the mayor of Marseilles in favoring a loose confederation, in which each component party or club would, for the immediate future, retain its personality and identity (and incidentally enable the SFIO to retain its present leadership structure). Finally, although Mollet and his supporters did not as yet favor any institutionalized united front with the PCF, they could not afford to alienate that party—because it threatened to split the Left by putting up its own candidate if Defferre's ideas, including the idea of a center-left federation, were officially endorsed by the SFIO.

The motion that the congress finally adopted quasi-unanimously provided for the creation of a *fédération démocratique-socialiste* and suggested that this federation pursue the following policies: (1) the control of parliament over the executive; (2) the introduction of comprehensive policies on education and youth; and (3) a change in the system of economic planning to provide for both more socialist content (e.g., greater social investments) and more democratic procedures (i.e., more meaningful workers' representation in planning bodies).[42] Further, the motion called for an effort to obtain agreement on a common presidential candidate. Finally, it provided that the new federation be composed of, and that invitations to a founding congress be issued to, the following groups in addition to the SFIO: the MRP; the Radicals; the UDSR; various leftist clubs (e.g., Horizon 80 and Jeune République); and about ten leftist trade unions and professional associations.[43] Superficially, it appeared as if Defferre's ideas were reflected in much of the motion, particularly the absence of official invitations to the PCF or its trade union, the CGT. Still, the hope was voiced that the new arrangement would influence the "evolution" of the PCF, presumably in such a way that the SFIO could collaborate with it in the near future.

Thus Defferre's "social democratic federation"—or at least his idea of its structure and its raison d'être—was stillborn. Defferre's two oaths that his candidacy was "irreversible" and that he would never negotiate with the Communists proved mutually incompatible as some kind of alliance between the SFIO and the PCF became virtually inevitable. Consequently Defferre was morally obligated to withdraw as a candidate for the presidency. The Permanent Bureau of the SFIO, at its meeting on July 1, went through the formality of congratulating Defferre on the way he had been conducting his campaign—in particular his fight against personal power—and "regretted that events have caused him to withdraw as candidate."[44] But partly in response to repeated pleas from the Communists, Mollet also declared at a National Council meeting on July 18 and 19 that it was absolutely necessary to restore the unity of all Socialists, and his call for (an as yet not clearly specified) unity with the Communists was approved by 2,028 to 881 votes. Since the resolution that was adopted also contained an attack on the MRP, it was clear that any new federation that Mollet and his supporters favored would exclude the clerical party.

The effort throughout the summer of 1965 to restore socialist unity culminated in the selection of a new candidate, François Mitterrand (September 9) and the establishment of a new group (September 10)—the Fédération de la Gauche démocratique et socialiste (FGDS). Both actions had been cleared beforehand with the PCF, the PSU, and the Radicals. The selection of Mitterrand, however, was not universally welcomed. The PSU, in particular, was less than fully enthusiastic because it felt that the new standard bearer of the Left, in the typical manner of many prominent French politicians, had too frequently adjusted his ideologies and allegiances on the basis of political convenience. Mitterand had originally been a conservatively inclined Independent; after World War II he became the leader of the UDSR, the party of the Resistance, and in that capacity he had moved closer to the Left. He was a frequent ally of the Radicals (and therefore acceptable to them). Ideologically he was perhaps closest to the SFIO, but that party, and in particular Mollet, perhaps resented Mitterrand's organizational independence of it.[45] The SFIO consoled itself in the belief that it could easily live with the new federation that was now led by Mitterrand. In addition to the SFIO, its most powerful component, the FGDS included only anticlerical formations, such as the UDSR, the Radicals, and the CIR, the last being itself a confederation of some fifty political clubs. Although the Communists were excluded from the FGDS, they supported its candidate, and they hoped that there would be a common program that would cement relationships between the two most important groupings of the Left.

The unity within the Socialist party, as well as the evolving rapport between the Socialists and the Communists, was impaired to a considerable extent by the "Pinay affair," which took place in the early fall of 1965. Some Socialists and others on the left and center-left feared that Mitterrand or any other non-Communist candidate of a united Left might not have enough electoral support to defeat de Gaulle in the forthcoming presidential elections; hence, they encouraged Antoine Pinay, a rather conservative Centrist, to campaign for the presidency to help divide the potential Gaullist electorate. Mollet himself, in a speech on radio station Europe No. 1 early in October, embraced this strategy when he appealed to Pinay to become a candidate. The Socialist secretary-general went even further when he stated that under certain conditions his party could support Pinay. For Mollet it was not a question of abandoning Mitterrand, but— should a Left candidate be unsuccessful—of a clear preference between two non-Leftists. If the choice were between de Gaulle and Pinay, he, Mollet, would choose Pinay.

The immediate reaction of the Communists was indignation. In the words of *L'Humanité*: "Can one choose between the plague and cholera?"[46] The Communists were not alone in questioning the good faith of Mollet. Many Socialist leaders, including Defferre, expressed fear that the secretary-general's support of Mitterrand was no less half-hearted than his earlier endorsement of the candidacy of the mayor of Marseilles. Mollet was criticized for his leadership by the National Council, but that criticism became muted and any immediate problem of dissension was shelved when Pinay indicated a lack of interest in a presidential candidacy.

At the opening of the campaign on November 17, Mitterrand appeared at a press conference in the company of Mollet and two other SFIO leaders, as well as Waldeck Rochet and Georges Marchais, the two top leaders of the PCF. Neither the SFIO nor the PCF had any difficulty in identifying with the common platform, which included the following points: the abolition of Article 16; the reform of the court structure; the loosening of government control of the public radio-television network ORTF (Office de radiodiffusion-télévision françaises); the replacement of the fifth modernization plan with a new, more progressive plan; the construction of 600,000 new housing units (including a large proportion of low-cost housing); the allocation of 25 percent of the budget for education; and the convocation of a round table between the government and the trade unions.[47] In a television address early in December, Mitterrand elaborated on these points and promised that, upon being elected president, he would dissolve the Assembly, "which no longer represents anybody." Pending the election of a new Assembly, he would appoint an interim government and abolish the "personal power" of one man.[48]

Although de Gaulle won the election, the electoral unity of the Left had proved viable enough to force the General into a second ballot. At the same time, the SFIO was acutely aware that it had become too weak to act alone, and there were many who wondered whether, despite what the *Comité directeur* called "the growing appeal of socialist democracy"[49] and despite the good showing of a more or less united opposition in the recent elections, socialism as traditionally conceived had much of a future. If there was a weakening of the socialist faith, its causes were many. The Marxist prophecies of the pauperization of the working class had not come true; the apparent contradictions of capitalism had not caused it to collapse; the image of socialism had suffered because Soviet Communism, its prototype of success, was being equated by many with Stalinist barbarism and naked power politics; and finally, there was the realization that nationalization and collectivization did not necessarily solve all problems of economic injustice.[50]

But for many Socialists, it was as yet too difficult to engage in a great deal of ideological speculation; they tended to look for more mechanistic and tactical reasons for their weaknesses. Some Socialists continued to blame Mollet for the progressive debilitation of the party's position; they wondered whether it would not be desirable to change the leadership, or at the least to reexamine the power of the secretary-general. Others wished that the party would come to a clear decision about its future choice of allies. Immediately after the election, several prominent members of the *Comité directeur* asked that a special congress be convened to deal with such problems. When the secretary-general refused to accede to this wish, these members made the symbolic gesture of resigning from the Permanent Bureau (while, however, choosing to remain in the *Comité directeur*).[51]

The problem of the direction of the party, and its choice of allies, was a difficult one; a good case could be made for either a centrist orientation or collaboration with the Communists. On the one hand, the loss of workers' votes to the PCF (at least in national elections), the muting of the clerical issue, the evolution of some centrist elements toward the Left, the perception of the PCF as a tool of Moscow, and the growing irrelevance of Marxist slogans—all these developments argued for Defferre's view that the party must broaden its base toward the Center. On the other hand, it could be argued just as convincingly that Communists, unlike many centrists, had not (or not yet) compromised with Gaullism. Moreover, the SFIO, because of its ideological traditions, was still sensitive to repeated Communist charges of clericalist tendencies. Because of the party's ideological traditions there were many Socialists who were still convinced that they had very few enemies on their Left. Finally, if the centrist thesis were adopted as the alternative to collaboration with the PCF, would that not vindicate Defferre's position and enhance his stature in the party and possibly threaten Mollet's leadership? It would be incorrect to discount the rivalry between the SFIO's secretary-general and the mayor of Marseilles, which transcended mere ideological divergences. On January 23, 1966, in a "letter to the militants," four of Mollet's closest collaborators in the bureau attacked Defferre for his alleged personal insults to the secretary-general and accused him of wanting to oust Mollet from his position. The Defferrists responded by attacking the "personalized" leadership of the party,[52] and a few of the supporters of the mayor of Marseilles even resigned from the *Comité directeur*.

The problem of Mollet's leadership was, however, less pressing than the problem of alliances. The Socialists decided, for the time being, to commit themselves neither to the Center nor to the Communists, but rather to pursue a dialogue with the latter and to collaborate with them in parliament whenever possible. At the same time, however, the SFIO wanted to continue its efforts at strengthening its organizational position in an enlarged non-Communist leftist grouping within the framework of the FGDS.

The SFIO had been almost persuaded by the PCF that a *functional* Popular Front was desirable in order to wage a more effective fight against Gaullism. This front implied, at least for the Communists, continued electoral and parliamentary collaboration. However, the elections were too far in the future, and the prospects for parliamentary cooperation proved hollow when, in April 1966, the PCF refused to associate itself with a Socialist-sponsored motion to censure the government for de Gaulle's decision to pull French forces out of NATO, a decision that the PCF considered "the only positive aspect of Gaullist policy."[53]

Meanwhile, attempts were made to fashion an effective instrument out of the FGDS. But the divisions within the SFIO, and between it and the Federation, were reflected in disagreements about the structure, orientation, and purpose of the FGDS. Both Defferre and Mitterrand—whatever their ideological disagreements—favored the rapid evolution of the FGDS toward a single party embracing the entire non-Communist Left; Mitterrand, at a press conference in February, 1966, had said that "the Federation is not merely a cover over the parties that desire to pass a dangerous phase, while waiting to regain their autonomy."[54] However, Mollet argued successfully against fusion. The reasons for Mollet's position were many. Perhaps he could not, or would not, choose between Defferre's proposal to include the MRP and Mitterrand's insistence that the MRP be excluded (at least in an organizational sense). Perhaps he feared that the FGDS, as a new party, would not be sufficiently socialist, since it included segments—such as some of the Radicals—with questionable progressive credentials.[55] One of the Radicals with whom Mitterrand had proposed discussions was Pierre Mendès-France, with whom Mollet had far from cordial relations, who appeared perhaps too *Defferriste*, and whose competition for leadership he had, no doubt, some cause to fear. Perhaps he also felt that in such a new party he would be eclipsed as a leader by Mitterrand, who would probably proceed rapidly toward an alliance with the PCF, and create a British-style shadow cabinet under his direction with himself as shadow prime minister.[56]

Mollet's fears were clearly reflected in the resolution, passed by the National Council on March 16, which emphasized that "the birth of the Federation would not serve as a pretext or reason [for the SFIO] to slacken its activities, to reduce its efforts, to moderate its propaganda, to slow down its recruitment. It must remain faithful to itself and its objectives; it must not resign itself to any obliteration; it must maintain its rules and its cohesion." The same resolution, however, invited "the delegates of the Party in the Executive Committee of the Federation . . . and the leadership of the Party to pursue their efforts at establishing departmental organs of the FGDS as soon as possible."[57] This apparent contradiction might be explained by Mollet's belief that the FGDS would not eclipse the SFIO on the local level where the SFIO had a strong foothold and where it would therefore not only manage to hold its own but also possibly exert effective control over the Federation.

Mollet's lack of enthusiasm for a shadow cabinet, in particular one led by Mitterrand, provoked considerable hostility toward the secretary-general within the CIR and other constituent groups of the Federation. When this hostility was clearly expressed at a meeting of the FGDS executive committee on March 24, Mollet reacted in a tone conveying injured innocence:

> I have been accused of having assassinated Mendès-France. One has also said that I have shot down Gaston Defferre. And now I am accused of wanting to stab Mitterrand in the back. All that is absurd. . . . There is a problem of direction of the Federation and there will be a problem of the presidency of the "shadow cabinet." Well, I propose that we say from now on that Mitterrand will remain our president and that, in the event of electoral victory, he will be our Prime Minister.[58]

Early in May a shadow cabinet of twelve members was established under the leadership of Mitterrand, consisting mainly of Socialist and Radical deputies.[59] Although Mollet was a member, he was perhaps justified in not having too many expectations about its efficacy or its socialist image. Without the PCF, such a shadow cabinet was doomed to impotence since legislative support on the part of Communist deputies had already proved unreliable. Moreover, the SFIO's *Comité directeur* issued a directive in June 1966 expressly forbidding Socialist deputies and senators to participate in any receptions of the president, premier, or members of the government, even on a local level.[60]

Attempts, undertaken elsewhere, to structure an extraparliamentary Popular Front were equally illusory. On May 1, 1966, there took place at Grenoble a "socialist encounter" to discuss the problem of the unity of the Left. Participants included Socialists, some dissident Communists, members of the PSU and CIR, in addition to representatives of the CGT and the CFDT. The participants failed to agree on a common program, not only because of their disparate political backgrounds, but also (and perhaps primarily) because the call for such a program had come from Mollet's rival Mendès-France.[61]

Opening to the Left

By the end of 1966 the attitudes of the non-Communist Left had evolved far enough in the direction desired by the Socialists that it could deal with the Communists from a position of both organizational unity and ideological equality—or so it seemed. In July the FGDS published its political program, which, inter alia, called for the revision of the constitution; the suppression of Article 16; the formalized parliamentary investiture of the prime minister; the obligatory dissolution of parliament in case of a ministerial crisis; the establishment of a constitutional court; the securing of freedom of information; the extension of rights for the trade unions (including more significant participation in industrial decisions); the reduction of the presidential term to five years; the renunciation of the nuclear *force de frappe;* the establishment of a supreme court to safeguard individual liberties; the strengthening of the Social and Economic Council. The FGDS program also called for planning for economic growth; a more egalitarian tax structure; a raise in workers' wages; and policies of full employment, low-cost housing, educational expansion and social justice. Certain differences within the FGDS were minimized or ignored: this was true with respect to the nationalization of industries, about which the SFIO was more enthusiastic than the CIR.[62]

Mollet appeared to have no objections to the institutional features of the FGDS program, as long as they implied a revision rather than a replacement of the Fifth Republic constitution, in the genesis of which he had, after all, played a part. For the secretary-general, the *après-Gaullisme,* which would hopefully commence after the anticipated electoral success of the united Left in

March, meant the application of the existing constitution in a better, more democratic fashion. As Mollet put it: "After de Gaulle leaves, the Constitution will, I fear, be swept aside; and that Constitution is not even so bad as some people say it is. I was one of its authors. It is the use that one has made of it that can result in the destruction of the Republic."[63] The significance of the FGDS program was that it stressed concrete issues rather than the ideological approach traditional for SFIO programs and in that sense it was a harbinger of the electoral platforms to be embraced later by the Parti socialiste.

The SFIO's National Council, meeting in October 1966, had little difficulty in approving the program. The council also approved a decision by the executive committee of the FGDS that all of its constituent parts collaborate in the forthcoming legislative elections, i.e., present common lists for the second ballot. At the same time, the council hoped that this new-found unity would facilitate an "opening to the left" toward the PCF and the PSU. In November Mollet announced to a group of journalists that it was even possible to envisage a common platform with the PCF for purposes of second-ballot collaboration. The executive committee of the FGDS confirmed this: it decided on joint electoral tactics with the Communists and the PSU, and appointed a nine-member delegation—composed of Mollet and two other Socialists, three Radicals, and three representatives of the CIR, including Mitterrand—to help work out the details. At the same time, the executive decided to widen the scope of general conversations with the PCF and the PSU.

A prompt electoral accord between the Federation and the Communists was seen as advantageous to both parties. For the PCF it would be an aid to overcoming its political isolation, and for the FGDS it would constitute a guarantee of massive electoral support by workers. But the accord eliminated neither the tactical nor the programmatic disagreements among the leftists. When the CGT (under PCF auspices) decided on a general strike on February 1 (1967) to protest low wages, the Confédération française démocratique des travailleurs (CFDT, the "deconfessionalized" successor of the CFTC) and the FEN (close to the SFIO) participated, but the FO (even closer to the Socialists) and the Confédération générale des cadres (CGC) refused, judging the time—a few weeks before the parliamentary elections—as inopportune.

Despite the disagreements within the camp of the Left, Mitterrand was able to wage a reasonably effective campaign. Mitterrand's slogan, "a school, a job, a roof" (as a counter to Pompidou's "progress, stability, independence"),[64] may have indicated a clear move by the Federation toward *travaillisme*; still, the Communists could not fault the slogan in terms of its obvious appeal to the electorate.

For the Socialists the Federation vindicated its existence during the parliamentary elections of March, 1967. In the first ballot (March 5) the FGDS obtained 18.79 percent of the votes, as compared to the 12.54 percent polled by the Socialists alone in the 1962 elections, and the Federation came out of the second ballot (March 12) with 116 parliamentary seats—a gain of 25 over the last Assembly. The electoral accord between the FGDS and the PCF of December had obviously proved advantageous to the Federation, for many of the seats it gained were attributed to second-ballot withdrawals by Communist candidates. For the PCF the electoral alliance had proved equally valuable, the party having increased its representation from 41 to 73.

In a burst of postelection optimism, the FGDS continued to express hope that organizational fusion of the entire non-Communist Left would be speeded up, and even Mollet was now vaguely in favor of the idea—provided, of course, that the ideals of socialism would be safeguarded. As the secretary-general put it, in the spring of 1967:

> We all wish that a great political force of the non-Communist Left would be formed, and that it attract in its wake the undecided. We wish this because that could enable us to defeat Gaullism, and to have discussions with the Communist party in a more comfortable situation. But that is the role of a coalition, of a confederation, yes, of the Federation; why pretend that one needs a fusion for that? . . . Why pretend that there is a chance for fusion without a prior agreement on doctrine, . . . without a socialist doctrine?[65]

Mitterrand was reelected president of the Federation, and good will, fortified by meetings and exchanges of letters between Mollet and the PCF's Waldeck Rochet, continued to prevail even in the relations between the Socialists and the Communists. To some extent, this era of good feelings was manifested in the relations between Federation and Communist deputies, who in May voted jointly—though unsuccessfully—to censure the government for its use of Article 38, under which the government enacted by decree the Vallon bill (which provided for asset-sharing by workers). The two groups also collaborated in mid-May when their trade unions (the CGT, FEN, FO, and CFDT) joined in a general strike and in mass demonstrations to protest against the reduction of social security payments.

This euphoria, to be sure, was never total because the SFIO continued to disagree with the PCF on foreign policy, notably on NATO and on European integration. Still, Mollet insisted, as late as May, 1967, that foreign policy issues separated the two parties much less than the PCF's "conceptions of democracy," and even these would not stand in the way of a rapprochement, because "the march toward unity had begun."[66] In fact the rather unorthodox pronouncements in favor of a humanized Marxism by Roger Garaudy, the chief of the PCF's research center, gave hope that perhaps the Communist party was in the throes of a positive ideological mutation. Earlier Mollet and Waldeck Rochet had agreed to discontinue their dialogues via the press and to pursue instead round-table conversations; consequently as spring ended there were frequent meetings between Socialist and Communist party delegates.[67]

The six-day Arab-Israeli war introduced a new crisis in Socialist-Communist relations, and also threatened the unity of the non-Communist Left. Most of the SFIO was quite openly pro-Israel, a position shared by most of the clubs, most of the Center, and most of French public opinion. The PCF's anti-Israel position was shared by a large percentage of PSU members, some MRP and CIR members, and most of the extreme Right. The almost automatic pro-Arab stand of the Communists (even before the outbreak of hostilities) impelled Socialist Pineau, for example, to say that "we are back to the time when . . . one could correctly describe the PCF as a mere branch of the Soviet Communist party."[68] Defferre echoed this sentiment, and Mollet himself wondered "whether our working hypothesis concerning the PCF is not wholly false."[69] The Communists were aware that their position might endanger the emerging FGDS-PCF rapprochement. During the parliamentary debate on the Middle East in mid-June when Mollet openly expressed pro-Israel sentiments, the Communist deputies were silent, and for several days thereafter both sides tried to avoid discussing the subject. Mitterrand appeared to be convinced that "we have passed the Mideast crisis with the requisite serenity."[70]

Nevertheless, at the Fifty-sixth National Congress, which took place in Suresnes at the end of June, Mollet, Moch, and Pineau continued to make pro-Israel speeches and attacked those who equated the Arab cause with socialism. Since in addition to the PCF many components of the FGDS (in particular some CIR members and some clubs) insisted on such an equation, one may assume that many Socialist delegates did not consider the time opportune to rush headlong into the kind of organizational fusion that Defferre (himself pro-Israel) had been demanding, but which Mollet had fought against.

The issue of Israel was not decisive here. The resurgence of a *patriotisme de parti* was in large part ideological: Defferre wanted a large social-democratic party, while Mollet, ever faithful to an ideological tradition, favored the restructuring of the party only if socialism were clearly its premise.[71] To complicate the situation, Mitterrand (who had only a few weeks earlier threatened to resign his leadership of the FGDS unless fusion occurred soon) was now less insistent and even hoped that fusion would be delayed. There was also the factor of personal ambition: Mitterrand realized that in a fused political organization, if the principle of proportionality were fairly applied, the SFIO would be overrepresented to the detriment of his own group, the CIR, and he might well lose the leadership to Mollet.[72] Indeed, in the executive committee of the FGDS, as reconstituted in May, 1967, the SFIO was already more strongly represented than the other components: of the 25 members, 11 were from the SFIO, as against 7 Radicals, 5 CIR members, and 2 representatives of miscellaneous clubs.[73]

Meanwhile though the dialogue between the SFIO and the PCF continued, it threatened to remain a merely perfunctory exercise, since the Socialists still doubted the seriousness of the Communists' opposition to Gaullism. The PCF had repeatedly asserted that its general anti-Gaullist ideology did not imply that the party would automatically reject all Gaullist policies: just as it had supported the General on the Arab-Israeli issue and on the issue of the withdrawal of French forces from NATO, so it supported him now on his position in favor of *Québec libre*.[74]

Nonetheless, the SFIO (via the Federation) continued its collaboration on domestic issues with the Communists. The Federation and the Communists, having decided in July on an ad hoc meeting to establish a common policy against any dismantling of the social security system (envisaged by the government in order to save money), had agreed also to remain in permanent contact. In October collaboration in parliament became more meaningful when the FGDS and PCF jointly sponsored a censure motion (which failed) on social and economic policy. Moreover, the two sides had effectively joined forces in the cantonal election campaign early in September; the PCF was heartened enough by this collaboration to demand a continuing "common platform" with the Federation.

However, before the Federation could commit itself definitely to any reliable form of collaboration with the PCF, it had first to decide about its future. In mid-1967 the executive committee had agreed to appoint a committee to make recommendations on fusion. Although the report of the committee favoring fusion was prepared by a non-Socialist (the secretary-general of the Club Moulin),[75] it appeared that the SFIO, and particularly its leadership, was now more amenable to fusion than before—and the Radicals less so. Mollet was probably heartened by the results of the cantonal elections of October 1: the fact that of the thirty-five presidencies of *conseils généraux* won by the FGDS, twenty-one had been assumed by Socialists, indicated that the latter would be able to hold their own in, and even control, the local structures of the Federation if it were transformed into a political party. Furthermore, in any future dealings with the Communists, the ideological bargaining stance of the SFIO would be strengthened —and conversely, the position of the Defferrists weakened—by the opportune demise of the MRP, which had been officially announced in mid-September. Finally, Mitterrand's own authority, which was based on the close rapport between the CIR and the

Radicals, would be undermined.

Meanwhile Mitterrand himself continued officially to work for fusion;[76] indeed, on November 15, the political bureau of the FGDS announced a "complete accord" among the three families on a gradual assumption of political leadership by the FGDS's executive committee. What that accord meant, however, was uncertain in view of the differing interpretations of fusion by Mollet and Mitterrand, and in view of a growing hesitation on the part of the Radicals, who feared that they would be under-represented in any future structural arrangement. Still, despite some feelings within the *Comité directeur* of the SFIO that the party had not yet accomplished its historic tasks, a special party congress held at the end of January, 1968, passed a resolution in favor of fusion. The congress thought that since the will to fusion had been affirmed by all the component parts of the FGDS, the time was near for the establishment of a new Social Democratic party.

The precise modalities of fusion were not yet fully established; therefore, Mollet could still hope that any unified party of the future would benefit the SFIO by making socialism a greater electoral force, and at the same time permit the Socialists to retain their old apparatus.

By early February both the CIR and even the Radicals (who earlier had been hesitant about fusion) accepted the Federation's proposals with respect to a new party, the latter perhaps persuaded by the fact that Félix Gaillard and Maurice Faure (two former Radical leaders) were to figure prominently in the new party's executive committee. But even before the new party materialized, the FGDS, on February 23, arranged an electoral and programmatic accord with the PCF. Their common platform embodied most of the institutional and economic features that had been hammered out for the FGDS during the preceding summer.[77] There was no agreement on foreign policy, with the FGDS (particularly its Socialist contingent) favoring NATO and British entry into the Common Market and the Communists opposed to both.[78]

Still, the consensus of the Left on domestic matters was clear enough to enable the Communist and Federation deputies in April, 1968, to introduce a joint motion of censure inspired by the legalization of commercials on television and the government's excessive control over ORTF, the national radio-television network. This consensus was also reflected in common activity by various trade unions, which protested jointly to the minister of social affairs against retrenchments in social security.[79] There were now many members of the Federation's constituent parties who considered the PCF respectable and responsible enough, and while there were no plans formally to affiliate the PCF with the Federation, there was increasing talk about continued political collaboration. In fact, according to an IFOP poll conducted early in 1968, 58 percent of those voting for the FGDS wanted the Communists to come to power together with the SFIO![80]

The "May Events" and Their Aftermath

The "May Events" of 1968, described in detail by the media at the time, put in question not only the permanence and reliability of whatever collaboration there was between the Communist party and the Federation, but also the viability of the traditional Left (Communist and non-Communist) as a whole. The "night of the barricades," the general strike of May 13, the demonstrations by workers, and the protest activities of students were engineered neither by the PCF nor the SFIO, and in fact caught both by surprise. Claude Estier, a spokesman for the FGDS, admits that "the FGDS did not figure prominently in the events" but "was not absent" because it had, since the end of 1967, been very attentive to the demands of the student movement and had been able, as no other leftist party, "to understand the depth of the student revolt."[81] On the eve of the general strike, the SFIO, the CIR, and the FGDS, separately and jointly, released communiqués expressing support for the release of arrested students. At the same time, the Federation issued a statement on the radio that "it favored all ideas conducive to thorough reform of the university . . . especially those relating to the participation of students on all levels."[82] Whether this declaration reflected the true sentiments of the leaders of the SFIO, or was merely a piece of rhetoric, remains uncertain. On the one hand, it could be argued that the SFIO, having lost the support of so many workers, now attempted to ingratiate itself with students. On the other hand, many Socialist leaders (for example, Guy Mollet and André Philip) had themselves been the products of the very elitist structures they were now criticizing. Moreover, among the civil servants, who were reliable supporters of the SFIO, were many university professors who were doubtless interested in preserving the status and privileges they possessed under the traditional university organization. It was therefore not surprising that for many students at the Sorbonne, the Socialists, as the main representatives of *"les pourris de la FGDS,"* were just as evil as the Communists—*"les crapules staliniennes"*[83]—who had become too establishmentarian and conservative.

Perhaps because misery loves company, the non-Communist Left and the PCF made, or pretended to make, a number of efforts at collaboration. Thus the Communists associated themselves readily with the FGDS in declaring support for the students and opposition to the police. Furthermore, the parliamentary groups of both the Federation and the PCF joined in sponsoring a motion of censure against the government although both groups were undoubtedly certain that the motion would not pass. When the political bureau of the Federation called for the resignation of the government and for general elections and the political bureau of the PCF associated itself with that demand, both groups did so with some trepidation.

The Socialists may have feared that in any general elections the PCF—which had garnered 5 million votes in the last elections as against 4.2 million for the Federation—would capture the pro-Left electorate. The PCF, fearing that it might be eclipsed by the Maoists, Trotskyists, and other, newer, anomic and amorphous "new left" groups *(groupuscules)* which threatened to become ever larger, took pains to caution students and workers against "adventurist" programs and methods. Furthermore, in the event of an electoral victory of the combined "old Left," it was far from certain that the PCF would be the main beneficiary because Mitterrand still refused to commit himself clearly to any meaningful form of governmental collaboration with the Communists. Instead, at a press conference he held on May 28, Mitterrand announced that he was prepared to become the head of a new "provisional" government and appealed to Mendès-France to join with him. (He also graciously told Waldeck Rochet that "at least one Communist" might be included.)[84]

Notwithstanding Waldeck Rochet's public declaration that "the Gaullist regime is finished and must disappear," it was far from clear whether the Communists wanted to see the departure of a government that had been conducting a pro-Soviet foreign policy. This interpretation is based primarily on two facts. First, at a meeting on May 20 between Socialist Claude Fuzier (who represented the Federation) and Georges Séguy, the leader of the Communist-oriented CGT, the latter refused to commit himself to any mass action that might result in unmanageable disorder. Secondly, there was the episode of André Barjonet, a prominent member of both the CGT and the PCF, who resigned from both organizations, charging that the Communists had deliberately declined to take advantage of an auspicious revolutionary situation.[85] The belief in law and order and the fear of revolution apparently gripped both the PCF and the non-Communist Left, for at the end of May, the leaders of the Communist as well as the non-Communist trade unions were persuaded to meet with the government and to accept a bargain (the Grenelle Accords) promising higher minimum wages and improved working conditions.[86]

The parliamentary elections, called in June in the wake of a noticeable pro-Gaullist backlash, proved a veritable disaster for the united Left. The PCF received only 20 percent of the first-ballot votes (as compared to 22.5 percent in 1967). The SFIO with its Radical and other republican allies received 16.5 percent (compared to 18.7 percent in 1967)—a loss of 600,000 votes—while their parliamentary representation was halved from 116 to 57 seats (42 of those occupied by SFIO deputies in contrast to the 76 they had held in the previous parliament). The postmortem of the election defeat provided by Jules Moch was as expected. He blamed the FGDS rather than the SFIO, because the Federation's structure was too heavy, its grass-roots organization too rudimentary, and its attitude toward the Communist party too ambiguous. On the one hand, the FGDS had considered the Communists as privileged allies, but on the other hand, it had failed to construct a common program with them specifically tailored for the 1968 parliamentary elections.[87] (But even Moch did not blame the FGDs for not having committed itself to a

government coalition with the Communists.) It was only natural
that the SFIO's Permanent Bureau and the Socialist deputies,
while approving the conduct of Mollet, heaped criticism upon
Mitterrand for his leadership of the Federation. But when some
Socialist deputies called for Mitterrand's resignation, Mollet
graciously supported his rival, affirming his "complete solidarity" with him. This timely support probably helped insure
Mitterrand's official reconfirmation on July 19 as head of the
FGDS.[88]

Many adherents of the Left tended to blame the "reflex of
fear"—generated by the "May Events" and exploited by the
Gaullists—for its election defeat. Others saw in this defeat a new
opportunity for the Left to reconstitute itself. But what was to be
the basis for this reconstitution? The election had shown that
since many Federation candidates had won only because of
second-ballot withdrawals by Communist candidates, the PCF
still held too high a mortgage on the success of the Left.
Furthermore, there was the question (referred to earlier) of how
serious the PCF was about replacing the Gaullist regime. The
only alternative was to transform the FGDS—which had by now
dissolved for all practical purposes into the old SFIO and the old
Radicals—speedily into a new political party. The Defferrists of
course hoped that the new party would move toward the Center—
if there was much of a Center still in existence that had not been
co-opted by the Gaullists, and if what remained after the
official demise of the MRP in September, 1967, still represented
anything or could even be clearly identified.

Conversely, the feasibility of retaining the FGDS as merely an
electoral instrument of collaboration with the PCF was
considerably reduced. And whatever remained of the Socialist-
Communist honeymoon was ended with the invasion of Prague
by Soviet forces in August, 1968. To be sure, the PCF immediately
criticised the Soviet Union, a reaction Mollet congratulated, but
its criticism was too mild and too vague. The *Comité directeur* of
the SFIO, which had expected an unequivocal denunciation of
the invasion, asked the Communists to choose between obedience
to Moscow and unity of the Left in France. When the PCF
defended the Moscow Accords imposed by the USSR on
Prague, Mitterrand declared himself satisfied, but the leadership

of the SFIO and CIR remained disenchanted and hostile. This division was apparent at the meeting of the Federation's political bureau held early in September, which had been convoked ostensibly to map out a doctrinal basis for the yet-to-be-created replacement party. At that meeting it was decided neither to debate the Czech events nor to issue a specific statement on them.[89]

Another factor also impeded collaboration with the PCF—the hardening of Communist dogmatism. When the Communists persecuted Roger Garaudy (the chief of the PCF's research section) for his advocacy of "Marxist humanism," the Permanent Bureau published the following communiqué:

> The Bureau of the SFIO does not wish to meddle in the internal problems of the French Communist party. Therefore it would not intervene in the discussion between Roger Garaudy and Lucien Mathey [a Stalinist hardliner] if an observation of the latter had not touched upon a central point of the doctrinal debate in which the Socialist party and the Communist party have been engaged for several years.[90]

If the SFIO, the CIR, and the Radicals, all suspicious of the Communists, agreed on the need to establish a new party of the Left from which the PCF would be institutionally excluded, they could not agree on the doctrinal and organizational bases of that new party. The CIR, which held its convention early in October, appeared to have accepted Mitterrand's thesis that a new party, to be viable, should not perpetuate the potential for dissension contained in the old party organizations, a situation that would place Mitterrand or any other leader in "the geometric center of contradictions between Mollet and Defferre, Billères and Gaillard."[91] As reported in *Le Monde,* Mitterrand warned the SFIO that "if the only purpose is to paint over a worm-eaten bench, we won't function as the paint." The CIR adopted a resolution that all the old parties of the Federation should be dissolved and that "the adherence to the new party must be on an individual basis without privileges for members of *old* political organizations." To sweeten the pill for the Socialists, Mitterrand promised that he would not seek any position of leadership in the new party. And to make the new party ideologically palatable to the SFIO, the CIR

delegates committed themselves to various principles of a socialism (including the nationalization of the means of production)
that "should be neither a constraining dogma nor an opportunistic ideology but a search and a creation of all militants."[92]

Toward a New Party and a New Leadership

At a meeting of its National Council at Clichy early in
November, the SFIO's delegates voted overwhelmingly in favor of
replacing the FGDS by a new party as of January, 1969, if such a
party would be "resolutely socialist," and affirmed that the SFIO
was ready to pursue negotiations to that end. The SFIO's notions
of socialism, which the council recapitulated, were presented in
terms of the traditional vague generalities. They included a call
for the liberation of the human person; the demand that each
person be assured the "free exercise of his rights and conditions
for the development of his personality"; the affirmation of the
party's attachment to democracy; and concern with the emancipation of the working class.[93]

Early in November the FGDS executive committee held its last
meeting. The main events were the resignation of Mitterrand as
president and the issuance of a "declaration of principles and
hopes" about socialism, which was defined as the progressive
nationalization of the means of production *and* a commitment to
political democracy. That the new party' commitment to socialism would be credible enough was emphasized by the Radical
party's refusal to associate itself with the declaration. Still the
SFIO participants were not satisfied. They wanted to go beyond
the declaration on political ideology to the establishment of
organizational and *procedural* principles, such as membership
cards, the distribution of seats and the nature of representation at
future congresses, and even the need for seniority in positions of
leadership. (The non-Socialist delegates at this last meeting of the
FGDS had no interest in examining such procedural problems,
and this fact gave rise to bitter polemics between the SFIO and the
CIR.)

Though many Socialists continued to talk about the need for
the modernization and renewal of the SFIO—particularly in
view of the fact that by the end of 1968 the party's membership had

declined to 30,000—and resolutions were introduced to seek a "reinforcement of party unity,"[94] Mollet was still hesitant about relinquishing the old structures of the SFIO. Nonetheless, the momentum for the establishment of a new party seemed irreversible, and at the SFIO party congress held on December 22 at Puteaux, it was decided by the overwhelmingly vote of 1,664 to 367 (with 836 absentions) to fuse the SFIO with, or replace it by, a new party and to hold the first constituent congress before May 1.[95] There was considerable argument about the name of the new party. Mollet appeared to have won a victory when he persuaded the congress to drop the designation of "Parti démocratique socialiste," but he seemed dissatisfied even with that concession (or any other that implied the disappearance of the old SFIO), because, as he said, the *"atmosphère"* for a new party was not there. But in part because he sensed the unavoidable and in part in response to the repeated insistence by Defferre and Alain Savary (a member of the *Comité directeur*) that there be a rejuvenation of the party leadership, he had announced in a *lettre aux militants* that although he would remain in the new party, he would refuse to serve as its secretary-general—a decision the congress dutifully regretted. The final motion adopted by the National Council "[noted] with satisfaction that an agreement had been reached regarding the principles proposed by the party, and [confirmed] that it would not accept the least modification of these principles."[96]

As the Radicals had refused to accept such a dogmatic declaration of socialism, they finally decided, at the end of November, not to participate in the formation of the new party; they did hope, however, to be able to associate with it in a kind of confederation.[97] The CIR and the UCRG (Union des clubs pour le renouvellement de la gauche, which had been founded a few years earlier) had no objections to the SFIO's principles and therefore agreed to join in the effort of party building—despite the uncertainties surrounding the new party's organizational arrangements—so long as no executive body was established before the forthcoming constituent congress that might give the SFIO premature control over its other partners.

In addition to the disagreements between the CIR and the SFIO, there were also clashing ideological and tactical perceptions within the SFIO. For Mollet (who was in this instance supported by Mitterrand), the socialism of the new party was to be construed rather narrowly, though it would be "modern in its methods, democratic in its functioning, open in its structures, and effective in its program."[98]

There was also some disagreement about the extent to which trade unions and other leftist organizations should be integrated into the new party and what this would imply for the SFIO. The SFIO's union, the FO, had become very weak. The CGT, the largest union, was still considered by many as a mere satellite of the PCF, and the CFDT, the second largest union, was not, in the eyes of many politicians of the Left, acceptably "deconfessionalized."

In any case, there was now sufficient momentum for the SFIO and CIR to lay the groundwork for a constituent congress to be held in May.[99] The preparatory committee consisted of twenty-eight members, with equal representation for each of the four participating groups: the CIR, the UCRG, the UGCS (the Union des groupes et clubs socialistes, established in 1967), and the SFIO. (The Socialist delegation included Mollet, Fuzier, Defferre, and Mauroy.) The collaboration of the non-Communist Left was also facilitated by the fact that virtually all its constituent parts and personalities agreed in opposing two aspects of Gaullist policy: the quasi-total embargo on arms shipments to Israel, announced in January, and the forthcoming referendum, announced in February, on the question of reforming French regional government and replacing the existing Senate by a corporative type of second chamber.

The failure of the referendum and the consequent resignation of de Gaulle as president of the republic constituted for the Left an opportunity to assert itself as a political force, provided that it could achieve the kind of organizational and ideological cohesion that had hitherto eluded it and unite behind a credible candidate.

Notes

1. *Année politique (AP) 1961*, pp. 130f.
2. *AP 1961*, pp. 160-165.

3. *AP 1962*, pp. 7-9.

4. Faucher, *La gauche française*, pp. 83-84.

5. Ibid., pp. 90-95.

6. *AP 1962*, pp. 98-99.

7. Ibid., p. 112.

8. Ibid., p. 128. On the second ballot the PCF supported the SFIO in 64 districts; the SFIO supported the PCF in 92 districts. For instances of Communist candidates' refusal to withdraw in favor of Socialist ones on the second ballot, see Jean Ranger, "L'évolution du parti communiste français et ses relations avec la SFIO," *Revue Française de Science Politique* 14, no. 1 (February 1964):78-79.

9. There were also second-ballot alliances in some localities between the SFIO and the PSU. Mollet himself was elected with the help of Communist votes.

10. *AP 1962*, p. 132.

11. Faucher, *La gauche française*, p. 109.

12. *AP 1962*, Annex, p. 689.

13. *Bulletin intérieur*, no. 128 (April 1963), pp. A1, A11-14.

14. *AP 1963*, p. 25.

15. Faucher, *La gauche française*, p. 110.

16. *AP 1963*, pp. 57ff. The unrealism of Mollet's anticlericalism was frequently attacked. As was brought out during a Socialist symposium, "many Catholics incline toward socialism, but stay away from the Socialist party because of fear that the latter wishes to stamp out religious education entirely." *La pensée socialiste contemporaine: Actes des colloques socialistes de 1964* (Paris: Presses Universitaires de France, 1965), p. 68. As was pointed out in the previous chapter, a significant proportion of the non-Communist Left electorate favored state support of Catholic schools.

17. *Bulletin intérieur*, no. 128 (April 1963), pp. A1, A11-14.

18. Raymond Barrillon, *La gauche française en mouvement* (Paris: Plon, 1967), p. 20. See also *AP 1963*, pp. 100-102.

19. Philip Williams, *French Politicians and Elections, 1951-1969* (London: Cambridge University Press, 1970), p. 162.

20. Georges Suffert, *De Defferre à Mitterrand* (Paris: Seuil, 1966), p. 27.

21. Serge Hurtig, "La SFIO face à la Ve République, *Revue*

Française de Science Politique 14, no. 3 (June 1964):552.

22. Ibid.

23. René Remond, "L'élection présidentielle et la candidature Defferre," ibid., p. 526.

24. *AP 1964*, pp. 13-14.

25. *La Revue Socialiste*, January/May 1964, p. 410.

26. Williams, *French Politicians and Elections*, pp. 165f.; and SFIO, *Bulletin intérieur*, no. 132 (February 1964), p. 4.

27. *AP 1964*, p. 147.

28. *AP 1964*, p. 16.

29. In conformity with its new openness, the bureau of the SFIO decided early in 1964 to send a delegation of six of its members (including Mollet and Defferre) on a visit to the USSR. *Bulletin intérieur*, no. 132 (February 1964), p. 15.

30. Barrillon, *Le gauche française en mouvement*, p. 20.

31. Institut français d'opinion publique poll cited in *AP 1964*, pp. 62-64.

32. *AP 1964*, pp. 84-85.

33. Ibid., p. 99.

34. *Ibid.*

35. *AP 1965*, pp. 4-5.

36. Ibid., p. 6.

37. Ibid., pp. 29-30.

38. Ibid., pp. 31, 35.

39. *Bulletin intérieur*, no. 137 (May 1965), p. 13. Among the members were Gazier, Jaquet, Brutelle, Pineau, Quilliot, Loo, Germain, Metayer, and Chandernagor.

40. Including Clubs Moulin, Tocqueville, Démocratie nouvelle, Citoyens 60.

41. *AP 1965*, pp. 46-49.

42. *La Revue Socialiste*, nouvelle série, no. 185 (July 1965), pp. 206ff.

43. Including CFDT, CFTC, FO, CTC, CNJA, FNSEA, UNEF, UGE. *Bulletin intérieur*, no. 139 (June 1965), pp. 2-3.

44. *La Revue Socialiste*, no. 185 (July 1965), p. 209.

45. Williams, *French Politicians and Elections*, p. 187.

46. Quoted in *AP 1965*, p. 82.

47. Ibid., pp. 95-97.

48. *Le Monde*, December 14, 1965, and *AP 1966*, pp. 68, 83-84, 95.

49. Barrillon, *La gauche française en mouvement*, p. 218; and communiqué of the *Comité directeur* of January 19, 1966 in *La Revue Socialiste*, no. 191 (March 1966), p. 270.

50. B. Lassudric-Duchêne, "Voie révolutionnaire ou réformisme limité?," *Le Monde Hebdomadaire*, February 3-9, 1966.

51. Serge Mallet, *Le Gaullisme et la gauche* (Paris: Seuil, 1965), p. 135.

52. *AP 1966*, p. 11.

53. Ibid., p. 30.

54. Ibid., pp. 22-23.

55. Barrillon, *La gauche française en mouvement*, p. 206.

56. Ibid., p. 52.

57. *Le Monde*, March 18, 1966.

58. Claude Estier, *Journal d'un fédéré* (Paris: Fayard, 1970), p. 69.

59. Mitterrand, (leader); R. Fabre, Radical deputy (Regional Development); Guy Mollet, Socialist deputy (Foreign Affairs and Defense); René Billères, Radical deputy (Education and Culture); Pierre Mauroy, Socialist (Youth); Christian Labrousse, Radical (Scientific Research); Gaston Defferre, Socialist deputy (Social and Administrative Affairs); Mlle Marie-Thérèse Eyquem, CIR (Women); Georges Guille, Socialist senator (Local Communities); Etienne Hirsch (Planning); Ludovic Tron, CIR senator (Economic and Financial Affairs); Michel Soulié, Radical (Human Rights). See *Le Monde Hebdomadaire*, 5-11 May 1966, p. 7.

60. *La Revue Socialiste*, no. 198 (December 1966), p. 495.

61. *AP 1966*, pp. 52-53.

62. Barrillon, *La gauche française en mouvement*, pp. 63-65; and *AP 1967*, p. 9.

63. *AP 1967*, pp. 11-21.

64. Faucher, *La gauche française*, pp. 223-224.

65. Barrillon, *La gauche française en mouvement*, p. 156. See also Estier, *Journal d'un fédéré*, p. 146.

66. Estier, *Journal d'un fédéré*, p. 146.

67. Barrillon, *La gauche française en mouvement*, p. 163.

68. Ibid., p. 170.

69. Faucher, *La gauche française*, p. 232.

70. Estier, *Journal d'un fédéré*, p. 149; and Barrillon, *La gauche française en mouvement*, p. 173.

71. Barrillon, *La gauche française en mouvement*, p. 158.

72. Faucher, *La gauche française*, p. 35.

73. Estier, *Journal d'un fédéré*, p. 139.

74. Barrillon, *La gauche française en mouvement*, p. 173.

75. Faucher, *La gauche française*, p. 236.

76. *Le Monde*, December 19, 1967, p. 8.

77. For text of the accord, see André Guerin, "Une opération 'charmé,' " *Revue politique et parliamentaire*, no. 787 (March 1968), pp. 90-91.

78. *New York Times*, February 25, 1968.

79. *Le Monde*, February 22, 1968.

80. *AP 1968*, p. 15.

81. Estier, *Journal d'un fédéré*, p. 206.

82. See *Le Monde*, October 4, 1968, for later position of the FGDS on university reforms.

83. *AP 1968*, p. 38.

84. Estier, *Journal d'un fédéré*, p. 232.

85. Ibid., p. 225. Cf. André Barjonet, *La révolution trahie de 1968* (Paris: Didier, 1968).

86. Patrick Seale and Brian McConville, *Red Flag, Black Flag* (New York: Ballantine Books, 1968), pp. 181ff.

87. Jules Moch, "Analyse des élections législatives de juin," *La Revue Socialiste*, no. 214-215 (June-July 1968), p. 563.

88. *AP 1968*, p. 62.

89. Estier, *Journal d'un fédéré*, p. 254.

90. *La Revue Socialiste*, no. 217-218 (November-December 1968), p. 958.

91. Pierre Viansson-Ponté, "A la recherche d'une opposition," *Le Monde*, October 6-7, 1968, p. 8.

92. *Le Monde*, October 8, 1968.

93. *Bulletin intérieur*, no. 159 (October 1968), pp. 7f. See also *AP 1968*, pp. 89-91; and *La Revue Socialiste*, no. 217-218 (November-December 1968), pp. 960ff.

94. *Bulletin intérieur*, no. 164 (December 1968), p. 3.

95. *Bulletin intérieur*, no. 165 (December 1968). In order to make the new party appear more dynamic and more credible to young leftists who were not then affiliated with any of the three components of the Federation, there were suggestions that the present executive of the FGDS be replaced by a collegial

directorate of young men (from which Mollet, Mitterrand, and Billères would be excluded) that would prepare the groundwork for fusion. *Express*, August 26, 1968, p. 19.

96. *AP 1968*, pp. 101-102; and *Bulletin intérieur*, no. 165 (December 1968).

97. See *Le Monde*, February 25, 1969.

98. *AP 1969*, p. 11.

99. Christiane Hurtig, *De la SFIO au nouveau Parti Socialiste* (Paris: A. Colin, 1970), p. 25.

8
The New Socialist Party:
Its Problems and Prospects

In the late 1960s, the French Socialists began their newest search for a model political party. Such a party would be socialist but pragmatic. It would be oriented toward industrial workers but hospitable to other social groups. It would be in favor of drastic economic changes but keep its commitment to traditional democratic principles. It would subject itself to an infusion of new blood into the leadership structure but not dispense with the counsel of old mentors who represented continuity. It would, finally, be equally receptive to collaboration with other forces of the French Left without being absorbed by them and losing its uniqueness.

Two Constituent Congresses

The first practical effort at the creation of such a party occurred at a congress in Alfortville on May 4-6, 1969. This congress was convoked by the *Comité directeur* of the SFIO, which had invited the party's regional federations and other interested political formations. There was uncertainty whether the new party would indeed be socialist, whether it was actually about to be established, and finally, whether the Alfortville group could be properly regarded as a constituent congress. The optimistic contention of André Laurens that the Socialist party was born officially on May 6, and that it was not merely the old SFIO wrapped in a new cloak, was lent some substance by the fact that in the weeks preceding Alfortville a number of departmental SFIO federations (such as that of Hauts-de-Seine) had formally dissolved.[1] Secondly, despite the fact that most of the leaders of the *vieille maison* (such as Defferre, Fuzier, Quilliot, and Chandernagor) figured prominently in the debates, there were many new faces of young persons having recently joined the party. Moreover, there were numerous representatives of the Radical party, the CIR, the UCRG, and several clubs, and even a few former members of the PSU. Altogether it was a delegation claiming to represent more than 87,000 members, as contrasted to the old SFIO's last membership of 30,000.

On the other hand, it could be plausibly argued that the gathering was, with a few adumbrations, essentially the same old SFIO. In the first place, most of the CIR, as well as the UCGS and the Radicals, had at the outset refused to participate in Alfortville. The Radicals still insisted that the old Federation was not quite dead and buried while the CIR contested the validity of the congress itself, arguing that a genuine constituent body could meet only if it consisted of delegates from specially elected departmental assemblies.

Secondly, the circumstances surrounding the selection of Gaston Defferre as the new party's candidate for president of the Republic made it seem as if that party was little more than the old SFIO in new clothes. Defferre had announced that he wished to be a candidate. In spite of Mollet's misgivings that Defferre would make any future alliance with the Communists difficult if not impossible, his candidacy had been approved by the *Comité directeur* of the SFIO (without prior consultation with the FGDS or the CIR).[2] Another name that was proposed was that of Alain Savary, a former member of the SFIO who had quit the party in 1958 in protest against Mollet's decision to support de Gaulle and his regime. Still, Mollet appeared to prefer Savary as presidential candidate because his outlook was reminiscent of the generalities embraced so often by the old SFIO. Savary favored "the restoration and the scrupulous defense of public liberties"; the building of a "modern economy"; the construction of a "just society," which would overcome the failures of capitalism in housing, education, and health; the allocation of priorities for national education; and the conduct of a foreign policy based upon impartiality, peace, and international cooperation.[3] This platform was obviously considered ideologically acceptable socialism, since Savary received the support of certain old SFIO leaders, notably Fuzier and Jaquet, who were against revisionism. Yet after considerable confusion, Defferre's candidacy —which he graciously announced was utterly dependent upon the congress' approval—was endorsed by 2,032 out of the total 3,370 votes.[4]

Notwithstanding this sizeable margin, it could in no way be said that Defferre was the best choice of the congress, that his candidacy was conducive to the unity or electoral effectiveness of the non-Communist Left, or that it augured well for the new Socialist party. The very choice of Defferre widened the split within the non-Communist Left. The Defferrists—led by Chandernagor, Quilliot, and other old members of the SFIO's *Comité directeur*—argued that a republican candidate of the stature of the mayor of Marseilles was necessary in order to obviate the danger of being too closely identified with, or dependent upon, the PCF, a party which had certainly not endeared itself to the electorate by its position on the events in Czechoslovakia. It was also argued that Defferre's candidacy would make it easier for the non-Communist Left to capture many moderate votes that might otherwise go to Alain Poher, the acting president of the Republic who had become the official candidate of the Democratic Center party.

The anti-Defferrists, led at Alfortville by Fuzier, contended that the new Socialist party would harm its image by opening itself too easily to the Center; that such an opening would make electoral collaboration with the Communists impossible and would make even a discourse with that party difficult; and that it was absolutely necessary, if the Gaullists were to be beaten, to have a common candidate for the entire Left as in 1965. It was also argued—just as in 1963 and 1964—that Defferre's conception of the presidency as a policymaking office was too close for comfort to that of the Gaullists. The anti-Defferrists and supporters of a common candidate for the Left included Savary (who, incidentally, shared Defferre's idea of the presidency); the president (Charles Hernu) and most of the other leaders of the CIR; the CGT and CFDT, the two most radical trade unions; the SFIO federation of Deux-Sèvres; the Fédération des groupes témoignage chrétien; François Mitterrand, the leader of the now defunct FGDs; the UGCS; and, of course, the PSU.

The PCF and the PSU immediately made good their threats to nominate their own candidates for the presidency. The CIR, which objected both to the premature establishment of a new party and to the choice of Defferre (which it had considered a fait accompli engineered by the old establishment of the SFIO) held its own congress at Saint-Gratien, at which the major event was a vigorous speech by Mitterrand defending his thesis of the need for a common candidate for the entire Left and attacking the exclusivist activities of the congress at Alfortville. A meeting hastily arranged between delegations of Alfortville and Saint-Gratien to achieve a compromise (which could only mean the withdrawal of Defferre's candidacy) was in vain—and all the CIR congress could do was to pass a resolution (by now quite meaningless) expressing confidence in Mitterrand.

Thus despite Pierre Mauroy's optimistic declaration that, as of May 6, "there no longer is an SFIO, a UCRG, or a CIR,"[5] there remained the old tactical confusions and opportunistic behavior of the separate formations and their leaders. This was particularly true of the old SFIO. Mollet (who had been relatively silent at Alfortville) now publicly favored Defferre's candidacy, irrespective of his disagreement with the mayor of Marseilles on his conception of the presidency. Before Alfortville, Mollet had refused to have any kind of entente with the Communists; now, however, his position became more *gauchisante*. Thus Mollet indicated that if there were to be a runoff between Pompidou and Duclos, the PCF candidate, Mollet would advise Socialists to vote for the Communist. This peculiar stand by Mollet was perhaps meant to weaken the appeal of the PCF; to curry favor with the Socialist party's militant rank and file (and thus to regain the leadership of the party); or to undermine Defferre's position, just as Mollet had been accused of doing in 1963. Perhaps he also needed to emphasize the new party's leftism in order to counterbalance Defferre's announcement in mid-May that, if elected president, he would choose Mendès-France, rather than a Socialist, as premier. If so, that tactic was surely nullified when Defferre hedged in answering the question whom *he* would support in the case of a second-ballot contest between Pompidou and Communist leader Duclos. Defferre persisted in his refusal to believe that either candidate could obtain a majority. However, the party, being more pragmatic, indicated somewhat prematurely that if Defferre failed to win on the first ballot or to get on the second ballot, it would support Alain Poher. Duclos immediately branded Defferre as "Poher's water boy."[6] The unity of the non-Communist Left, and therefore Defferre's potency as a candidate, were certainly not enhanced by the fact that many federations of the old SFIO and many local sections still refused to adhere to the new party. They considered Defferre's nomination null and void and hoped that a unitary candidate of the entire Left would be chosen at the last moment.

The result of the first ballot, on June 1, was an absolute disaster for the Socialist party and its candidate, who received slightly over 5 percent of the total vote and was thus effectively eliminated from the second ballot. Nor did the "provisional executive committee's" definite second-ballot endorsement of Poher help the party's socialist image.

Pompidou's victory on June 15 was due in large measure to the PCF's decision to abstain on the second ballot. It was also due to the disorganization of the non-Communist Left. Charles Hernu, the leader of the CIR, said: "If I were in Pompidou's place, I would send a telegram to those who had assembled at Alfortville, because it is due to them . . . that he has been elected. They had provoked the division of the Left. They had thought that a centrist candidate would do better."[7] Other, more forward-looking leaders were ready to start anew. While Mitterrand announced his intention to undertake a tour of France to gather up all Socialist groupings at grass-roots levels, the leaders of the old SFIO and the organizers of the Alfortville congress decided to hold another, and presumably more decisive, constituent congress.

That congress, held at Issy-les-Moulineaux on July 11-13, definitely established the organizational framework of the new Socialist party (Parti socialiste—PS). One of the first decisions of the congress was to retain the basic structure of the SFIO, with its National Congress, whose delegates were chosen by constituent regional federations, its Permanent Bureau, and its *Comité directeur*.[8] The congress elected a *Comité directeur* of sixty-one individuals, about fifty of whom had belonged to the SFIO, and thirty-three of whom were holdovers from the SFIO's *Comité directeur.* Four members came from leftist clubs, two had been Radicals, and one had belonged to the CIR.[9]

The position of secretary-general (now called "first secretary") was retained, but it was understood that he was to be less a leader than a mouthpiece of a collective leadership reflecting the diversity of elements within the new PS. The newly appointed first secretary, Alain Savary, embodied that diversity. Like so many other Socialists, he had abandoned the SFIO in opposition to Mollet's acquiescence to the Gaullist regime and had joined the PSU. He subsequently led a leftist organization, the Union des clubs pour le renouvellement de la gauche (UCRG), which he brought into the newly formed PS.

There was some disagreement about whether Savary was "Mollet's man," and about the extent to which the Mollet aura pervaded the reconstituted executive. By his own choice Mollet occupied no formal position in the national offices of the PS, but there is little doubt that he continued to function as an *éminence grise.* Furthermore, the fact that most of the CIR and Radicals had boycotted the constituent congress and had decided against adherence to the PS, made it easier for that party to conform to Mollet's preferred image of it as a socialist rather than a social-democratic organization.

Actually the policy preferences of the PS could be described as either socialist or social-democratic, depending upon one's taste for semantic distinctions. In its action program adopted in July 1969, the PS did not go far beyond a recapitulation of its rejection of capitalism. It repeated the traditional Socialist demands for a more redistributive economic policy, the improvement of the condition of the worker, the construction of public housing, the expansion of worker participation in factory management, and an increase in the power of parliament. In sum, these were not so much new policies as reaffirmations of the platform embraced earlier by the now defunct FGDS.

There was good reason for the ideological open-endedness of the PS, for despite its (officially claimed) membership of 88,000— to some extent the consequence of the adhesion of additional leftist clubs—the PS could not be effective in future elections without allies. But which allies? A left-center alliance of course presupposed a collaboration of the working class and the petite

bourgeoisie. Such collaboration was now theoretically possible in view of the claim of the PS that it included, "without
making distinctions among beliefs or religious philosophies, all
intellectuals and workers, all city or rural people who accept the
ideals of socialism."[10] Unfortunately for the PS, a left-center
alliance was not feasible because part of the Democratic Center
(led by Jacques Duhamel) was being co-opted into the
government majority of President Pompidou while the part that
remained in opposition (led by Jean Lecanuet, a former leader of
the MRP) was too weak and troubled by indecision. There were,
however, a number of Socialists who considered an alliance with
the Radicals. In view of the dynamic leadership of the Radical
party under Jean-Jacques Servan-Schreiber and in view of its
program, *Ciel et Terre* (Heaven and Earth),[11] some Socialists in
fact wondered whether the Radicals of 1970 were more
revolutionary than the Socialists of 1946, and whether the
Radicals, "no longer having a choice between risk and death,"
would wish to seek an alliance with the PS.[12]

As a practical step in building a system of alliances with
progressive non-Socialists, André Chandernagor, an anti-Communist deputy, established Démocratie socialiste, which was not
another party but rather an umbrella group made up of interested
Socialists, Radicals, and Democratic Centrists. At the same time,
the PS accepted Mitterrand's suggestion of continued discussions
with the Communists. Although the PCF favored close cooperation and even hoped for a common platform, the PS was more
cautious at this stage; it was interested mainly in a "dialogue"
and "common activities in certain areas."[13] Mitterrand, however,
was concerned primarily with tactics. In an interview he declared
that while theoretical discussions were necessary, the masses were
not much interested in them.[14]

The Epinay Congress: The New Shape of the Party

The need for an electoral alliance with the Communists was
based on an optimistic assessment of the strength of the PS. Party
leaders calculated that the growth in membership and the
expanded appeal of the PS would be enough to insure that it

would not be absorbed by the Communists. Furthermore, they reasoned, since the Communists had been able to capture no more than 23 percent of the popular vote since the end of World War II, they should welcome cooperation with another party. And the fact that only the Socialists were capable of helping the Communists out of their political ghetto would almost insure that the PS would ultimately emerge as the most important component of a united Left. This thesis, which had been steadfastly advocated by Mitterrand, dominated the discussions at the PS congress that met in June 1971 at Epinay-sur-Seine. Its acceptance by the congress coincided with Mitterrand's transfer of the entire CIR, an organization which had once been noted for its anticommunism, into the reconstituted Socialist party.

Mitterrand was elected to replace Alain Savary as the first secretary of the party. The choice of Mitterrand was fortunate. He was viewed as a person who combined a desire for a Popular Front with convincing credentials as a moderate who knew how to adapt himself to changing circumstances. It is of course true that in his political mobility (referred to in the previous chapter) Mitterrand was not much different from his predecessor. But Mitterrand was a proven vote-getter: it will be recalled that in the presidential elections of 1965 he had received 45.5 percent of the vote against General de Gaulle.

Mitterrand's assumption of the leadership did not mean that only one tendency would henceforth be articulated. In fact the PS was divided into the following broad groups: (1) the old supporters of Mollet, who fluctuated uneasily between hardline socialism and anti-Communism and who were interested in preserving a role for the old-time leaders of the SFIO; (2) the social-democratic and vociferously anti-Communist faction organized around Gaston Defferre and Pierre Mauroy; (3) the supporters of Savary's leftist clubs, which were formerly united in the UCRG; (4) the group organized around Jean Poperen, who had for many years devoted his energies to uniting the Left, and for that purpose had established the UGCS which professed to be more leftist than the UCRG; and (5) the supporters of Mitterrand, who were concerned more with a successful electoral strategy than with dogma.

Another faction within the PS was the Centre d'études, de

recherches et d'éducation socialistes (CERES). Established in June 1967, it described itself as *"réformiste révolutionnaire"* and favored from the very beginning a reform of economic structures, the reconstitution of the Socialist party primarily on the basis of a reliance on the working class, and the establishment of a union of all left-wing movements (including the PCF) supported by a common platform.

This diversity was reflected in the PS *Comité directeur:* its expanded membership of 81 included 23 Defferrists, 13 supporters of Mitterrand, 10 who were identified with Poperen, 7 adherents of CERES, a few who were still nostalgic about Mollet's long-time leadership, and a miscellany of individuals who had their own unique approaches to Marxism. The *Comité directeur* continued to have a bureau, which had been expanded to 27 members and 14 national secretaries to assist the first secretary. The national convention, which was to meet every two years and to appoint the executive officers, was selected, as before, by the department federations, with the largest federations (Nord and Bouches-du-Rhône) furnishing the largest number of delegates.

This complex democratic structure put the PS at a disadvantage vis-à-vis the PCF, which retained its highly centralized and disciplined organization. In order to overcome this disadvantage and maintain internal unity, the PS national secretaries had to participate constantly in the deliberations of the subnational party organizations. The first secretary had to attempt to arrest the tendencies of factions to recruit their own members on local levels. CERES was particularly noted for its independent activities. In the early 1970s CERES managed to found its own regional federations and to implant itself in factories. Its successful recruitment of CFDT unionists, ex-PSU elements, "laic progressives," and even "revolutionary Christians"[15] enabled it to more than double its representation in the *Comité directeur* by 1973 and to exert considerable influence on the other executive organs of the party.

Although its independent local activities were not unusual, CERES was considered troublesome. In the eyes of many, the "leftism" of CERES and its belief in the class struggle were not fully credible since a significant proportion of its leaders were middle-class technocrats and intellectuals. While the CERES faction controlled the Paris federation of the PS, Defferre controlled the Marseilles (Bouches-du-Rhône) section even more tightly. In fact Defferre, with his local patronage and his grass-roots committees *(comités d'intérêts)* in the municipal districts of Marseilles, frequently acted like a Tammany Hall boss.[16] But although Defferre supported Mitterrand's leadership, CERES continued to fight against it.

At the PS National Congress in Grenoble (June 1973), there were intensive discussions about changing the method of electing the *Comité directeur* so that CERES' influence could be reduced. Under the existing method, each faction had been automatically represented (by at least one person) in the party's executive organs if it had a minimum of 5 percent of the delegates at a party congress. Savary proposed that the congress itself determine the composition of the *Comité directeur,* but to no avail. At the subsequent congress in Pau (January 1975), Mitterrand, whose support had increased dramatically, responded to the challenge of CERES. Mitterrand juxtaposed his own aims to CERES' notions concerning a "revivified Marxism" as follows:

> I want to build the organization of the party so that it will end up opening itself to the working class; so that it will be financially sound; so that it will be able at the proper time to respond to ill-advised government measures. At the same time [one must] continue to build a clear theory, an original vision of socialism.[17]

Mitterrand was interested above all in developing the PS into an effective electoral machine, and therefore he viewed as counter-productive CERES' insistence on remaining a distinct faction within the party. He succeeded in getting anti-CERES programmatic resolutions passed by 68 percent of the delegates.[18] At the same time, by expanding the *Comité directeur* to 130 members, the CERES component was reduced to an insignificant minority; it responded by quitting the secretariat for the next two years.

The ideological diversity of the PS and its inherent factionalism were a reflection of the changed composition of party membership. The new Socialist of the early 1970s was, according to an inside observer, between 30 and 40 years old; was likely to have been a political activist during the events of May and June 1968; possessed "youthful political enthusiasm"; and

had become disillusioned with both Gaullism and Communism.[19] The party had begun to add to its ranks not only "young
gauchistes who love the warmth of the masses,"[20] but also an
increasing number of trade unionists. In particular the "decon-
fessionalization" of the CFTC and its reappearance as the CFDT
in the mid-1960s were to have a favorable impact on the PS.
Whereas the old CFTC had more or less supported the MRP, the
new CFDT, which became decidedly leftist after 1969, had moved
fairly close ideologically to the PS. In addition the PS added to its
ranks a miscellany of moderates who saw little future in the
Radical or centrist parties, which appeared to be disintegrating if
not moribund. These new members included old notables,
engineers, employers, "well-dressed bourgeois types," and even
"peasants whom Socialism had long neglected."[21] The extent of
the *embourgeoisement* of the PS was confirmed by an inquiry
conducted in the early 1970s which revealed that 21.5 percent of its
members were farmers or farm laborers (compared to 22 percent of
Gaullist party members); nearly 20 percent were entrepreneurs or
shopkeepers; nearly 32 percent workers; and nearly 20 percent
belonged to middle-management and white-collar sectors.[22]

The Common Program and the Revival of the Popular Front

Despite the diverse social composition of the Parti socialiste,
virtually all of its members were unhappy with the existing forms
of capitalism and were committed to altering the system of
economic relations by standard democratic methods. However,
several approaches to socialism were in contention. A small
faction (concentrated primarily within groups belonging to the
CGT and to CERES) favored a Soviet-style wholesale abolition of
the capitalist system through a comprehensive nationalization
policy. Others (found especially within the leadership of the
CFDT and among individuals formerly associated with the PSU)
preferred the more gradualist approach of factory self-management *(autogestion)*. Most Socialists were interested only in
fighting the overconcentration of economic power and, beyond
that, in promoting the transformation of capitalism from within
(as the Swedes had been doing rather successfully) by a
redistributive policy aimed at achieving as much equality as

possible without a drastic and sudden abolition of the capitalist system.

The PS platform, *Changer la vie*,[23] presented by Mitterrand and adopted· in 1972, was an attempt to combine all of these approaches. This document of over 240 pages was hardly revolutionary. Mitterrand's Introduction contained the usual references to "ending the exploitation of man by man," the fight against monopoly capital, and the need to make French society more egalitarian, both in terms of income and opportunity. The program was remarkable for its detailed attention to minimum wages, sliding scales, the return to the 40-hour work week, the support of farmers' incomes, aid to shopkeepers and artisans, the abrogation of the "Debré Law," tax reforms, the abolition of the death penalty, the democratization of the process and content of planning, the establishment of local democracy, the nationalization of certain enterprises, as well as steps to be taken "in the direction of factory self-management." There was, in addition, a demand for the return to the electoral system based on proportional representation that had been in effect during the Fourth Republic. Furthermore, the PS program—possibly as a gesture to party members with centrist inclinations—called for the replacement of the prefects by general council presidents as provincial chief executives.

Since the PCF accepted most of this program, it could form the basis of a joint platform with the PS. Furthermore, the Communists seemed to have come around to accepting at least implicitly the position of the PS, as contained in its program, that "the defense of liberties is compatible only with democratic institutions. The PCF had already given up its view of elections as "treason"; after the "May Events," the "domestication" of the PCF had evolved even further with the appearance of numerous publications by Communist politicians and intellectuals expostulating new approaches. The culmination of this development was the appearance of the 1971 PCF program,[24] in which there were no references to the dictatorship of the proletariat; which favored the achievement of socialist goals by parliamentary means; and which seemed to accept free elections, free speech, and interparty competition. In this program, the PCF also publicly committed itself to the acceptance of the principle that, once in power, it would be willing to step aside peacefully if it lost an election. These developments produced a softening of popular antagonisms toward the Communists, and made a Socialist rapprochement with them less risky. And since by 1972 PS membership was already close to 100,000, the PS could finally deal with the PCF from a position of relative strength.

On June 27, 1972, the two parties signed a Common Program.[25] This document, which took several months to fashion, was on the surface a compromise between the Communist and Socialist party platforms. Most of its 150 pages read like a typical social-democratic platform, calling for the extension of social benefits, the strengthening of trade-union rights, the gradual elimination of parochial schools, the abolition of the death penalty, the rescission of Article 16 of the constitution, and the return to proportional representation. The PCF's acceptance of civil liberties—which was to be reaffirmed three years later at the party's twenty-second congress when it issued a "declaration on liberties"—was matched by the Socialists' acceptance of *autogestion* of factory workers and the nationalization of industries. The PS benefited directly from the first of its compromises. Since *autogestion* had been a major concern of the PSU and the CFDT, its acceptance by the PS led these two groups to associate themselves with the PS and support Mitterrand in subsequent parliamentary and presidential elections. This development also led to the partial integration of the leadership of the CFDT into the decision-making structure of the PS and culminated two years later in the PSU leadership and a large proportion of its membership joining the PS.

In spite of the Common Program, the Socialists and Communists still disagreed on several major points (which will be discussed in more detail in the next section). First of all, though the PS in principle favored the nationalization of the very largest, monopolistic enterprises, it could not go along with the Communists' more far-reaching designs. Secondly, both parties agreed on raising the minimum wages of the lowest-paid industrial workers, but the PS preferred to narrow the differential between the highest and lowest wages somewhat less than the PCF. The Socialists' more moderate stand was to make it easier for the Left Radical movement (the Mouvement des radicaux de gauche—MRG), which contained a significant petit-bourgeois element and which opposed nationalization, to join the leftist alliance.[26]

There were certain other issues on which the two parties were divided. For instance, the PS held a generally favorable view regarding the prospects of European integration, while the Communists resembled the Gaullists in harboring suspicions about the Common Market. On the Middle East dispute the PS, which included many supporters of Israel, tended to be neutral, while the Communists, again like the Gaullists, held one-sided pro-Arab views. As the parliamentary elections approached, such disagreements were deliberately underemphasized. In addition the PS and PCF agreed on certain ad hoc elaborations of the Common Program: specific housing units to be built per annum, specific minimum wages, and a lowered retirement age for men and women.

The Left made impressive gains in the parliamentary elections that took place on March 4 and 11, 1973. The Socialists in particular had succeeded in appealing to centrist voters who were frustrated with Pompidou's policy immobilism and insufficiently convinced of the reformist zeal of the *Réformateur* movement, a new alliance of the Democratic Center and Radical parties. The PS even made inroads in a number of traditionally Gaullist areas, e.g., Lorraine and Western France, where it received 8 percent more votes than in the previous parliamentary elections. Conversely the PS lost votes in Southern France, where electors were fearful of the consequences of Socialist collaboration with the Communists. In any case the PS together with its Left-Radical ally received 20.4 percent of the popular vote (as compared to the Communist share of 21.3 percent) on the first ballot, and 25.1 percent of the second-ballot votes (compared to 21.3 percent for the PCF.)[27] The Socialists sent 94 deputies to parliament, and their Left-Radical ally, 9 (compared to 73 Communists), thus nearly doubling their representation. It is clear that the PS benefited from the agreement among the Common Program parties that the leftist candidate who had the weaker first-ballot performance would withdraw in favor of the stronger on the second ballot.

The leadership of Mitterrand had proved decisive. He was duly rewarded for his performance when he was overwhelmingly reelected as first secretary of the party at the PS congress in Grenoble (June 1973). Mitterrand's leadership and the unity of the Left alliance continued to hold when, as a consequence of Pompidou's sudden death on April 2, 1974, France was plunged into a presidential campaign. Unlike the situation in previous presidential elections, there was no competition for the party's standard bearer: Mitterrand was selected almost unanimously as the candidate of his own party and endorsed without difficulty by the MRG and the PCF.

Mitterrand went into the election campaign with several advantages. The petroleum crisis that followed in the wake of the October 1973 Mideast War had caused severe economic problems for France. The restlessness of workers over the loss of real income had given rise to wildcat strikes, and Pompidou, already ill, had appeared to be irresolute and confused about what policies to pursue. In addition the opponents of the Left were divided, with the Gaullists and the centrists each putting up their own candidates, Chaban-Delmas and Giscard d'Estaing, respectively.

To face his opponent without difficulty on the second ballot, Mitterrand had to make a good showing on the first ballot. In order to draw first-ballot votes away from Giscard in particular, whom the Democratic Centrists and Radicals were inclined to support, Mitterrand avoided saying too much about the prospects of nationalization or the future of the French commitment to the Western alliance in the event of his victory. Instead he emphasized the Left's concern for the workers and the poor. Mitterrand reiterated the Left's well-known position on institutions: a reinvigoration of parliament and a corresponding reduction of presidential prerogatives. At the same time, to reassure un-committed and suspicious voters, he promised that *he* (rather than the premier) would select the cabinet—thus endorsing the Gaullist view of presidential powers—and that, if elected, he would not give certain delicate portfolios to Communists.[28]

On the first ballot Mitterrand received the largest number of votes in what was essentially a three-cornered race: he obtained 43.4 percent against Giscard's 32.8 percent and Chaban's 14.8 percent (with the rest of the vote divided among nine other candidates). This result was not quite good enough for the Left, which had hoped to get at least 45 percent. Mitterrand (and to a lesser extent Communist leader Marchais), in an attempt to draw a few crucial left-wing Gaullist voters to the leftist alliance and weaken Giscard's second-ballot chances, emphasized Giscard's conservative and business-oriented political background, and even briefly endorsed the Gaullists' exaggerated nationalism.[29] But this tactic proved fruitless; the Gaullists overwhelmingly flocked to Giscard's support, with the result that Mitterrand (with 49.3 percent of the popular vote against Giscard's 50.7 percent) once again failed to bring the Left to power.

The presidency of Giscard, apart from constituting a severe blow to the hopes of the Left, proved to be embarrassing for another reason: the preemption of much of the Socialists' program. There was a considerable revival of the power of parliament as that body was increasingly consulted on social and economic legislation. In the spring of 1974, the PS introduced some forty bills calling, inter alia, for the lowering of the voting age to 18, the raising of the minimum wage, the granting of equal pay for men and women, the liberalization of abortion laws, and the exemption of the aged from medical-care payments. Such reforms, and others, were enacted during the following three years not as Socialist legislation but largely as a result of the government's own bills, for which the Giscardian deputies took most of the credit.[30] As a result of Giscard's politics of reformism, a number of progressive Centrists and Radicals who might have been drawn to the Socialists were instead being attracted to Giscardism. Although certain Radicals (such as Servan-Schreiber) would have preferred an understanding with the Socialists, such an option was for the time being foreclosed by the continuation of the Common Program alliance.

The Problems of Senior Partnership

Nevertheless, the Parti socialiste continued to strengthen itself. By 1975 the party membership, swelled by the adhesion of former PSU members, former Democratic Centrists and even renegade Communists, had reached 140,000, and by mid-1977, 164,000.[31] The federations of Bouches-du-Rhône, Nord, and Pas-de-Calais accounted for about one-fourth of the total membership. A large proportion of FO and FEN members had over the years been Socialist supporters; in addition the CFDT leadership was solidly in the Socialist camp, and an increasing number of CGT members switched their loyalties from the PCF to the PS. Much of this achievement was the result of assiduous recruiting. By early 1977 the PS had established some 900 sections in factories.[32] The party publications were now addressing themselves to a diversity of social sectors; they included the journal *L'Unité*, which contained features on agriculture, the communes, women, and youth; *Le Poing et la Rose*, a monthly dealing with party matters; *La Nouvelle Revue Socialiste*, containing articles on ideology; *Socialisme et Entreprise*, intended for employers and industrial managers; and *L'Université Socialiste* (published under the auspices of the Cercle Jean Jaurès) for students.

Among the most hopeful signs of the rejuvenation of the PS was the fact that more than 40 percent of the membership was under 35 years of age.[33] There was also an increase in the number of militants, who campaigned, organized, propagandized, and participated regularly in party gatherings. Although the percentage of PS activists was smaller than that of the PCF,[34] the Socialist activists must have done their work well. In the nineteen parliamentary by-elections held between 1973 and 1977, the PS increased its vote in all fifteen constituencies in which it had fielded candidates, while the PCF gained votes in only five.[35] After the cantonal elections of March 1976, the PS controlled 528 cantons, a gain of 202.[36] Similar results were achieved in the municipal elections a year later when the Left won impressively over the Gaullists, with the largest share of the gains accruing to the PS. That party captured control of 81 out of 220 cities (a gain of 35) compared to Communist victories in 72 cities (a gain of 22).[37] In terms of overall popular support, the PS, by mid-1977, had reached first place with 30 percent of the voters as compared to 20 percent for the PCF.

Objectively these figures augured well for the prospects of a victory of the Left in the forthcoming parliamentary elections. Throughout 1977 most public-opinion polls predicted that the Left would dominate the Assembly by a two or three percent margin. Unfortunately the unity of the Left had already begun to erode. Disputes between the two major parties of the leftist alliance, primarily over the nature of the Common Program, had in fact occurred a short time after the presidential elections but were not then considered serious. They gained steadily in volume and acerbity in the spring of 1977, however, and continued up to the parliamentary elections a year later.

As we have seen, the Common Program had included references to nationalization and wage equalization but had omitted both specific details and a timetable for their implementation. Now that a Left victory was within reach, the PCF insisted that these policies be clearly defined. The Common Program had named only nine firms as candidates for takeover; but now the Communists were insisting that more than a thousand firms be nationalized, including domestic *and* foreign subsidiaries. The Socialists were reluctantly prepared to nationalize about a hundred companies, including the main deposit banks, as well as about a dozen industrial giants (among them large steel and automobile firms). The Common Program had proposed differential forms of nationalization, not all of them amounting to complete takeovers by the government. Thus, full nationalization was envisaged for some giant firms with insufficient private capital (e.g., the Dassault aircraft manufacturing firm) or under foreign control (e.g., Honeywell-Bull), while for other sectors (e.g., certain steel firms), the government was to become merely the majority stockholder. The Communists, however, preferred outright nationalization.

The PCF and PS also disagreed on means of indemnification: the Communists wished to base the amount of indemnification on the value of shares during the three years prior to nationalization, while the Socialists wished the sum to be determined by the fair market price. Furthermore, the PCF favored the spreading of indemnification payments over a twenty-year period, while the PS preferred an exchange of shares with stockholders. Another point of contention was the management of the nationalized firms: the PS insisted that aptitude and expertise be the chief criteria in the selection of managers, while the PCF favored their selection by the trade unions (hoping thereby to increase the power of CGT, still the strongest union and still heavily controlled by Communists).[38]

The two parties also disagreed on the matter of wage

redistribution. The PCF favored a reduction of the existing income gap of 1:10 between the lowest and the highest decile of wage earners to a 1:5 ratio, while the PS preferred a 1:8 ratio. Both parties demanded a raise of minimum wages, but the Socialists' figures, which represented a compromise between the positions of the CFDT and the MRG, were somewhat lower than those of the Communists. Furthermore, the Communists insisted on a specific timetable for the implementation of the Left's platform that the Socialists were unable to accept.

A further difference of opinion revolved around the electoral system. All three parties of the Left favored a return to proportional representation, at least for Assembly and Senate elections, as well as for elections to the councils of larger municipalities. The PS and its ally, the MRG, however, wished to exempt the smaller communities from this reform for the simple reason that these parties were in a better position than the PCF to make alliances with centrist parties in such communities.[39]

An additional disagreement involved foreign policy. The Common Program had included a demand for the phasing out of the independent French nuclear force *(force de frappe)*. While the PS held fast to that plank, the PCF now embraced the Gaullist position favoring the maintenance of such a force—not because the Communists had come to believe in its defense efficacy, but in order to demonstrate their continuing hostility to Atlanticism. Similarly, the PS was inclined to favor a system of direct popular elections to the European Economic Community's parliament, while the Communists, essentially hostile to European integration, were unenthusiastic.

There were differences of opinion on other matters as well. The PCF demanded a number of cabinet seats in the event of a Left victory. While Mitterrand was not opposed to such demands, he still carefully refrained from specifying the portfolios to be assigned to the Communists. However, it was generally understood that the PCF would not be given such sensitive ministries as interior (which controls the police), justice, defense, or foreign affairs. In addition the PCF demanded the right to veto any policy that might be promoted by Mitterrand once he assumed the premiership, but Mitterrand refused to have his hands tied.

Mitterrand was pressured by the CERES wing of his party (and by certain elements of the CGT) to be more forthcoming in his concessions. (CERES did not agree with every Communist demand, but it was concerned with maintaining the unity of the Left at almost any cost.) At the same time, the moderates in his own party and his allies from the Left Radicals felt that he had already conceded too much.

A number of meetings between the two parties were held in attempts to narrow the gap. The PCF's list of firms to be nationalized was reduced to 729, and the PS's list was expanded to 227. The PS also tried to defuse the conflict over the nuclear strike force by suggesting that a referendum be held on this matter after the elections.

All attempts at compromise failed, and at the end of September further discussion ceased. The PCF stepped up its campaign of vituperation against the Socialists, who were accused of playing a centrist game and of neglecting the interests of the masses.[40] The PS responded in kind. In an article in *Le Monde*, a member of the party's bureau suggested that the Communists had no right to berate the PS, or to speak for the French, since the PCF represented only 20 percent of the total electorate, less than half of the pro-Left electorate, and not even the entire working class. Moreover, he argued, the PCF showed a disquieting conception of multipartism and an intolerance of diversities of opinion. Finally, he reminded the PCF that whereas it arrived at its positions without internal debates, the PS made its decisions on the basis of intensive discussions.[41]

The hardened position of the PCF vis-à-vis the PS had much less to do with programmatic considerations than with the realization that the PS had emerged as the senior partner in the Left alliance. Public opinion polls throughout 1977 had shown that the Socialist party was the choice of 30 to 33 percent of the electorate, as against 20 percent for the PCF. It is probably true that the PS' increased popularity derived from its tactical advantage: its ability to play the role of a mediator between the extreme Left and the progressively inclined centrists. This was illustrated by the fact that for at least a year the leadership of the Radical party and the Democratic Centrists (the

Centre des démocrates sociaux) had suggested an alliance with the Socialists if only they would break with the Communists. The acceptability of the PS was also illustrated by the decision of the MRG not to compete with Socialists in over 200 constituencies in the forthcoming parliamentary elections.

There is some reason to believe that by provoking the rift with the Socialists, the PCF hoped to exploit whatever dissatisfaction existed with the leadership of Mitterrand. An IFOP poll[42] had shown that only 52 percent of Socialist voters were completely satisfied with Mitterrand's leadership, while 15 percent were sensitive to arguments that the Socialist leader had been insufficiently concerned with the plight of the working class.

While Mitterrand and the PS continued to be committed to socialist economic goals, they were equally committed to the continuation of parliamentary methods. They were not entirely convinced that the PCF had been fully converted to such methods, or that it had de-Stalinized itself completely.[43] On the contrary, the PCF had been heavily criticising Helmut Schmidt and James Callaghan, the Socialist prime ministers of Germany and Britain with whom Mitterrand maintained good relations, but avoided criticism of the repressive regimes of Czechoslovakia and other Eastern European countries. The Socialists also feared that a programmatic convergence too close to the PCF might alienate many of the newly acquired members of their party.

The Embourgeoisement of the Parti socialiste

In terms of its social composition and attitudes, the present-day Socialist party is roughly comparable to the social-democratic parties of other Western European countries. According to recent commentators, "the PS appears today as the only large interclass party, which . . . faithfully reflects the image of the French social structure. [But] it is doubtlessly younger, more working-class . . . and more masculine than French society as a whole."[44] Among the party's newcomers the following have predominated: supervisory white-collar personnel *(cadres supérieurs)*, managers, free professionals, the self-employed, and even practicing Catholics. A poll conducted at the end of 1974 revealed this breakdown of

Socialist party supporters:[45]

Factory workers and domestics	37%
Unemployed (including retired)	19%
White collar	18%
Farmers	10%
Liberal professions and upper echelon white collar	9%
Industrialists, shopkeepers, and artisans	7%

Though workers constitute the largest category, it has been estimated that about three-fourths of these are skilled workers or foremen.[46] There is, as before, a heavy representation of civil servants, technicians, and school teachers among the membership. A sample survey for the Gironde (Bordeaux) region in 1974 revealed that of those Socialists who were members of interest groups (62 percent of the total party membership), 53.6 percent belonged to one of the three major trade unions, but more than 17 percent belonged to the teachers' union (FEN) and about 20 percent to agricultural associations.[47]

As with the old SFIO, this social diversity is only imperfectly reflected in the PS leadership structure. At a typical national party congress (Grenoble, 1973), only one in thirty delegates was a worker; 8 percent were white-collar workers, and 6 percent were teachers.[48] Free-lance intellectuals, academics, and professional politicians have continued to dominate the executive organs of the PS, and such domination has undoubtedly had an impact on the party's orientation. Although Marxism has always fascinated French intellectuals, who delight in endless restatements of the meaning of socialism, the *programmatic* orientations of many economists and most of the professional politicians among the national leadership of the PS have been guided more by hardnosed realism or technocratic considerations than dogmatism. Thus Jacques Attali, one of the chief economic advisors of Mitterrand, in opposing extensive nationalization, cited its dubious effects on productivity, capital formation, and the balance of payments, and questioned the capacity of the national treasury to pay for it.[49] Michel Rocard, a graduate of the prestigious National School of Administration, as a leader of the

PSU (which considered itself more leftist than the PS), had been concerned more with interpreting social phenomena than questing after power. Finally realizing the futility of his political isolation, he rejoined the PS and became a member of its bureau.[50] Michel Charzat and Jean-Pierre Chevènement were both representatives of the CERES faction in the bureau, and as such pressured Mitterrand to make concessions to the Communists for the sake of the unity of the Left. At the same time, both rejected the PCF's totalitarianism. Chevènement was proud of the fact that he belonged to a party where "all varieties and nuances of opinion are tolerated."[51] And Charzat sounded very much like a Lecanuet type of centrist in his advocacy of a fusion of secular progressivism and Left-oriented Christianity.[52]

The professional politicians were guided by other considerations also. They opposed extensive nationalization and excessive wage equalization because they were aware of the fact that the trade unions that supported the PS themselves contained skilled-worker and white-collar elements that insisted upon wage differentials and, more important, because they knew that by such opposition they could entice additional support from shop-keepers and entrepreneurs. Politicians such as Defferre, the long-time mayor of Marseilles and chief of the PS parliamentary faction, also realized that in the case of many old members of the PS, Socialist expressions were often divorced from instrumental actions. Thus, although the PS supported the minimal national-ization and education planks of the Common Program, the bulk of the Socialist electorate opposed it. By 1968 only 23 percent of Socialists had favored a reduction or elimination of governmental subsidies to parochial schools.[53] In 1963 only 37 percent of Socialist voters had supported an extension of nationalization; in 1977 between 44 and 70 percent favored nationalization, depending on the type of industry in question,[54] but only 17 percent had sympathy for the Socialist economic program as a whole.[55] Additional public-opinion polls revealed that many more Socialists adhered to humanist socialism than to Marxism;[56] that 19 percent of the anticipated PS electorate had supported Giscard in 1974; and that of those Socialists who had voted for Mitterrand in that year, 68 percent placed themselves on the center-left on a right-left ideological spectrum, 20 percent on the left, and none on the extreme left.[57]

In response to the ideological diversity of the Socialist electorate, and in order to dispel the impression that the PS was hopelessly "antiliberal," Mitterrand had for several years been engaged in a hesitant dialogue with elements of the business community.[58] This effort must have been at least partly successful. An opinion poll conducted in the autumn of 1976 revealed that 40 percent of the entrepreneurs belonging to the Association of Small Businesses (Petites et moyennes entreprises) held a favorable opinion of the PS, and that 25 percent of the leaders of firms employing more than 500 workers held positive views.[59] This indicated that at least some entrepreneurs doubted somewhat whether the PS held completely to the nationalization plank of the Common Program, or whether the party would be capable of implementing it.

The 1978 Parliamentary Elections and After

The *embourgeoisement* of the PS as such was not the primary reason for the continued bitter relations with the PCF. The PCF was not only worried about the postelectoral commitments of the Socialists with respect to implementing the Common Program, but also about whether the support of Mitterrand by the Communists would pay them sufficiently in terms of office. The fear that Mitterrand would cast them off as allies in favor of Democratic Centrists was based on the fact that Mitterrand had unabashedly labeled himself a reformist Social Democrat who "would not hesitate to sacrifice the union of the Left" if freedom were threatened.[60]

There were additional grounds for the Communists' suspicions. A poll conducted in the autumn of 1977 had revealed that only 29 percent of Socialist voters hoped for a postelection coalition with the PCF. The other preferences were as follows: a Socialist-Left Radical coalition, 27 percent; a Socialist-Centrist alignment, 16 percent; and Socialist participation in a Gaullist-Giscardian-Centrist government, 24 percent![61] Communist suspicion was also based on the social-democratic rhetoric emanating with increasing volubility from the Democratic Centrists and Giscardians and on the network of close personal relations between Socialist and Centrist politicians that had been built up since the days of the Fourth Republic. Such relationships had been particularly important on local levels, with the result that Socialist-Communist electoral agreements arrived at nationally had been translated with doubtful effectiveness locally. Nevertheless, in most of the smaller communities, the PS had had little difficulty in reaffirming its agreement with the PCF concerning second-ballot withdrawals, in the foreknowledge that the Socialist candidate would almost invariably do better on the first ballot than the Communist one.

At a congress eight years earlier, the Socialist party had specifically rejected alliances with "forces representing capitalism," or the quest for "centrist combinations."[62] Nevertheless, in practice such alliances were never foreclosed at the local level. As Defferre put it, "there is no Common Program for municipalities."[63] On this matter Defferre reflected the attitude of the national leadership of the PS. In 1973—a year after the signing of the Common Program—Communist leader Marchais had critically noted the continued tendency of Socialists to cooperate with centrists locally. Claude Estier, a member of the *Comité directeur,* had responded with the assertion that "the ambition of the Socialist party to develop its audience . . . is not incompatible with its will to [the] unity [of the Left]."[64] The misunderstandings between Socialists and Communists engendered by such an attitude sometimes had interesting consequences. At Reims, for instance, where the Left had gained control of the city council in March 1977, Socialist councilmen refused to vote for the budget submitted by the Communist mayor, charging that he had been using his office to favor his Communist comrades over Socialists in the distribution of local offices.

Nevertheless, during the parliamentary election campaign, Mitterrand remained publicly committed to his party's electoral (i.e., second-ballot withdrawal) agreement with the PCF. Marchais however refused to make such a commitment until after the first ballot.

The results of the first round of the parliamentary elections, which took place on March 12, 1978, were a severe disappointment for the entire Left. Together its three parties garnered only 45.3 percent of the popular vote, as against 46.5 percent for the

Gaullists and the Giscardian electoral alliance, the Union pour la démocratie française (UDF). The outcome of the second ballot a week later was even less encouraging: the Left received 49.3 percent of the vote against 50.7 percent for the majority parties. The result in terms of the allocation of parliamentary seats was worse still: 200 for the Left to 287 for the majority.

It is not clear why the PS and its Left-Radical ally gained only 9 seats compared to the PCF's 12. It is possible that the PCF sabotaged the success of Socialist candidates in some constituencies by "sitting out" the second ballot; it is equally possible that centrist voters, whose support might have gone to the Socialists, punished them for having made an alliance with the Communists. Still, the PS emerged with 104 parliamentary seats, 18 more than the Communists, and could look forward with certainty to the support of the 10 Left-Radical deputies. Moreover, the elections confirmed that, with 28 percent of the total second-ballot vote, the Socialist party had become the most popular party in France. Perhaps the PS might have done better had its disagreements with the PCF been resolved at the last moment; perhaps it was precisely these disagreements that swelled the vote for the PS because many voters had become convinced of the party's commitment to a policy of responsibility and moderation.

As of mid-1978, the implications of the elections for the political future of Mitterrand were still not clear. According to a poll conducted immediately after the elections, the blame for the Left's defeat was attributed largely to Communist leader Marchais;[65] yet the continuation of Mitterrand's leadership and the direction of the party may remain in doubt for some time. The Popular Front he had fashioned, and to which he owed his continued leadership, has been shaken to its foundations, and the PS appears likely— despite the leftist illusions of CERES—to become more decisively social-democratic, like its sister parties elsewhere in Western Europe. The Common Program, too, will probably be abandoned. The MRG was the first to consider itself no longer bound by this document which, as one Radical of the Left put it, might now be put "into the museum of the political history of the Left."[66]

The election results have put an end to the long-held myth that French politics had become irreversibly bipolarized in an Anglo-

American fashion. If the first ballot of the presidential elections of 1974 had begun as a tripolar contest, the parliamentary elections of 1978 produced a four-party system, which in turn might well be translated into a tripolar constellation dominated by a programmatic alignment with a center-left flavor. If Giscard and his centrist UDF supporters are serious about promoting the socioeconomic reforms they promised, they will have to distinguish themselves more decisively from the Gaullists. This would, in turn, require the Giscardians to establish a new programmatic majority based on collaboration with the Socialists. If such a realignment comes to pass, the Socialist party will finally have succeeded, after twenty years in the wilderness, in gaining a share in government while remaining true to its traditions.

Notes

1. Christiane Hurtig, *De la SFIO au nouveau Parti Socialiste*, p. 18.
2. *Le Monde*, May 6, 1969.
3. Ibid.
4. *Le Monde*, May 3, 1969.
5. *Le Monde*, May 6, 1969.
6. Ibid. See also *New York Times*, May 25, 1969.
7. *Le Monde*, May 16, 1969.
8. "Statuts du parti," *Bulletin intérieur*, no. 1 (September 1969).
9. Cf. Dorothy Pickles, *Government and Politics in France* (London: Methuen, 1972), vol. 1, pp. 383-84.
10. "Statuts du parti," *Bulletin intérieur*, no. 1 (September 1969). Cf. André Philip, "Les impératifs d'un socialisme moderne," *Le Monde*, June 11, 1970.
11. Jean-Jacques Servan-Schreiber and Michel Albert, *Ciel et Terre: Manifeste Radical* (Paris: Denoël, 1970).
12. *Le Monde*, February 13, 1970.
13. *Le Monde*, January 13, 1970.
14. *Le Monde*, February 27, 1970.
15. Jean-François Bizot, Léon Mercadet, and Patrice van Eersel, *Au parti des Socialistes: plongée libre dans les courants*

d'un grand parti (Paris: Grasset, 1975), pp. 338, 486ff. See also Michel Charzat, Jean-Pierre Chevènement, and Ghislaine Toutain, *Le CERES: un combat pour le socialisme* (Paris: Calmann-Lévy, 1975), pp. 16f, 263-66.

16. Bizot et al., *Au parti des Socialistes*, pp. 180-84.

17. Quoted in Ibid., p. 14.

18. The vote was 2,500 against 500. François Mitterrand, ed., *Parti socialiste* (Paris: Marabuto, 1977), pp. 37-38. On the differences between Mitterrand's resolutions and those of CERES (which emphasized the class struggle), see Charzat et al., *Le CERES*, pp. 108-109.

19. Bizot et al., *Au parti des Socialistes*, p. 13.

20. Ibid., p. 14.

21. Ibid.

22. Jacques Lagroye et al., *Les militants politiques dans trois partis français* (Paris: Pedone, 1976), pp. 5, 22-23.

23. Parti socialiste, *Changer la vie: programme de gouvernement du parti socialiste* (Paris: Flammarion, 1972).

24. Parti communiste français, *Changer de cap: programme pour un gouvernement démocratique d'union populaire* (Paris: Editions Sociales, 1971).

25. Partis communiste et socialiste, *Programme commun de gouvernement du parti communiste et du parti socialiste* (Paris: Editions Sociales, 1972).

26. The MRG's joining led to an updated program, *Programme commun du gouvernement: Parti socialiste, parti communiste, et mouvement des radicaux de gauche* (Paris: Flammarion, 1973).

27. *Le Monde*, March 6 and 13, 1973. Jean Blondel (in "The Rise of a New-Style President," Howard R. Penniman, ed., *France at the Polls: The Presidential Election of 1974* [Washington, D.C.: American Enterprise Institute, 1975], p. 43) gives slightly different statistics for the second ballot: PS and allies, 26.4%; PCF, 20.6%.

28. Ibid., p. 53.

29. See reports on and excerpts of speeches in *Le Monde*, May 15, 16, and 17, 1974. Note that significant transfers of first-ballot Gaullist voters to Mitterrand on the second ballot occurred only in two departments of West-Central France, in several south-

western departments, and in Corsica (*Le Monde,* May 21, 1974).

30. For examples of legislative activity in the spring of 1977, see *Journal officiel,* May 27 (pollution control); June 29 (increase in pensions); and July 6 (employment of young people).

31. Figures—which must be used with caution—from François Mitterrand, ed., *Les socialistes* (Paris: Flash-Actualité-Marabout, 1977), p. 42.

32. Howard Machin and Vincent Wright, "The French Left Under the Fifth Republic," *Comparative Politics* 10, no. 1 (October 1977):58. On the political activities of the CFDT, see *Syndicalisme Hebdo,* no. 1435 (March 8, 1973) and no. 1498 (May 30, 1974).

33. Mitterrand, *Les socialistes,* p. 55.

34. According to one estimate for 1975, 17% of PS members were activists, compared to 26% of PCF members. Lagroye et al., pp. 11-12.

35. Machin and Wright, "The French Left," p. 56. On the PCF's reaction to the PS advance, see also Jean-Claude Colliard and Gérard le Gall, "L'Union contre le pessimisme," *Nouvelle Revue Socialiste,* no. 19 (1975).

36. *Le Monde,* March 9, 1976.

37. *Le Monde,* March 22, 1977.

38. Georges Mamy and Franz-Olivier Giesbert, "Les quatorze dossiers du 15 septembre," *Nouvel Observateur,* August 29-September 4, 1977, pp. 24-25. See also François Renard, "L'éventuel application du Programme Commun," *Le Monde,* February 12, 1977.

39. See "L'actualisation du programme commun," *Le Monde,* August 11 and September 14, 1977.

40. See, for example, *L'Humanité,* September 28, 1977.

41. Lionel Jospin, "La stratégie du soupçon," *Le Monde,* August 18, 1977. See also *L'Unité,* June 10 and September 8, 1977.

42. Published in *Le Point,* October 24, 1977.

43. See Fernand Claudin, "La dimension pathologique du PCF," *Le Monde,* October 5, 1977.

44. Roland Cayrol and Jerôme Jaffre, "Y a-t-il plusieurs électorats socialistes?," *Le Monde,* March 22, 1977.

45. Based on citations in *World Opinion Update* 1, no. 1 (September 1977):5; and Michele Cotta, "Les nouveaux social-

istes," *L'Express*, May 10-16, 1976, p. 31.

46. Lagroye et al., pp. 22-23.

47. A more precise breakdown of union membership is as follows: CGT, 12.4%; CFDT, 12.4%; FO, 28.8%; FEN, 17.6%. Ibid., p. 144.

48. François Goguel and Alfred Grosser, *La politique en France* (Paris: A. Colin, 1975), p. 110.

49. See Jacques Attali, "Faire peur, faire croire, faire taire," *Nouvel Observateur*, March 4-10, 1978, pp. 51-52.

50. See Michel Rocard, *Le parti socialiste unifié et l'avenir socialiste* (Paris: Seuil, 1969).

51. Jean-Pierre Chevènement, *Les socialistes, les communistes, et les autres* (Paris: Aubier Montagne, 1977), pp. 76-77. See also Charzat, *Le CERES*, pp. 246ff.

52. Bizot et al., *Au parti des socialistes*, p. 31. Bizot himself had been a Maoist until 1968 and a member of the PSU until 1970. Thereafter he had been a "libertarian of the Left," p. 12.

53. Fougeyrollas, *La conscience politique*, p. 93.

54. Cayrol and Jaffre, "Y a-t'il plusieurs électorats socialistes?" Curiously workers tended to be more hostile to nationalization than certain types of middle-echelon white-collar elements. For tables, Denis Lindon and Pierre Weil, *Le choix d'un député* (Paris: Editions de Minuit, 1974), pp. 27-77.

55. *World Opinion Update 1*, no. 1 (1) September 1977:5. According to the same poll, 13% of respondents were not sure why they inclined to the Socialist party!

56. Lagroye et al., p. 95.

57. Societé française d'enquêtes par sondages (SOFRES), September and November, 1977.

58. See *Le Monde, Dossiers et documents*, no. 47 (January 1978).

59. *SOFRES*, September 1976.

60. Bizot et al., p. 56. Cf. Mitterrand's own views in his *Un socialisme du possible* (Paris: Seuil, 1971).

61. SOFRES poll cited in *Nouvel Observateur*, January 16, 1978, pp. 32-33.

62. Jean Poperen, *L'unité de la gauche, 1965-73* (Paris: Fayard, 1975), p. 267.

63. *Le Monde,* October 28, 1975.

64. *Le Monde,* May 29, 1973.

65. *Le Matin,* March 21, 1978. Twenty percent blamed Mitterrand for the defeat of the Left alliance, and 41% blamed Marchais.

66. *Le Monde,* March 22, 1978.

9
Comparisons and Perspectives

It is difficult to argue that an essentially descriptive analysis of one political party from its genesis in 1905 to the present can provide a meaningful basis for empirical theories about political parties in general, or socialist parties in particular. Definitions of socialism vary with time and place, and the conditions under which socialist parties have arisen, flourished, and declined are peculiar to the sociopolitical and historical contexts of a country.

The uniqueness of the SFIO can be seen first of all in the mixture of Jacobin, utopian, anarcho-syndicalist, and Marxist traditions that informed it. By participating early in bourgeois government coalitions, the SFIO saw its "antisystem" attitudes challenged much earlier than was the case in Britain and West Germany, where the Labour and Social-Democratic parties, respectively, entered cabinets only after World War I. Nevertheless, the slow pace of socioeconomic change in France, in comparison with Britain and Germany, kept the SFIO's belief in the class struggle and in revolution alive longer. Moreover, the presence of a strong Communist party forced the SFIO to adhere to a relatively rigid dogmatism. Such dogmatism has been attributed by some scholars to the prevalence of a peculiarly French "absolute-value rationality,"[1] which has prevented communication among social sectors and hampered the development of an Anglo-American type of two-party system based on compromise.

The SFIO fancied itself as a workers' party, but its preoccupation with ideology was designed to appeal to intellectuals who insisted on adhering to Marxist dogma because it was fashionable. In Britain, by contrast, both Fabian socialism and democratic Toryism—embodying noblesse oblige, the civic responsibility of the educated, and pragmatic adaptation—have always been respectable ideologies for intellectuals; while in West Germany the Marxist vogue among intellectuals had to compete with equally widespread ideologies of etatism, Catholic communalism, and liberalism.

However, the French Socialist party has shown itself to be no less pragmatic than social-democratic parties elsewhere in its support of nationalist policies, especially in wartime, in its budgetary compromises, in its moderate stand regarding nationalization, and in its adherence to traditional republican institutional values. This moderation reflected the desire of the SFIO, and even more the PS, to expand the Socialist electoral base and to appeal especially to the bourgeoisie. In Germany the Social Democratic party (SPD) provided the classic model for Robert Michels' "iron law of oligarchy."[2] In Britain more recently, the Labour party was the object of criticism for its utopian dogmatism.[3] The SFIO's adherence to the *Union sacrée* after the outbreak of World War I and the abandonment of Socialist principles of pacifism by Mollet's government during the Suez crisis echo the SPD's conversion to *Burgfrieden* during World War I and, much later, Kurt Schumacher's exaggerated nationalist pose in the early years of the Bonn Republic. Britain furnishes a similar parallel: the antiimperialist stance of the Labour Party when forming the opposition did not seem to be relevant for Ernest Bevin's imperialism in the Middle East; nor did the vaunted imperialism of the Labour party prevent the articulation of anti–Common Market sentiments on the part of prominent leaders of that party.

The conflicts between principle and personal ambition, between ideology and pragmatism, and between strategy and tactics that have beset the French Socialist party have been experienced also in Britain and Germany. The fear of a civil war that prompted Mollet to support de Gaulle in 1958 and the desire to hold back the Communists that caused the Socialists to support a Democratic Centrist (Poher) on the second ballot of the presidential elections of 1969—both of these actions reminded one of the decision by the SPD to support Field Marshal

Hindenburg, an archconservative, for president in 1925.

The SFIO's participation in coalition cabinets with the MRP during the Fourth Republic, the nomination of a centrist-oriented politician (Defferre) as presidential candidate, and the chronic alliances between Socialists and Democratic Centrists on local levels all could be cited as examples of a betrayal of socialist principles of *laïcité* for electoral considerations. In these instances, too, the French Socialists were not unique. In its Godesberg Program of 1959, the SPD dropped its nationalization plank in order to widen the party's appeal to the bourgeoisie; and in 1969 Socialist leader Willy Brandt quietly shelved his party's "codetermination" plank in order to enable him to enter into a coalition with the liberal Free Democratic party. Similar behavior is found in Britain, where Socialist Ramsay MacDonald made common cause with the Conservatives in the early 1930s to keep himself in power.

In view of its political realism, the ideological nostalgia of the French Socialist party, as exemplified by Mollet's frequent insistence on a *socialisme pur et dur,* appeared to be artificial and irrelevant. But such nostalgia has been found also in the argument among British Labourites about whether there is "too much or too little" socialism, and in their decision in 1961 to retain Clause Four of the Labour party constitution despite their large-scale abandonment of the nationalization option. Similarly in Germany, the SPD has retained certain Marxist symbols and rituals despite its ideological modernization, and that party's youth wing (the Young Socialists) has continued to use revolutionary rhetoric.

The preservation of organizational cohesion and proven leadership has often been given higher priority than the sorting out of internal ideological or programmatic disputes. This is clearly seen in the repeated reelection of Mollet as secretary-general of the SFIO and of Mitterrand as first secretary of the PS despite criticisms of the ideas and the conduct of these leaders. But such behavior was seen in Britain, too, where Gaitskell was reelected leader of the Labour party in 1961 despite his opposition to Clause Four.

Yet the French Socialists have had much greater ideological difficulties: they could not ignore Marxism as cavalierly as could the British Labourites or the German Social Democrats. Neither the Labour party nor the SPD needed to fear the taunts of rival Communist parties regarding excessive clericalism or the selling out of the working class. In both countries anticlericalism has been weak, owing to the successful depoliticization of the religious issue as a consequence on the one hand of rapid industrialization and urbanization, and on the other, of the general acceptance of historic arrangements for the legitimation of churches. Moreover, in both countries the Communist parties were too insignificant to be able to entice the working class away from democratic socialism. In Britain attempts to establish Marxist mass movements had foundered in the second half of the nineteenth century; in West Germany the Communist party, discredited in any case because of the division of Germany, was unconstitutional in the years 1956 to 1968.

In France, by contrast, the Communist party remained strong throughout the Fifth Republic. It was estimated that in 1968, 33 percent of the workers voted for the PCF, and only 18 percent for the FGDS; while the PCF retained about 20 percent of the total electorate, the FGDS appealed to only 12 percent.[4] Hence it was clear that the Socialist party needed an expanded electoral base. But in its quest for allies, the Socialist party was caught in a "Catch-22" situation. It was committed to laicism, but it was also aware of the growing importance of support from Catholic voters. Not wanting enemies on the Left—although in the middle of the 1950s it was among the most anti-Communist of French parties[5]—it constantly entertained the possibility of collaborating with the PCF. Unfortunately the Socialist party could not have any reliable prognosis about the effects of such collaboration on its own position. On the one hand, it could be argued that if the voters distrusted the Communist party, then the Socialist party would be hurt by collaboration. On the other hand if voters were no longer so distrustful, the PCF as the larger of the two parties might benefit to the detriment of the non-Communist Left. The Socialist party would clearly benefit only if it emerged as the more important of the two parties—a condition that did not occur until the early 1970s. But the PS's recent electoral strength also provoked resentment on the part of the Communists and threatened to undermine the Popular Front. This is clearly illustrated by the elections of 1978. Although the PS emerged as the largest party of France in terms of popular support, such support was still not quite enough to overcome the polarizing impact of the (single-member) constituency system of the 1958 electoral reform.

In the various elections of the 1970s, the electoral support of the PS had become as disparate as that of the British Labour party and the SPD. But the price the PS has had to pay for this development has been greater than that demanded of its British and German counterparts. Both the Labour party and the SPD have retained the working class as a reliable nucleus of support, because each of the two parties has had more or less institutionalized connections with a monolithic trade-union movement, and because industrial workers have had no place else to go, despite the adaptiveness of the Conservative party in Britain and the Christian Democratic Union in Germany. In France, however, the trade union movement has been fragmented, and the working class has had a leftist alternative to the PS. Furthermore, the working-class appeal of the PS was weakened by that party's attempts to accommodate the small farmers and shopkeepers (who lacked class consciousness) and the civil servants (who have been etatist by profession and have therefore lacked a serious commitment to a thorough transformation of society). Finally, many of the French Socialist party's regional federations have been led by local notables, who have tended to reflect an opportunistic small-town provincialism that has been anti-Parisian and therefore anti-proletarian—a fact that has accounted for the persistent conservatism of Socialist senators in the Third, Fourth, and Fifth Republics. In contrast, the leaders of the Labour party and the SPD have always been more consistently urban and national in orientation.

The continued meaningfulness of the socialist, or social-democratic, faith, and of ideological cleavages in general, has been related to the persistence of relatively rigid class systems in Western Europe democracies—even if there has never been a one-to-one correspondence between a particular class and a particular ideology—and to relatively restricted opportunities for upward social mobility. To the extent that Socialist parties recognize this problem as paramount, it makes little difference what label they attach to themselves. It has recently been argued that in Western Europe the distinction between socialism and communism has become obliterated.[6] In France, Italy, and Spain this is said to be exemplified by the electorate's shameless flirtation with the Communists, by the Socialists' insistence that they have the same long-range economic ideas as the Communists, by a growing indifference, if not hostility, to the Western alliance, and by a reluctance to defend liberty. The French PS is particularly berated for having signed a Common Program with the PCF.

Such an argument ignores the democratic institutional values of the PS as well as the persistent discomfort of most of its leaders with the party's Communist connections—themes discussed in some detail in the last three chapters of this study. That discomfort led the Socialists in the early days of the Fifth Republic to look for signs of progressivism within de Gaulle's entourage, and later led to repeated attempts at alliances with Radicals and Democratic Centrists, and throughout this period to a desire to see in a British-type of *travaillisme* a feasible alternative to Marxism.

The developments described above do not prove conclusively that the *embourgeoisement* of the working class has been significant enough to produce a general depoliticization, or "the end of ideology."[7] Yet there have been sufficient changes in the French political and social climates to make the Socialist party more comparable to social democratic parties in other European countries. For instance there are signs that the traditional antagonism between socialism and Catholicism in France, as elsewhere, is receding. In 1973 many practicing Catholics voted for the PS, and Mitterrand openly avowed the fact of his Catholicism.[8] It is now estimated that about half of the electorate of the French Socialist party consists of committed Catholics,[9] which is roughly the same proportion of the religiously observant as in the German SPD.

The comparison of the French Socialist party with other European social-democratic parties may be taken even further. Socialist dominance, or participation, in government in France has had roughly the same programmatic consequences as has social-democratic dominance elsewhere. In fact France has been less successful in democratically restructuring the tax system or in eliminating the income gap between the middle class and the working class than have the Netherlands, Denmark, Austria, and even Britain (with its historic class system), despite a revolutionary commitment to equality and despite several periods of Socialist influence or dominance (e.g., 1936-38, 1944-47, 1955-57). Perhaps it is because the leaders of the parliamentary Left in France have themselves been products of the bourgeoisie and have had little concrete understanding of the problems of the masses they have purported to represent. Perhaps, too, the leaders of French democratic socialism, as teachers, humanists, intellectuals, and esthetes, had persuaded themselves that a serious intellectual commitment to socialism as a meaningful ideology could substitute for a lack of persistent and successful agitation for concrete social changes and redistributive policies. It is curious that while some Socialists castigated the SFIO for being too intellectual and not concrete enough,[10] and thus for forfeiting the support of the workers who cared little about ideas, others berated the party for having an inadequate intellectual foundation.[11] Perhaps those leaders of the SFIO who insisted on the importance of dogmatism have been the more realistic after all in their conviction that *expressive* politics was more in tune with the spirit of Frenchmen than *instrumental,* or pragmatic, politics. Seymour Martin Lipset, referring to an attitude survey conducted in the mid-1950s, remarked that in France (as elsewhere in Western Europe) "the actual sentiment favoring a 'socialist solution' to economic and social problems is much lower than the Socialist or Communist vote."[12]

In this respect the SFIO has by no means been unique among Center-Left parties in Western Europe. When Socialists participated in Netherlands coalition governments between 1951 and 1957, Dutch unions were forced to acquiesce in wage cuts; the *apertura a sinistra* in Italy, which in 1963 opened the door to Socialist participation in the government, was followed by a policy of wage restraints; in West Germany the establishment of the Grand Coalition in 1966 was followed by the passage of antiunion emergency legislation two years later. Even in Great Britain—where due to the two-party system that normally prevails, a Labour party, once in power, would not be under the coalition restraints characteristic of multiparty systems—the Labour government of Harold Wilson presided over wage freezes, attempted to control trade unions and wildcat strikes, and evinced a traditionally bourgeois interest in productivity, currency stabilization, and governmental supervision of collective contract negotiations. Just as in France many of the SFIO's socialist policy positions were inspired by the pragmatic consideration of anticipating the Communists, Italy's nationalization of the electricity industry, promoted by the Socialists, was inspired less by socialist dogma than by the desire to strengthen the patronage potential of the Ministry of State Participation, which was a Socialist stronghold.

The SFIO, particularly when in power, could not always promote the kind of policy that its ideology theoretically imposed on it. In 1946 in France, the SFIO had become, according to official interpretations emanating from the party congress, "a party of fundamental and irreducible opposition to the ensemble of the bourgeois class, and to the state whose instrument it is."[13] But this aspect of the SFIO's ideology became meaningless because certain programs flowing from it might, if implemented, have become dysfunctional for the party itself. Irrespective of the party's belief in class war and the antagonism between the working class and the bourgeoisie, the very existence of the SFIO as a significant electoral force depended upon the party's success in bridging the gulf between the working class it still claimed to represent, and the bourgeoisie, which came to constitute the majority of the SFIO's electorate and parliamentary leadership.

In view of the *embourgeoisement* of the leadership of the SFIO and of other European social-democratic parties, and in the face of the internal and external constraints imposed upon *any* party in government—such as international competition, the scarcity of resources, currency pressures, and the dangers of domestic violence—the redistributive inclinations of Socialist parties must often be sacrificed in the interest of "saving the Republic" or maintaining social stability. What divided the SFIO from other parties in the 1950s was not so much the conflict over the distribution of economic resources but the question of maintaining the French colonial interests and the problem of preserving parliamentary government. Similarly, in Britain of the mid-1960s, the economic elements of the electoral platforms of the two major parties were not always easily distinguishable, and what most divided the Labour party from the Conservatives was the issue of British membership in the Common Market. What divided the German SPD from the CDU in the late 1940s and early 1950s was not so much economics as the question of Atlantic collaboration. What divided the Labour party in Israel from the right-wing opposition in the 1960s and 1970s was not socialist as opposed to free enterprise economics, but the question of whether or not to pursue a hard-line foreign policy. What divided the Australian Labour party from the Liberals, particularly between the early 1920s and 1950, was not economics but the question of the compulsory military draft, which the ALP opposed, and what divided them later was the question of governmental support of parochial schools.

When Socialist parties participate in the government, they have a stake in the success of the democratic political system and in political stability. When these parties are in the opposition, they have a similar stake because they must prove their legitimacy in order to gain power. Despite the fact that Socialists frequently define the ideal democratic polity as one in which capitalism has been eliminated, their commitment to the existing polity implies support (albeit temporary) of certain of its components, including the current industrial structure, a strong currency, labor peace, productivity, and the stability of the social system. Thus every republican party, right or left, is committed to the maintenance of neo-capitalist systems but views itself as a better system manager than its opponent—striving to gain its managerial legitimacy via democratic elections.

It could be argued that the French Socialists' agreement to a Common Program with the Communists was an indication that the PS was seriously interested in abolishing capitalism. But as one scholar noted even before the Common Program was signed, "the gap between Right and Left has been . . . eroded by the de facto disinclination of the Left to make any considerable extension of the public sector a real political issue."[14] Furthermore the nationalization scheme proposed by the Common Program hardly went beyond those already obtained in several other Western European countries. It was estimated that in 1977 the nationalized sector in France accounted for only 8 percent of industrial salaries as compared to 14 percent in Austria and 12 percent in Italy, and that the Common Program would, if implemented, have increased the proportion in France to less than 17 percent. One may therefore conclude that the PS' agreement to the nationalization plank was largely campaign rhetoric and—in view of the subsequent disagreements with the PCF on this issue—a tactical aberration.

Socialist party leaders—who, like Harold Wilson, tend to dismiss ideological questions as "theology"—cannot be strictly bound to party platforms. Frequently French Socialists, desirous of promoting certain politicians and goals, have had to settle for the less undesirable of two unpleasant options. The ideological hard-liners within the SFIO tried (successfully) to stop Defferre's presidential candidacy in 1963, just as the urban Democrats tried (unsuccessfully) to stop Carter in the American presidential election of 1976. In 1969 the traditional Socialists, after Defferre's first-ballot failure in the presidential election, supported Poher, a Democratic Centrist, against Pompidou, just as in the United States in 1976 the traditional Democrats, after the primary failures of Humphrey and Jackson, supported Carter against Ford.

But despite this pragmatism and opportunism, there are ideological dispositions "that point to certain options and exclude others."[15] And there is no question that left-wing parties tend on the whole to be more humane and more interested in efficiency than right-wing parties. These differential predispositions that distinguish one party from another are the elements that render a political party, on occasion, quite dynamic. However, due to a variety of circumstances, the "parameters of the possible" are constantly restricted, leaving less and less room for party dynamism. Socialist parties can no longer be viewed as politicization devices par excellence for the following reasons: (1) since most adults already have the right to vote, there are no longer many opportunities for bringing additional sectors of the population into the political system and taking the credit for it (or in British parlance, for "dishing the Whigs"); (2) the economy, due to external factors, has become stagnant; (3) a politics of imagery and circuses is played out and no longer compensates for redistributive failures; and (4) internal "enemies" pose no threat and external ones cannot be vanquished.

Moreover, there is some question whether socialist parties in

Western Europe are seriously viewing themselves as socio-economic conflict-muting instruments. The traditional liberal parties have been committed to autonomous conflict aggregation between capital and labor by means of collective bargaining, whereas socialist parties, recognizing the weakness of autonomous bargaining and the imbalance of power between trade unions and organized business, have been *ideologically* committed to political—i.e., parliamentary—solutions to problems of aggregation. But such a commitment has doubtful functional relevance in view of the progressive weakening of the decision-making role of parliament. The bureaucracy and technocracy (including the planners), who are the real initiators and controllers of policy options, cannot be relied upon to promote the kind of redistributive policies required in an economy of limited growth. The bureaucracy, whose important members (even Socialist ones) tend to be elitist, is inclined to use standards of efficiency and productivity rather than social justice.

There remains, theoretically, the possibility of a reversion to anomic mass action for the promotion of Socialist policy goals. But the Socialist party frowns upon anomic action, not only because such action tends to strengthen the hand of the Socialist party's competitors to its Left, but also because violence has the effect of subverting the parliamentary approach to managing the republican system itself. In order to concentrate upon system maintenance (that is, "saving the Republic"), the Socialists in France, and Social Democrats elsewhere in Western Europe, have done what they could to disengage their parties from the task of resolving conflicts between the disadvantaged and the privileged economic sectors. These parties have often promoted indicative economic planning, the decentralization of social welfare administration, and "co-management" at the factory level—although these could all be viewed as instruments for the maintenance of capitalism.

It is a paradox that in those European countries where social-democratic parties have made the greatest electoral gains since the end of World War II, the development of extraparliamentary and extrapartisan devices for the resolution of economic conflicts—especially between labor and management—has gone furthest. Mass parties have not objected to, and have often encouraged, devices as price-wage councils in Austria, the Foundation of Labor in the Netherlands, the labor-market boards in Sweden, central wage accords in France, and even the "social compact" in Britain. To the extent these devices have worked properly, they have contributed to the functional decomposition of political parties, including social-democratic ones. The growing policy disengagement by political parties has in part accounted for the decline of registered party memberships, the reduced programmatic expectations voters have of mass parties, and the fact that voters' choices have been made increasingly on the basis of the personal qualities of candidates.[16]

European countries are sometimes said to be systemically different from the United States, where, we are told, the aggregative functions of political parties—including moderately progressive if not socialist parties—are facilitated by a pragmatic political culture. Yet the experience of the French Socialist party can be quite easily compared with that of the American Democratic party. Leaving aside the obvious differences in electoral systems, history, and social support bases, in addition to the fact that the Democratic party hardly pretends to socialism, one may discover striking similarities between the two parties. The regionalism prevailing within the French Socialist party (despite the unitary nature of the French political system) can be compared to the localism of the American Democratic party: in terms of their impact on the national party, the strong Democratic party machines in Chicago, Boston, and New York City are roughly comparable to the dominant Socialist federations of Nord, Pas-de-Calais, Seine, and Bouches-du-Rhône.

The PS and its predecessor, the SFIO, are said to have been much less effective as aggregative mechanisms than the Democratic party. Yet neither the more restrictive electoral base nor the ideological commitment of the SFIO prevented it, during the Fourth Republic, from entering coalitions at the parliamentary level with such manifestly incompatible allies as the MRP, or from voting in a manner inconsistent with its traditional ideology, or from permitting Defferre to turn to the Center in the early 1960s. Of course the unifying capabilities of the PS were diminished by the presence of a large Communist party, which in effect meant the presence of a mass of alienated working-class voters whom the PS found difficult to entice. But the agglutinative properties of the Democratic party have not been totally successful either: the Democrats have had difficulty incorporating the demands of Blacks, Chicanos, and other minorities.

Both the PS and the Democratic party have been informed, or encumbered, by a plethora of myths: the former by the myths of laicism and egalitarianism, and the latter by the myth of "urban progressivism." In neither case has the operative myth prevented accommodation, cynicism, opportunism, or electoral pragmatism. The red flag periodically unfurled by the SFIO did not keep that party from collaborating with Radicals or cause it to merge with the PCF; just as the "waving of the bloody shirt" in reminiscence of the Civil War has not prevented the Southern Democrats from entering congressional coalitions with Northern Republicans. For the sake of party unity, the Democratic party's progressivism has often been underemphasized. The party's tactical conservatism has on occasion led it to adopt a "Southern strategy," which has been reflected in the assignation of legislative committee chairmanships and in a concern with law and order. Similarly, the French Socialists' egalitarianism has on occasion been underemphasized in order to enable them to keep the status-conscious *fonctionnaires* reliably within the fold, and the party's laicism has not precluded attempts, no matter how half-hearted, to fashion electoral strategies with the clericalist Center. In the case of the Democratic party, the law-and-order issue was picked up in 1968 to prevent George Wallace's American Independent party from making even deeper inroads into the Democratic electoral base, just as Mollet and other leaders of the SFIO had considered it opportune, in the years 1958-62, to support the Fifth Republic in order to prevent too many defections to Gaullism by traditional Socialist voters. Similarly, events forced Mollet to opt for a war strategy during the Suez crisis of 1956, just as ten years later Johnson and Humphrey were forced to opt for military policies in Indochina that contradicted their party's platform and ideology.

Both parties have been beset by a number of problems. Splinter groups whose aggregation into party mainstreams has not been completely successful act as gadflies. Blocked on both sides, the

SFIO could ill afford to disregard the PSU on its left or the Defferrists (and Radicals) on its right. Similarly the Democratic party could disregard only at its peril the Eugene McCarthy contingent on the one hand, and the Dixiecrats, or supporters of George Wallace, on the other. Both parties have on occasion been prodded by statements of ideological orthodoxy and programmatic imperatives from "idea groups"—the Democrats by the Americans for Democratic Action, and French Socialists by the Jacobin, Jaurès, and similar clubs. Prominent party renegades have defected temporarily or permanently—for example, Soustelle and Mitterrand from the SFIO, and John Connally and Strom Thurmond from the Democratic party. Nor has either party been able to prevent traditional electoral supporters from "crossing over"—whether because of a commitment to law and order," concern for the protection of property, the fear of left-wing radicals, or hero worship. Thus in 1968 many French Socialists turned to de Gaulle, and in 1972 many American Democrats—including hard hats and even trade-union leaders—defected to Nixon.

The distinction that is sometimes made between presidential and congressional parties in the United States[17] has, since the advent of the Fifth Republic, applied in some measure to France. The persistence of a Democratic congressional majority in the face of Republican presidential victories (as in 1952 and 1956, and in 1968 and 1972) was paralleled in France, where (except in 1958 and 1968) the parliamentary strength of the combined Left was nullified by the conservative presidents who had gained their victories by making plebiscitarian appeals that transcended political ideologies. To make the point somewhat differently: efforts at aggregation and integration were impeded in both countries because of unforeseen political events and the irruption of atypical political behavior. Just as the SFIO could control neither a defection to Gaullism in 1958 nor the threats of the protagonists of an *Algérie française,* the Democratic party could prevent neither the "Chicago Riots" nor the defection of its traditional supporters.

The greater pragmatism and aggregative potential of the Democratic party have not, in the long run, rendered it more instrumental in producing particular policy outputs than the

French Socialist party. Just as one may cite the fact that in France, the SFIO from the time of the Popular Front government of 1936 was part and parcel of an inflexible political system and participated in occasional "crisis" legislation to safeguard the system, one may also cite the failure of the Democratic party many years after the New Deal to promote meaningful employment legislation, medical insurance laws, antipollution measures, or tax reform. Notably, after 1963 the Democrats helped enact civil rights provisions largely to preserve the established constitutional order and to neutralize extraparliamentary radical forces. The programmatic changes for which the two parties have taken the credit have also been promoted in order to preserve traditional myths: in the case of the Democrats, the myth of economic and racial equality, and in the case of the French Socialists, the myths of anticlericalism, social progressivism, and a commitment to radical structural change. The apparent revival of the political fortunes of the two parties in 1974 was not, however, due primarily to the parties' greater programmatic commitments, nor to the longevity of the aforementioned myths. It was due to certain accidental elements: for the Socialists of France the desanctification, departure, and demise of de Gaulle, boredom with the leadership of his immediate successor, and the partial disintegration of a scandal-ridden Gaullist party; for the American Democrats the corruption of Watergate, the distrust of the national Republican establishment, and the fall of President Nixon.

It seems to be the fate of social-democratic and other moderately progressive parties, because of their belief in the feasibility and desirability of reforms within the system, to be led by *responsible* elements. These leaders are committed to an ethos of a responsible politics because they have grown old in a system in which they have found respectable places for themselves, and which they therefore regard in a less negative light than more radical groups or than younger and less patient members of their own party. Caught between the Scylla of socioeconomic reformism and the Charybdis of electoral opportunism or personal ambition, they embrace attitudes and positions to which the parties they lead are supposed to be ideologically ill-suited. The strike-breaking policies of French Socialist Alexandre

Millerand early in the twentieth century and Mollet's defense of
the new Gaullist order are no less inconsistent ideologically than
Ramsay MacDonald's coalition with the Conservatives in Britain;
the monarchist inclinations of Friedrich Ebert, the leader of the
SPD early in the Weimar Republic; Willy Brandt's coalition with
ex-Nazi Kurt Kiesinger in 1966; the preelection coalition
agreement between Bruno Kreisky, the Socialist chancellor of
Austria, and the leader of the neo-fascist Freedom party in the
early 1970s; and in the United States, the racial elitism of
Woodrow Wilson, the hawkishness of Henry Jackson and Hubert
Humphrey, and the ambiguities of most Democratic leaders
around the issue of school busing.

The best that can be said is that, despite their positions, the
leaders of the French Socialist party—as well as the leaders of
similar parties—have been loyal to their *maison politique*
because they have considered it to be a better framework for the
achievement of democracy, equality, and social justice than
competing political organizations.

The axiom sometimes suggested for French political parties,
that they originate on the left and end on the right, can of course
be applied to the French Socialist party. That party was caught by
socioeconomic developments and by episodic factors that (1) it
could not predict, (2) its ideological tradition prevented it from
recognizing, (3) competition from the Communist party prevented it from adjusting to, or (4) its basic interest in preserving a
democratic constitutional order forced it to disregard. In the 1950s
the SFIO was more interested in preserving the regime than in
competing with the PCF for electoral advantage; in the first few
months of the Gaullist regime, it was more interested in
preventing civil war than in exploiting what might have been
revolutionary opportunities. To be sure, the existence of a strong
Communist party on its Left caused the loss of most of its
traditional working-class supporters at the same time that the
bourgeois attitudes of its remaining reliable adherents, the *petits
fonctionnaires,* caused it to deemphasize its antisystem orientations.

But the dilemma of the SFIO has by no means been unique. Just
as the *embourgeoisement* of many of its supporters created
difficulties for its ideological traditions, so the suburbanization of

many of the traditional supporters of the Democratic party moderated the preoccupation of that political group with the underdog. Similarly the phenomenon of a party ostensibly appealing to the working class being led by well-educated bourgeois or well-to-do esthetes such as Blum, Philip, and Mollet finds its parallel in many other social democratic parties: Schumacher in Germany, Saragat in Italy, Wilson in Britain, Kreisky in Austria, and Palme in Sweden. One reason why the SFIO lost much of its credibility with, and support from, the working class was that the party could not compete with the PCF, whose leaders were "true sons of the people," or with the charismatic and populist appeals of a de Gaulle. In contrast, social democratic parties in other countries could maintain themselves much better than the SFIO either because (as in West Germany, Britain, Austria, and Sweden) there has not been a significant party to the Left of them, or because (as in Italy, Germany, or Austria) charismatic irruptions from the Right have been suspect for historic reasons.

In view of the foregoing, the SFIO's insistence upon a nostalgic attachment to Marxist principles and upon the preservation of its *vieille maison* appears unrealistic. But a merger of all non-Communist Left parties into one giant, electorally significant party proved impossible: the Radical Socialists were too liberal, too individualistic, too opportunistic, and too prone to compromise their political principles (except for anticlericalism); the UDSR was too small and its raison d'être too much the fading memory of the Resistance; the CIR, too recent and too loose a group; and the PSU, too doctrinaire and too much given to flirting with the Communists. This inability to merge with other leftist groups, in the face of pressure from the PCF on the left and the Gaullists on the right, constituted the essential dilemma of the SFIO and eventually led to its formal demise. But the circumstances surrounding that demise proved, in a sense, a vindication of the SFIO, because other parties increasingly adopted some of the positions of the Socialists: the PCF began to acquire a parliamentarist and pseudoreformist orientation; the Radicals, under J.-J. Servan-Schreiber, adopted a new program incorporating many Socialist features; and even the Gaullists, after the accession of Pompidou and Chaban-Delmas, moved leftward in an attempt to become a *parti des électeurs*. Thus it can be said that as the old SFIO departed from the French political scene, its basic outlook was being perpetuated.

To a very large extent, the French Socialist party has been propelled recently in a more pragmatic reformist direction and has therefore become more "modern." The parliamentary elections of 1973 and 1978 and the presidential elections of 1974 have shown that the Socialists can give a better account of themselves than the Communists can, and that they are able to come close to winning elections. The PS is no longer too preoccupied with the extremist ideological challenges to its Left, because the PCF needs the PS more than the PS needs the PCF, and because the extreme-leftist extraparliamentary forces are too fragmented to mount effective electoral challenges. Conversely, the neo-liberal, progressive, and even neo-socialist orientation of Giscard d'Estaing is likely to evoke a positive response among French Socialists. Such a response will have the effect of liberating the PS from its historic ideological constraints, of enabling it to widen its electoral appeal even more than before, and ultimately of transforming it into a typically Western European social democratic party.

Notes

1. Gabriel Almond and G. Bingham Powell, Jr., *Comparative Politics: A Developmental Approach* (Boston: Little, Brown & Co., 1966), pp. 263-66.

2. Robert Michels, *Political Parties* (Glencoe, Ill.: Free Press, 1949).

3. C. A. R. Crosland, *The Future of Socialism* (London: Jonathan Cape, 1956), especially Chapter 4.

4. Jean-François Petitbon, "La crise de la gauche française," *Socialisme* (Brussels), no. 95 (September 1969), p. 5.

5. Frank L. Wilson, *The French Democratic Left in Search of a Role, 1963-1969* (Stanford, Calif.: Stanford University Press, 1971), p. 167.

6. Stephen Haseler, "Europe: The Collapse of the Social Democrats," *Commentary* 64, no. 12 (December 1977):42-46.

7. Léo Hamon, "Partis politiques et dépolitisation," in Georges Vedel, ed., *La dépolitisation: mythe ou réalité?*, Cahiers de la Fondation Nationale des Sciences Politiques, no. 120 (Paris: A. Colin, 1962), pp. 115-46.

8. Stanley Hoffmann, *Decline or Renewal? France Since the 1930s* (New York: Viking Press, 1974), p. 478.

9. William E. Paterson and Ian Campbell, *Social Democracy in Post-War Europe* (New York: St. Martin's Press, 1974), p. 35.

10. E.g., Alain Savary's warnings against "revolutionary verbalism," in *Le Monde Hebdomadaire*, June 10-16, 1971. See also François Mitterrand, *Ma part de la vérité* (Paris: Fayard, 1969), p. 79; and Roger Jacques's critique of Socialists as excessively idealistic, in *La pensée socialiste*, pp. 91-92.

11. Philip, *Le socialisme trahi*, p. 196; Petitbon, "La crise de la gauche," p. 7. See also Vincent Auriol (*Journal du septennat* 7, p. 82), who criticizes the SFIO because, for most of its politicians, "narrow interests dominate ideals."

12. Seymour Martin Lipset, *Revolution and Counter-Revolution* (New York: Anchor Books, 1973), p. 282.

13. Marabuto, *Les partis politiques*, p. 119.

14. Pickles, *Government and Politics in France*, vol. 1, p. 167.

15. *Le Monde*, March 9, 1977, p. 34.

16. For a discussion of party "decomposition," see Samuel H. Beer, *The British Political System* (New York: Random House, 1974), pp. 202-204.

17. James MacGregor Burns, *The Deadlock of Democracy: Four-Party Politics in America* (Englewood Cliffs, N.J.: Prentice-Hall, 1963), pp. 257-64.

Selected Bibliography

Selected Bibliography

This bibliography includes books that have been consulted by the authors in the preparation of the present study. The periodical and serial titles cited in the Notes are not listed separately below. Among these, the following have been found most useful: *L'Année politique (AP), Bulletin intérieur du parti socialiste, Combat socialiste, La Documentation socialiste, Le Figaro, Le Matin, Le Monde, New York Times, Le Populaire, La Revue Socialiste* and *La Nouvelle Revue Socialiste, Socialist International Information,* and *L'Unité.*

Association Française de Science Politique, dir. Maurice Duverger. *Paris politiques et classes sociales en France.* Paris: A. Colin, 1955.

Auriol, Vincent. *Journal d'un septennat.* 2 vols. Paris: A. Colin, 1970, 1974.

Avril, Pierre. *Le régime politique de la Ve République.* Paris: Librairie Générale de Droit et de Jurisprudence, 1967.

Barjonet, André. *La révolution trahie de 1968.* Paris: John Didier, 1968.

Barrillon, Raymond. *La gauche française en mouvement.* Paris: Plon, 1967.

Bilger, Pierre. *Les nouvelles gauches de janvier 1956 à mai 1958.* Paris: Fondation Nationale des Sciences Politiques, 1960.

Bizot, Jean-François; Mercadet, Léon; and van Eersel, Patrice. *Au parti des Socialistes: plongée libre dans les courants d'un grand parti.* Paris: Grasset, 1975.

Blum, Léon. *For All Mankind,* trans. William Pickles. New York: Viking Press, 1946.

———. *Les problèmes de la paix.* Paris: Stock, 1931.

Chapsal, Jacques. *La vie politique en France depuis 1960.* Paris: Presses

Universitaires de France, 1966.

Charlot, Jean, ed. *Quand la gauche peut gagner*. Paris: Alain Moreau, 1973.

Charzat, Michel; Chevènement, Jean-Pierre; and Toutain, Ghislaine. *Le CERES: un combat pour le socialisme*. Paris: Calmann-Lévy, 1975.

Chevènement, Jean-Pierre. *Les socialistes, les communistes, et les autres*. Paris: Aubier Montagne, 1977.

Clark, James M. *Teachers and Politics in France: A Pressure-Group Study of the Fédération de l'Education Nationale*. Syracuse, N.Y.: Syracuse University Press, 1967.

Club Jean Moulin. *Un parti pour la gauche*. Paris: Editions du Seuil, 1961.

Cole, G. D. H. *Socialist Thought: The Forerunners, 1789-1850*. London: Macmillan, 1953.

_____ . *Socialist Thought: Marxism and Anarchism, 1850-1890*. London: Macmillan, 1954.

_____ . *Socialist Thought: The Second International, 1889-1914*. London: Macmillan, 1956.

Colton, Joel. *Léon Blum: Humanist in Politics*. New York: Alfred A. Knopf, 1966.

Criddle, Byron. *Socialists and European Integration: A Study of the Socialist Party*. New York: Humanities Press, 1969.

Defferre, Gaston. *Si demain la gauche*. Paris: Laffont, 1977.

_____ . *Un nouvel horizon: le travail d'un équipe*. Paris: Gallimard, 1965.

Depreux, Edouard. *Le renouvellement du socialisme*. Paris: Calmann-Lévy, 1960.

Douël, Annie. *L'accession du Général de Gaulle au pouvoir et la SFIO*. Paris: Fondation Nationale des Sciences Politiques, 1960.

Dreyfus, François. *Histoire des gauches en France, 1940-1974*. Paris: Grasset, 1975.

Droz, Jacques. *Le socialisme démocratique, 1864-1960*. Paris: A. Colin, 1966.

Duverger, Maurice, ed. *Partis politiques et classes sociales en France*. Paris: A. Colin, 1953.

Earle, Edward M., ed. *Modern France*. Princeton, N.J.: Princeton University Press, 1951.

Ehrmann, Henry W. *Politics in France*. 3rd ed. Boston: Little, Brown and Co., 1976.

Einaudi, Mario; Byé, Maurice; and Rossi, Ernesto. *Nationalization in France and Italy*. Ithaca, N.Y.: Cornell University Press, 1955.

Estier, Claude. *Journal d'un fédéré*. Paris: Fayard, 1970.

Faucher, Jean-André. *La gauche française sous de Gaulle*. Paris: John Didier, 1969.

Fauvet, Jacques. *Les forces politiques en France*. Paris: Editions Le Monde, 1951.

_____. *La France déchirée*. Paris: Fayard, 1957.

_____. *Histoire du parti communiste français*. 2 vols. Paris: Fayard, 1964, 1966.

Fauvet, Jacques, and Mendras, Henri, eds. *Les paysans et la politique*. Paris: A. Colin, 1958.

Fougeyrollas, Pierre. *La conscience politique dans la France contemporaine*. Paris: Denoël, 1963.

Furniss, Edgar S. *France, Troubled Ally*. New York: Praeger, 1960.

Godfrey, E. Drexel, Jr. *The Fate of the French Non-Communist Left*. Garden City, N.Y.: Doubleday, 1955.

Goguel, François. *France Under the Fourth Republic*. Ithaca, N.Y.: Cornell University Press, 1952.

_____. *La politique des partis sous la IIIe République*. Paris: Editions du Seuil, 1946.

Goguel, François, and Grosser, Alfred. *La politique en France*. Paris: A. Colin, 1975.

Graham, B. D. *The French Socialists and Tripartism, 1944-1947*. Toronto: University of Toronto Press, 1965.

Grosser, Alfred. *La IVe République et sa politique extérieure*. Paris: A. Colin, 1961.

Guidoni, Pierre. *Histoire du nouveau parti socialiste*. Paris: Tema-Editions, 1973.

Halévy, Elie. *Histoire du socialisme européen*. Paris: Gallimard, 1948.

Hurtig, Christiane. *De la SFIO au nouveau Parti Socialiste*. Paris: A. Colin, 1970.

Jaurès, Jean. *Anthologie de Jean Jaurès*, ed. Louis Lévy. Paris: Calmann-Lévy, 1946.

Joxe, Pierre. *Parti socialiste*. Paris: Editions de l'Epi, 1973.

Lagroye, Jacques; Lord, Guy; et al. *Les militants politiques dans trois partis français*. Paris: Pedone, 1976.

Landauer, Carl A. *European Socialism*. 2 vols. Berkeley, Calif.: University of California Press, 1959.

Laurens, André, ed. *Les élections législatives de mars 1978*. Paris: Le Monde, Dossiers et Documents, supplement, March 1978.

Leites, Nathan. *On the Game of Politics in France*. Stanford, Calif.: Stanford University Press, 1959.

Ligou, Daniel. *Histoire de socialisme en France 1871-1961*. Paris:

Presses Universitaires de France, 1962.

Lipset, Seymour Martin, and Rokkan, Stein, eds. *Party Systems and Voter Alignments.* New York: Free Press, 1967.

Louis, Paul. *Histoire de socialisme en France.* 5th ed. Paris: M. Rivière, 1950.

MacRae, Duncan, Jr. *Parliament, Parties and Society in France, 1946-1958.* New York: St. Martin's Press, 1967.

Mallet, Serge. *Le gaullisme et la gauche.* Paris: Editions du Seuil, 1965.

Malterre, Jacques, and Benoist, Paul. *Les partis politiques français.* Paris: Bibliothèque de l'Homme d'Action, 1957.

Marabuto, Paul. *Les partis politiques et les mouvements sociaux sous la IVe République.* Paris: Sirey, 1948.

Micaud, Charles. *Communism and the French Left.* New York: Praeger, 1963.

Mitterrand, François. *La paille et le grain.* Paris: Flammarion, 1975.

_____. *Ma part de verité.* Paris: Fayard, 1969.

_____, ed. *Parti socialiste.* Paris: Marabout, 1977.

Mollet, Guy. *Bilan et perspectives socialistes.* Paris: Plon, 1958.

_____. *13 mai 1958-13 mai 1962.* Paris: Plon, 1962.

Noland, Aaron. *The Founding of the French Socialist Party, 1893-1905.* Cambridge, Mass.: Harvard University Press, 1956.

Parti communiste français. *Changer de cap: programme pour un gouvernement démocratique d'union populaire.* Paris: Editions Sociales, 1971.

Parti socialiste. *Changer la vie: programme de gouvernement du parti socialiste.* Paris: Flammarion, 1972.

Partis communiste et Socialiste. *Programme commun de government du parti communiste et du parti socialiste.* Paris: Editions Sociales, 1972.

Paterson, William E., and Campbell, Ian. *Social Democracy in Post-War Europe.* New York: St. Martin's Press, 1974.

Penniman, Howard R., ed. *France at the Polls: The Presidential Election of 1974.* Washington, D.C.: American Enterprise Institute for Public Policy Research, 1975.

La pensée socialiste contemporaine: Actes des colloques socialistes de 1964. Paris: Presses Universitaires de France, 1965.

Philip, André. *Le socialisme trahi.* Paris: Plon, 1957.

_____. *Les socialistes.* Paris: Editions du Seuil, 1967.

_____. *Pour un socialisme humaniste.* Paris: Plon, 1960.

Pickles, Dorothy. *Government and Politics in France.* 2 vols. London: Methuen, 1972.

Poperen, Jean. *La gauche française: le nouvel age 1958-65.* Paris: Fayard, 1972.

_____. *L'unité de la gauche, 1965-73.* Paris: Fayard, 1975.

Pour le socialisme: le livre des Assises du socialisme. Paris: Stock, 1974.

Prélot, Marcel. *L'évolution politique de socialisme français, 1789-1934.* Paris: Spes, 1939.

Quilliot, Roger. *La SFIO et l'exercice du pouvoir.* Paris: Fayard, 1972.

Rocard, Michel. *Le parti socialiste unifié et l'avenir socialiste.* Paris: Editions du Seuil, 1969.

Savary, Alain. *Pour le nouveau parti socialiste.* Paris: Editions du Seuil, 1970.

Servan-Schreiber, Jean-Jacques, and Albert, Michel. *Ciel et Terre: Manifeste Radical.* Paris: Denoël, 1970.

Simmons, Harvey G. *French Socialists in Search of a Role, 1956-67.* Ithaca, N.Y.: Cornell University Press, 1970.

Suffert, Georges. *De Defferre à Mitterrand.* Paris: Editions du Seuil, 1966.

Tiersky, Ronald. *French Communism, 1920-1972.* New York: Columbia University Press, 1974.

Vedel, Georges, ed. La dépolitisation: mythe ou réalité, Cahiers de la Fondation Nationale de Science Politique. Paris: A. Colin, 1962.

Willard, Claude. *Socialisme et communisme français.* Paris: A. Colin, 1967.

Williams, Philip M. *Crisis and Compromise: Politics in the Fourth Republic.* Garden City, N.Y.: Anchor Books, 1966.

_____. *French Politicians and Elections, 1951-1969.* London: Cambridge University Press, 1970.

_____. *Politics in Postwar France.* London: Longmans, Green, 1954.

Wilson, Frank L. *The French Democratic Left, 1963-1969.* Stanford, Calif.: Stanford University Press, 1971.

Wright, Gordon. *Rural Revolution in France.* Stanford, Calif.: Stanford University Press, 1964.

Zévaès, Alexandre. *Histoire du socialisme et du communisme en France de 1871 à 1947.* Paris: France-Empire, 1947.

Index

Index

Adler, Friedrich, 12
Affair of the generals (1949), 26
Agriculture and SFIO, 17, 98-100, 115, 163, 171. *See also* Farmers
Alfortville Congress, PS, 211-214
Algeria, 1, 31-32, 113, 131, 134, 137-140, 146, 149, 150, 153, 156, 157, 159, 161, 163, 169, 170, 171, 256
Allemanists. *See* Parti ouvrier socialiste révolutionnaire
Alliance communiste révolutionnaire, 11
Antarctic Treaty of 1959, 127
Asian Socialist Conference, 123
Assembly of the French Union, 80, 135
Attali, Jacques, 232
Auriol, Vincent, 36, 116, 120, 146, 147, 159; elected president, 23; resignation from SFIO, 160, 165
Australia, 251
Austria, Socialist party in, 103, 249, 251, 254, 258, 259
Autogestion. See Industrial democracy

Babeuf, François, 7, 8
Bakunin anarchists, 9
Barangé Law, 28, 101
Barjonet, André, 199

Bebel, August, 12
Ben Bella, Mohammed, 32
Bevin, Ernest, 244
Bidault, Georges, 26, 29, 105, 164
Billères, René, 201, 209
Blanc, Louis, 11
Blanqui, Louis Auguste, 8
Blanquists, 8, 9, 10, 39
Blum, Léon, 1, 16, 20, 21, 23, 24, 36, 40, 41, 49, 50, 53, 54, 55, 69, 82, 84, 94, 95, 97, 259; death of, 26; on dictatorship of the proletariat, 50; elected premier of Fourth Republic, 23; leader of new SFIO, 18; on party discipline, 69; policy of wage stabilization, 24; and popular front, 82, 99
Bolshevik revolution, 15, 16
Bonnel, Pierre, 42
Boulloche, André, 158
Bourgès-Maunoury, Maurice, 33, 36, 130
Brandt, Willy, 245, 258
Braunthal, Julius, 121
Briand, Aristide, 19
Brousse, Paul, 11
Broussists. *See* Fédération des travailleurs socialistes
Brussels Pact. *See* Western European Union (WEU)
Brutelle, Georges, 149, 175

Cachin, Marcel, 16, 17
Cartel républicain, 163
Catholicism, Catholics, 8, 48, 165, 182, 187; and socialism, 101, 179, 205, 233, 248
Catroux, General Georges, 31, 138
Centre de la réforme républicaine, 148
Centrism, Centrists, 17, 106, 113, 180, 181, 200, 213, 221, 225. See also Democratic Center, MRP
Cercles Jean Jaurès, 66. 69
Cercle Tocqueville, 171
CERES, 218-220, 221, 230, 233, 236, 238
CFDT, 191, 204, 213, 219, 221, 227, 229; and Federation of the Left, 190; and support of Mitterrand, 229
CFTC, 162, 169, 170, 175, 191, 221
CGT, 12, 20, 34, 60, 67, 96, 102, 103, 111, 116, 162, 169, 170, 183, 190, 191, 213, 227, 228, 230
Chaban-Delmas, Jacques, 225, 259
Chandernagor, André, 155, 173, 212, 213, 217
Charzat, Michel, 233
Chevènement, Pierre, 233
CIR, 178, 181, 184, 189-191, 194-197, 203, 212, 213, 215, 216, 259; and fusion, 193, 202, 218
Civil servants and Socialist party, 78, 79, 80, 81, 109, 173, 232, 247, 255, 258
Club des Jacobins, 175, 180
Club Jean Moulin, 171, 175, 180, 195
Clubs, 171, 175, 180, 182-183, 184, 193, 194, 195, 206, 212, 216, 218, 256; and Defferre candidacy, 176
Colin, André, 170
Collectivism, 46-47
Combes, Emile, 11
Comintern. See Communist International
COMISCO, 121
Comité des démocrates, 178-179
Comité directeur, PS, 215-216

Comité directeur, SFIO, composition of, 80-82; and de Gaulle investiture, 147, 148-149; and parliamentarians, 64, 69-73, 133; structure and function of, 61-65, 133
Comité révolutionnaire central, 10, 11
Comités d'entreprise, 103, 110
Commission nationale d'études. See National Studies Commission
Commission nationale ouvrière. See National Workers' Committee
Committee of Nine, 121
Common Market, 33, 130; British membership in, 196
Common Program of the Left, 223, 224, 226, 228-230, 234, 235, 236, 251, 252
Communist International, 16-18, 124
Compromise Declaration of 1905, 38
Congrès national. See Party congress
Constitution of the Fifth Republic, SFIO and, 21-22, 92-94
Constitution of the Fifth Republic, 148-151, 190-191; Article 16 of the, 52, 162, 163, 164, 185, 190, 223
Consultative Committee of the International Socialist Conference. See COMISCO
Coty, René, 36, 147
Council of Europe, 128-130
Criddle, Byron, 132, 142
Czechoslovakia, invasion of, 200-202

Daladier, Edouard, 20
Debré, Michel, 153, 155, 156, 159, 163; fall of government, 171, 172
Debré Law, 157, 158, 159, 222
Declaration of Principles, 1946, 41, 53, 119, 121, 127
Defferre, Gaston, 77, 101, 147, 149, 151, 153, 156, 159, 161, 163, 172, 173, 175, 176-189, 193-194, 218, 220, 232, 235, 254, 256; as presidential candidate, 212-213
De Gaulle. See Gaulle, Charles de

Democratic Center, 224, 225, 226, 230-231, 234, 235
Democratic socialism, aims and tasks of, 122-123
Démocratie socialiste, 217
Denmark, 249
Depreux, Edouard, 104, 147, 149, 156, 178
Disarmament, 20, 134
Dreyfus affair, 11
Duclos, Jacques, 29, 214
Duhamel, Jacques, 217
Dumas, Charles, 120
Duverger, Maurice, 71-72, 108, 147

Ebert, Friedrich, 258
Education, reform of, 157, 175
Elections, cantonal, of 1967, 195; of 1976, 227
Elections, municipal, of 1959, 153, 155; of 1961, 163; of 1965, 180, 181; of 1977, 227
Elections, parliamentary, of 1914, 13; of 1928, 18; of 1936, 20; of 1945, 21, 74; of 1946, 22, 74, 84, 92; of 1951, 27, 74-75; of 1956, 31, 74; of 1958, 74, 151; of 1962, 74, 172, 205n; of 1967, 76, 192, 198; of 1968, 199; of 1973, 224, 260; of 1978, 226, 231, 234-237, 247, 260; parliamentary by-elections, 1973-1977, 227
Elections, presidential, of 1965, 185, 186, 218; of 1969, 212, 213, 214-215, 252; of 1974, 225, 233, 238, 260
Elections, system of, 25, 27, 31, 92, 151-152; reform of, 26-27, 31, 112, 171, 223, 229
Embourgeoisement of Socialist electorate, 180, 221, 234, 244-250, 258-259
Engels, Friedrich, 10
Estier, Claude, 197, 235
Etudiants socialistes. *See* Student Socialists
European Defense Community (EDC), 28, 72, 131-133

European integration, 130, 160, 175, 193, 224, 229
Executive Committee. *See Comité directeur*

Farmers, 99, 160, 222, 247; in Socialist party, 78, 79, 81, 221, 232. *See also* Agriculture
Faure, Edgar, 27-28, 30, 31, 113
Faure, Maurice, 170, 172, 179, 196
Fauvet, Jacques, 109
Fédération des travailleurs socialistes, 11, 38
Fédération nationale Léo Lagrange, 68, 69
FEN, 83, 100, 162, 169, 191, 227, 232. *See also* Teachers
Ferri, Enrico, 12
FGDS, 51-52, 57, 66, 72, 184-200
Finance Control Committee, 64-65
First International, 7, 8, 9, 12, 120; Brussels Congress (1868), 9
FO, 96, 103, 104, 162, 169, 170, 191, 227
Fourier, Charles, 7, 8
French Political Science Association, 79, 87
French Union, 28, 108, 131, 135
Frossard, L. O., 16, 17
Fundamental Program (1962), 41-42, 44, 46, 47, 55
Fuzier, Claude, 160, 179, 199, 204, 212, 213

Gaillard, Félix, 33, 114, 154, 196, 201
Gaitskell, Hugh, 245
Garaudy, Roger, 193, 201
Gaulle, Charles de, 1, 2, 23, 33, 91-92, 125, 126; and Algeria, 137-138, 150, 156-159, 170-171; provisional government of, 21-22, 91-93; return of, 145-147; resignation of, 204
Gaullism, Gaullists, 23, 26, 27; and the Left, 105, 112, 149, 153-159, 164, 171, 174, 177, 179-180, 187,

199; of the Left, 155, 162
Gazier, Albert, 149, 151, 153-155, 156, 158, 161, 163, 164, 171; and Popular Front, 172, 174
Geneva Conference of 1954, 136
Germany, 9, 11, 15, 28, 103, 131-134, 243-249, 251, 258-259
Giscard d'Estaing, Valéry, and Giscardists, 225, 226, 234, 236, 237, 260
Godesberg Program, 245
Gouin, Félix, 22
Great Britain, 8, 9, 12, 59, 60, 120, 122, 123, 154, 243-254, 258-259
Grenelle Accords, 199
Grosser, Alfred, 85
Grumbach, Salomon, 120
Guesde, Jules, 10, 14, 15. *See also* Parti ouvrier français

Halévy, Daniel, 13
Halévy, Elie, 40
Hernu, Charles, 213, 215
Hindenburg, Paul von, 244-245
Hitler, 20, 120
Ho Chi Minh, 135
Horizon 80, 183
Hungarian uprising, 127

Immigrants and SFIO, 110, 111
Indépendants, Les, 11
Independent Socialists, 20
India, 123
Indochina, independence movement in, 135-137
Industrial democracy, 97, 190, 216, 221, 223, 253,
Intellectuals, intellectualism, and the Socialist party, 109, 217, 219, 232, 243, 249
International Council of Social Democratic Women, 121
International Union of Social Democratic Teachers, 123
International Union of Socialist Youth, 121, 123

Isaac, Jules, 134
Israel, 193-195, 204, 251
Italy, 248, 249, 250, 259

Jaquet, Gérard, 175, 177, 213
Jaurès, Jean, 1, 13, 14, 39-40, 41, 42, 48, 53, 54, 82, 119; assassination of, 13, 14, 16; leadership of PSU, 13-14; philosophy of, 39-40
Jeune République, 183
Jeunes Agriculteurs, 162, 170
Jeunes Patrons, 176
Jeunesses socialistes, 67, 160
Julliard, Jacques, 139-140

Kautsky, Karl, 12
Kiesinger, Kurt-Georg, 258
Kreisky, Bruno, 258, 259

Lacoste, Robert, 31, 96, 138, 140, 151
Lafargue, Paul, 10
Laïcité, 28, 48, 100-102, 107, 108, 172-173, 174, 223, 245, 246, 255, 257
Laniel, Joseph, 29, 36
Lapie, Pierre-Olivier, 157, 158
Laurens, André, 211
Laurent, Augustin, 85, 149, 155
Lecanuet, Jean, 217
Leenhardt, Francis, 149, 153, 175
Lejeune, Max, 72, 161
Lenin, Vladimir Ilyich, 37, 42
LeTroquer, André, 36, 151
Lévy, Louis, 120, 124
Lie, Trygve, 126
Lipset, Seymour Martin, 243
Longuet, Jean, 15
Lussy, Charles, 29

MacDonald, Ramsay, 245, 258
MacRae, Duncan, Jr., 36, 79
Malroux, Mme Paul, 80
Marchais, Georges, 185, 226, 235, 236, 241
Marie, André, 29
Marshall Plan, 104, 128

Marx, Karl, 9, 10, 15, 37, 38, 39, 40, 42, 43, 49, 53, 119

Marxism, 9, 37, 38-40, 53, 94, 219, 233, 243-244, 259

Mauroy, Pierre, 204, 214, 218

Mayer, Daniel, 21, 26, 147, 149; as minister of labor, 105; as secretary-general, 83-85, 94

"May Events" of 1968, 197-200

Mendès-France, Pierre, 29, 30, 31, 32, 108, 117, 136, 139, 164, 188, 190, 198, 214; government of, 29, 111; and PSA, 156; and Socialist voters, 113

Merlat, Odette, 135, 143

Micaud, Charles, 65-66, 108

Michels, Robert, 244

Middle East, 224, 225

Military credits, 19, 25, 54, 107, 109, 110

Millerand, Alexandre, 11, 257-258

Mitterrand, François, 1, 114, 140, 156-157, 162, 178, 184, 188, 202, 214, 217, 218, 248; on Common Program, 229-230; on presidential powers, 225. *See also* FGDS

Moch, Jules, 25, 26, 42, 104, 105, 116, 120, 155, 157, 163, 173, 194, 199; on disarmament, 125-126; as minister of interior, 110

Mollet, Guy, 1, 24, 26, 27, 31-33, 48-49, 75, 79, 83-85, 106, 110, 120, 121, 124, 126-127, 129, 130, 132, 146-159 *passim*, 161, 172-174, 218; on Algeria, 32, 137-140; career of, 82-85; and Defferre, 176-178, 214; on democratic socialism, 41-42; and Fifth Republic constitution, 147-149, 159, 164; and de Gaulle, 146-153, 156, 158, 159, 173, 179, 212, 216; on *laïcité*, 113, 151, 174, 205; becomes party secretary, 61, 64, 94; as premier, 31, 108, 112, 113

Monnet Plan, 97

Morocco, independence of, 136-137, 138

Moutet, Marius, 135

MRG, 223-224, 225, 229, 231, 236

MRP, 21, 22, 152, 157, 158, 159, 170, 171, 174, 176, 180; demise of, 200; attitude to Fifth Republic, 179; relations with Socialist party, 28, 92, 93-95, 104-105, 112, 114, 148, 153, 164, 254

Mutualists. *See* Proudhon

Naegelen, Marcel-Edmond, 35n, 131-132

Napoleon III, 9

Nasser, Gamal Abdel, 32, 127, 140

National Bloc of 1924, 19

National Commission of Socialist Women, 67-68

National Conflict Committee, 69-70

National Council, 62-63, 72

Nationalization, nationalized industry, 9, 13, 20, 25, 46-47, 57, 95, 96, 115, 175, 186, 190, 202, 221, 222, 223, 225, 228, 230, 232, 234, 244, 245, 251, 252

National Studies Commission, 68, 69

National Workers' Committee, 67

NATO, 131, 172, 188, 193, 195, 196

Netherlands, 249, 254

Nuclear weapons, 110, 127, 161, 175, 190, 229, 230

ORTF, 185, 197

Palme, Olaf, 259

Paris Commune, 8, 9, 10

Parti ouvrier français, 10, 11, 38, 41

Parti ouvrier socialiste révolution-naire, 11

Party congress of PS: of 1969 (Alfort-ville), 211-214; of 1969 (Issy-les-Moulineaux), 215-216; of 1971 (Epinay), 217-218; of 1973 (Gre-noble), 220, 225, 232

Party congress of PSU: of 1906 (Chalon-sur-Saône), 59; of 1910 (Nîmes), 13; of 1915 (Paris), 15; of

1920 (Strasbourg), 16-17; of 1920 (Tours), 18
Party congress of SFIO, 64, 66, 70, 72; functions of, 61-63; of 1926, 19; of 1944, 35; of 1945, 92, 94; of 1946, 84; of 1948, 128; of 1949, 25, 26, 101; of 1950, 126; of 1951, 137; of 1952, 106; of 1953, 126; of 1954, 63, 132, 133; of 1955, 62, 63, 72, 111, 136; of 1958, 149; of 1959, 155; of 1960, 160; of 1961, 163; of 1963, 173, 174, 177; of 1965, 182; of 1967, 194; of 1969, 203
Party membership, PS, 216, 220-221, 223, 226-227, 231, 232
Party membership, SFIO, 156, 157, 202-203
Party sections, 60-61, 65
PCF, founding of, 16
Periodicals, Socialist, 68-69, 84, 98, 227
Permanent Bureau, 63-64
Pétain, Marshal Henri-Philippe, 20-21, 99
Pflimlin, Pierre, 33, 36, 114, 146, 147
Philip, André, 64, 72-73, 79, 95, 97, 106, 108, 109, 110, 113, 120, 124, 128, 147, 198, 259
Philips, Morgan, 122
Pinay, Antoine, 28-29, 156, 158, 170, 185
Pineau, Christian, 155, 160, 161, 163, 193, 194
Pisani, Edgard, 171
Planning, economic, 46-47, 96-98, 175, 183, 185
Pleven, René, 27, 110
Poher, Alain, 213, 215, 244, 252
Police, 170, 198
Pompidou, Georges, 192, 214, 217, 224, 252, 259; appointment as premier, 171; death of, 225
Poperen, Jean, 218, 219
Popular Front, 19-21, 23, 82, 169, 174, 175, 187, 189-190

Poujadists, 31, 109, 140
Proudhon, Pierre Joseph, 8, 9, 12, 40
PS, founding of, 215-217
PSA, 147, 156, 159
PSU, 159, 162, 164, 169, 170, 172, 179, 180, 212, 216, 219, 233, 256, 259; and FGDS, 184, 190; and Middle East, 193; and support of Mitterrand, 223
Public-opinion poll: on Algerian independence, 139; on coalition with PCF, 197; on coalition preferences, 234; on government power, 150; on ideological identification, 233; on Mitterrand leadership, 231; on Mollet as leader, 117; on nationalization, 115, 233; on parochial schools, 157, 158, 233; on presidential preferences, 178; on republican liberties, 150; on social composition of party electorate, 231-232; on voting intentions, 1978, 227, 230

Queuille, Henri, 26, 105
Quilliot, Roger, 212, 213

Radical-Socialists, 11, 19, 20, 101, 104, 106, 107, 110, 112, 114, 115, 147, 154, 157, 159, 162, 170, 179, 212, 216, 226; disintegration of, 221; fusion with the Left, 195, 196; and Gaullism, 171; and progressivism, 188, 217; and Socialist party, 148, 153, 163, 164, 203, 256, 259; and 1967 elections, 199. *See also* MRG, *Réformateurs*
Ramadier, Paul, 23-25, 95, 116, 151
Referendum of 1969, 204
Réformateurs, 224
Renaudel, Pierre, 15, 16
Resistance, 21, 83
Revue Socialiste, La, 69, 131, 135
Rey, André, 57
Reynaud, Paul, 20, 29

Ribière, Henri, 21
Rimbert, Pierre, 52-53
Rocard, Michel, 232
Rochet, Waldeck, 185, 193, 198, 199

Saint-Simon, Claude-Henri de, 7, 8
Saragat, Giuseppe, 259
Savary, Alain, 147, 150, 203, 212, 213, 216, 218, 220
Schumacher, Kurt, 244, 259
Schuman, Robert, 25, 110
Second International, Stuttgart Congress (1907), 54
Séguy, Georges, 199
Sembat, Marcel, 15
Servan-Schreiber, Jean-Jacques, 176, 217, 226, 259
SFIO, founding of, 18
Shadow cabinet, 188, 189, 207
Shopkeepers and small businessmen, 104, 106, 221, 234, 247
Simmons, Harvey G., 67-68, 79, 80-82
Social Democratic Federation, 176, 182-183
Socialist Enterprise Groups, 66-67, 69
Socialist Parliamentary Group, 152, 172; composition and function of, 64-65, 71
Soustelle, Jacques, 150, 256
Stalin, Joseph, 37
Strikes, 29, 104, 111, 116, 162, 169, 173, 193, 197
Student movement, 197-198
Student Socialists, 67
Suez crisis, 32, 127, 139-140, 244, 255
Sweden, 103, 254, 259
Switzerland, 15, 52

Tanguy-Prigent, François, 99, 115, 156
Taxation policy and reform, 20, 105, 107, 108, 109, 112, 190

Teachers, 66, 72, 78, 79, 80, 81, 100, 232. *See also* Education, FEN
Teitgen, Pierre-Henri, 104
Témoignage crétien, 213
Thomas, Albert, 1, 15
Thomas, Eugène, 152
Thorez, Maurice, 173, 179
Tours, Schism of, 16-18
Trade unions, 12, 13, 17, 20, 102-103, 169, 173, 175, 183, 190, 191, 193, 197, 199, 204, 233, 247, 250, 253. *See also* CFDT, CGT, FO
Travaillisme, 180, 182, 192, 248
Tripartisme, 21-24, 104
Troelstra, Pieter J., 12
Tunisia, 28, 136-137, 138
Twenty-one Conditions, 17, 18

UCRG, 203, 204, 212, 216, 218
UDF, 236-237
UDSR, 27, 101, 147, 157, 184, 259
UGCS, 204, 212, 214
UNEF, 162, 169
Union sacrée, 14, 244
United Nations, 123, 125-128, 135, 140
United States, Democratic party of, 254-257; Socialist party of, 123
University, reform of, 197
UNR, 1, 151, 154, 158, 172, 180. *See also* Gaullism

Vaillant, Edouard, 10, 13, 15
Vedel, Georges, 49
Verdier, Robert, 147
Veterans, 104, 107, 112, 162
Vichy government, 21
Vietnam Socialist party, 123
Viviani, René, 14

Wages policies, 23, 26, 97, 105, 107,

199, 222, 223, 226, 233; Common Program and, 224, 228-229

Waldeck-Rousseau, René, 11

Weill-Raynal, Etienne, 56, 160

Western European Union (WEU), 133-134

Williams, Philip M., 84

Wilson, Harold, 249, 251, 252

Working class, 102-109; *embour-geoisement* of, 106, 108; and nationalization, 240; and Socialist party, 10, 12, 16, 29, 38, 67, 76-80, 106, 162, 172, 187, 211, 216, 219, 221, 231, 232, 250

Zimmerwald Conference, 1915, 15

Zinoviev telegram, 18